THE WILDLIFE PARKS OF AFRICA

Nicholas Luard is the author of nine novels and two works of non-fiction: *The Last Wilderness, A Journey across the great Kalahari Desert*, and *Andalucia, A Portrait of Southern Spain*.

THE WILDLIFE PARKS OF AFRICA

Nicholas Luard
in conjunction with the
World Wildlife Fund

SALEM HOUSE
SALEM, NEW HAMPSHIRE

First published in the United States by Salem House, 1986
a member of the Merrimack Publishers' Circle,
Salem, New Hampshire 03079.

Originally published in Great Britain by
Michael Joseph Ltd, 1985

ISBN : 0 88162 156 0

Library of Congress Catalog Card Number 85-62184

Filmset and printed by BAS Printers Limited,
Over Wallop, Hampshire, Great Britain
Bound by Butler and Tanner Ltd,
Frome, Somerset, Great Britain

DEDICATION

To all who work for the conservation of
the African wilderness

CONTENTS

ILLUSTRATIONS

Colour Plates

Black and White Photographs

Martial eagle (*p* 19), ARDEA – *Clem Haagner*; baboon (*p* 22), WWF – *Norman Myers*; nyala bull (*p* 25), ARDEA – *Clem Haagner*; lion (*p* 32), ARDEA – *JS Wrightman*; Thomson's gazelle (*p* 37), WWF – *Norman Myers*; Defassa waterbuck (*p* 41), WWF – *P Géroudet*; bat-eared fox (*p* 45), ARDEA – *JS Wrightman*; bushbuck (*p* 49), WWF – *CAW Guggisberg*; springbok (*p* 52), ARDEA; marabou storks (*p* 57), WWF – *J Allan Cash*; crowned cranes (*p* 59), WWF – *JF Ormond*; impala (*p* 64), WWF – *JF Ormond*; addax (*p* 68), WWF – *Thane Riney*; oribi (*p* 71), ARDEA – *Clem Haagner*; honey badger (*p* 74), WWF – *Mark N Boulton*; serval cat (*p* 77), WWF – *Mark N Boulton*; nyala (*p* 81), WWF – *P Macartney*; tsessebe (*p* 84), ARDEA – *Clem Haagner*; red lechwe (*p* 91), WWF – *CAW Guggisberg*; spotted hyena (*p* 94), WWF – *Mark N Boulton*; reticulated giraffe (*p* 99), WWF – *Norman Myers*; impala (*p* 102), WWF – *Emil Schulthess*; sable (*p* 109), WWF – *Centro de Informaçao de Angola*; lechwe (*p* 115), ARDEA – *Clem Haagner*; Buffon's kob (*p* 131), ARDEA – *P Blasdale*; Uganda kob (*p* 135), WWF – *CAW Guggisberg*; vervet (*p* 145), WWF – *Norman Myers*; fringe-eared oryx (*p* 152), ARDEA – *Kevin Carlson*; bush pig (*p* 159), WWF – *Peter Jackson*; lesser kudu (*p* 164), WWF – *Dr F Vollmar*; tawny eagle (*p* 168), WWF – *Mark N Boulton*; black-backed jackal (*p* 175), WWF – *Dr F Vollmar*; wildebeeste (*p* 183), ARDEA – *Clem Haagner*; waterbuck (*p* 188), WWF – *Eugen Schumacher*; topi (*p* 193), WWF – *J Allan Cash*; caracal (*p* 202), WWF – *Norman Myers*; eland (*p* 207), WWF – *CAW Guggisberg*; ostriches (*p* 219), ARDEA – *Clem Haagner*; bontebok (*p* 223), WWF – *SA National Parks Board*; greater kudu (*p* 226), ARDEA – *Clem Haagner*.

FOREWORD

Forty years ago, as a small child, I arrived at the little Kenyan town of Nyeri one hundred miles north of Nairobi. The Second World War was approaching its end and I was on my way home to Britain with my family from Iran.

We intended to spend a few weeks in Kenya as a break in the long and difficult journey back. The few weeks stretched into a year which we spent at Nyeri's Outspan Hotel. In 1943 the Outspan and its wilderness lodge, Treetops, where Queen Elizabeth II was staying the night her father died nine years later, was owned by a legendary figure in Kenya's colonial past, a buccaneering former hunter and soldier of fortune named Eric Sherbrooke Walker.

A few miles west of Nyeri lie the hills of the Aberdares, today within the Aberdares National Park. To the north the snow-capped peak of Mount Kenya rises above the plains. East and south are the rich savannas of central Kenya. On every side the landscape teemed with animals. The hotel had few other guests and Sherbrooke Walker, restless and bored with time on his hands, decided to show us the country's wildlife. For most of that year, bucketing beside him in an ancient car or trudging after him on foot across the plains, we did little else.

We watched the huge migrating herds of wildebeest. We saw prides of lion asleep in the midday heat, and leopards sinuously climbing down from trees to hunt at dusk. We heard the mewing calls of fish eagles and listened to the barking of antelope. We spent long hours waiting at water-holes for herds of elephant to come down to drink. We found the huge tracks of rhino and followed them late into the day as the light faded. More than once the car broke down after dark and we slept out huddled together for warmth on the seats beneath the forest's canopy, waking at intervals to the clamour of the African night.

The indelible impression of those expeditions has taken me back to Africa many times since then. The delight in its landscape and animals

11

remains as vivid as ever, but over the succeeding years the African wilderness has undergone immense changes. For a time the pressure of post-war human settlement threatened to destroy vast areas of it entirely, together with their rich and intricate communities of wildlife. Then, late in the day for the wild, came a growing acknowledgement of the truth in a message that a few far-sighted individuals had been stubbornly proclaiming for more than a century – that something unique and lovely was vanishing from Africa. The tide of conservation began to flow and a systematic effort was made to save what was left of the wilderness.

The attempt came only just in time. As late as the early sixties Africa only had a handful of Parks and reserves. Today there are well over three hundred under some form of national or provincial administration, and perhaps three times as many again in private hands. Although most ecologists would say it is still nothing like enough, it is none the less a considerable achievement for which the credit belongs in large measure to black Africa's recently-independent nations. Throughout the continent at least some representative facet of all the major habitats and eco-systems is now protected.

In the first part of this book I have tried to give these Parks and reserves, the surviving vignettes of Africa's ancient landscape, a context – to outline how they came into being against the continent's historical background and how they function and are managed today. The second part lists all the present African National Parks south of the Sahara on a country-by-country basis, together with their most striking animals, birds, plants, and natural features. Although there are a number of Parks and reserves in countries north of the Sahara they have long since lost their former populations of Africa's larger animals, and tend to be of interest to the specialist rather than the ordinary visitor.

As the book has been written for the general reader I have almost entirely, and unapologetically, avoided using scientific names for the species mentioned. To follow each reference to a 'lion' with the explanatory *Panthera leo* seems to me cumbersome and unnecessary – even, dare I say so, in the case of certain academic textbooks which slavishly obey the convention on every page. In the relatively few instances where there may be some uncertainty about which particular sub-species is being referred to, the African specialist is likely to know in any event. If an individual race or form of some animal does occur in a certain reserve, the ordinary visitor will almost always be told about it by the professionals on the ground – the wardens, rangers and scouts, normally the best of all sources of local information.

I have inevitably consulted many books and papers on African wildlife and conservation, and owe something in greater or lesser degree to all of them. In particular I would like to acknowledge the late Leslie Brown's monumental and scholarly *Africa*, Bernhard Grzimek's moving account of his work with his son Michael in *Serengeti Shall Not Die*, C. A. W. Guggisberg's *Man and Wildlife*, S. K. Eltringham's *Ecology and Conservation of African Mammals* and J. G. Williams' *Field Guide to the National Parks of East Africa*. In addition I owe thanks to many individuals and organisations — so many that in attempting to name them all I would risk unintentionally overlooking some particularly valuable contribution. I would however like to single out the Natal Parks Game and Fish Preservation Board, its director John Geddes-Page, and all its staff for their courtesy in allowing me to observe and take part in modern wildlife management at its most thoughtful and effective.

Finally, while its views and opinions are my own, the book would have been impossible to produce without the co-operation of the World Wildlife Fund in the United Kingdom, and the International Union for the Conservation of Nature and Natural Resources, whose data register at Kew Gardens provided the basis for the detailed information on the African reserves. To everyone involved in their vital work I, on behalf of the hundreds of thousands all over the world who love Africa, its wildernesses and its animals, extend my thanks.

PART I

Conserving the Wilderness

ONE
The History of a Continent

Africa is both vast and immensely old. Those two seemingly self-evident facts, the first apparent on any world map, the second noticeable only to a trained geologist on the ground, have played an important role in the evolution of the continent's wildlife as it exists today.

Its size first: covering an area of 30.3 million square kilometres it is, after Asia, the world's second largest continent, a huge landmass stretching from the southern shores of the Mediterranean down to the approaches to Antarctica. It contains the world's biggest desert, the Sahara, three thousand miles in length and a thousand in width, and its longest river, the Nile. Its climate ranges from searing heat – a surface temperature of 76°C has been recorded in Libya – to the icy cold of the snow-flanked Ethiopian highlands. In certain places and at certain times of the year the temperature can fluctuate wildly within twenty-four hours. During winter in the Kalahari Desert, for example, blazing sun at midday can be replaced soon after dusk by several degrees of frost.

Straddling the equator, embracing both the tropical zones and extending far beyond them to the north and south, Africa's range of landscape and vegetation is as varied as its climate. Apart from deserts and mountains it includes mangrove swamps, steppes and scrub, tropical rainforests, grassplains, thornbush, wooded savanna, delta, marsh and valley. Unsurprisingly this wealth of different living conditions supports an aray of life that is extraordinarily rich, both in sheer numbers and in different types. North America has about twenty species of land mammal bigger than a dog; Africa has well over eighty. They include one large form of wild cattle, one deer, four pigs, three sheep and goats, five of the huge 'thick-skinned' animals called pachyderms, four wild horses, three man-like apes unknown in North America, and more than sixty species of ungulate, the hollow-horned vegetation-eating ruminants commonly known as antelopes or gazelles.

In addition, the African lakes and rivers contain some 2,000 species of fish, compared with fifty in Europe, while on land the continent supports about 1,850 species of bird. A species broadly defines a creature distinct enough from any other so that, under natural conditions at least, it cannot breed successfully except with members of its own kind. For groups of animals with a common ancestor to evolve into separate species requires an immense amount of time under reasonably stable conditions. If conditions change abruptly, if forests disappear or valleys are flooded, the animals evolving within them will normally disappear. Equally time, measured in millions or even tens of millions of years, is needed for the animals to develop and pass on the characteristics that eventually differentiate them from their relatives. In Africa, in contrast to many other parts of the world, both time and a reasonably stable landscape have been available to the wild.

Evidence of Africa's great age comes from the fact that in certain places on the continent large areas of the earth's foundations, the underlying stone of the pre-Cambrian basement rocks dating back thousands of millions of years, are still exposed to the air. The landscape round them has obviously undergone a whole series of changes since the rocks were formed. Even quite recently deserts and savannas were expanding or contracting, forests were shrinking or growing, rivers changing course and altering the shape of the land. The process is natural and continues today. In spite of this, conditions for Africa's animals remained remarkably constant until the modern era. At times when the forests or savannas retreated, enough of the 'nursery' environment always remained to support stocks of the creatures which were growing and developing there. When the trees and grasses expanded their range again, the animals were able to increase with them.

The fearsome decline of African wildlife, different not merely in degree but in kind from even the worst natural catastrophes of the distant past, started with the great human migrations of Bantu peoples towards the south, which began two thousand years ago and gradually changed the face of the continent. The upheaval caused by man was violently accelerated in the nineteenth century by the spread of the Europeans with their guns and their apparently limitless desire and capacity for slaughter. Today a visitor to an African reserve could well think he was looking at one of the last little pockets of the primal landscape, of Africa as it was at the dawn of life – unknown to and untouched by man, black or white. In fact man and his ancestors have been a factor in sculpting the face of Africa and helping determine how its wildlife emerged for at least a million years. To understand how it happened one has to go

18

Martial eagle, Botswana

as far back as one can with any reasonable certainty to Africa's beginnings.

175 million years ago all the world's continents were fused into a single great block of land, a vast sea-encircled island which modern geologists have named Pangaea. Africa formed part of the block's lower lobe, Gondwanaland, a landmass which included the future South America, Antarctica, Australasia, India, Iran, and southeast Asia. At about the same time the first important group of warm-blooded animals, the pouched marsupials, appeared on earth. Then, some fifteen million years after their arrival, Gondwanaland began to break up. Antarctica and Australia floated away first, taking some of the original marsupials with them. On the remaining landmass the placental mammals began to develop. The placental method of rearing young, allowing them to develop in the protection of the womb, proved more efficient than the pouch technique used by the marsupials. More of the young survived and survived in better health. In Gondwanaland the marsupials died out and the placental mammals took over. Among the placental groups were the early apes, the prosimians, which were eventually to lead to man.

Madagascar was next to break away from Gondwanaland, taking with it the lemurs, which still inhabit Madagascar today and at that stage were the most advanced of the early monkeys. South America followed, carrying what are now the New World monkeys, the marmosets and spider monkeys. Meanwhile simian development continued in the Old World with the appearance of the baboons and the catarrhine group of monkeys (which had nostils close together and facing downwards), both of them further steps towards man's emergence. Five million years ago, in its last major geological convulsion, Africa was parted from Arabia. The Red Sea and the Gulf of Aden were formed, and Africa was left precariously joined to Asia at Suez. Two more spasms in the turmoil at the earth's core created the two rift valleys. One led from the Afar Triangle at the Gulf down to the east of Lake Victoria, and the other from the Nile's source at Lake Albert south through the system of the great African lakes – Albert, Edward, Kivu, Tanganyika, Rukwa, and Nyasa (known today as Lake Malawi). Lake Victoria is really a huge shallow pond formed by the overlap between the two rifts. All the other lakes are deep and narrow, following the scars of the rifts.

Three million years later, or two million years ago, the world's climate settled into its present pattern. In Africa the arid and drifting dunes of the Sahara created an impenetrable barrier against movement by most land animals. The equatorial rainforests contracted. Grassland plains spread out in the south and east. Climbing down on to them from the

20

vanishing trees came a group of apes which had learned to walk upright. *Australopithecus*, early 'southern man', made his appearance. The time of his descendant, *Homo sapiens*, was swiftly approaching.

One million years ago a branch of *Australopithecus* had doubled his brain size and become a capable maker of tools. He could also probably talk and use fire. As *Homo erectus* he was able to cross the Sahara and settle throughout Europe and Asia. Behind him in southern Africa the older and less adaptable *Australopithecines* died out. Quite how and when their heirs, the spreading *Homo erectus*, evolved into modern man, *Homo sapiens*, is largely a matter of guesswork. The palaeontologists struggling to find the answer still have little raw material to work on, and each of their new discoveries, a skull or a collection of bones unearthed in some African gorge, provokes fresh debate and argument.

The first major modern search for man's origins was carried out in South Africa by Professor Raymond Dart. He decided, on an interpretation of fossil evidence most later investigators find severely flawed, that early man was a ruthless and aggressive predator. More recently researchers like the Kenyan Leakeys, husband, wife and son, and the American Don Johanson working in Ethiopia, have come to the conclusion that modern man derives from an essentially peaceful member of the animal kingdom who is in turn descended from nomadic groups of primitive hunter-gatherers. Whichever interpretation is correct, it seems clear that by the end of the last European Ice Age, or about 8000 BC, man's neanderthal brow had gone and his brain had become fully developed. He had, in fact, acquired his present physical and mental equipment as *Homo sapiens*.

In Africa five distinct races of *Homo sapiens* appeared at about the same time: the Negroes, the Nilo-Saharans, the Semites, the Pygmies, and the San people or Bushmen. Like the Negroes, the Nilo-Saharans are tall and black, but tend to be thinner in both body and face. The tiny black Pygmies are still confined, as apparently they always were, to the rainforests of the Congo Basin, the habitat in which they evolved. The paler-skinned Semites became dominant in the north beyond the barrier of the Sahara. The San people, the Bushmen, small and apricot-skinned hunter-gatherers, were for thousands of years the sole and unchallenged human occupants of all southern and southeastern Africa.

During the old and middle Stone Ages, the grey mist-sheathed zone in time between early and modern man, human survival depended on a combination of hunting and gathering. Hunting could produce substantial rewards. Animals were rich in protein and a large mammal could supply the needs of an entire human group for a week. On the other

Baboon with infant, East Africa

hand, large mammals were strong, swift, and well-equipped to defend themselves. Hunting was always difficult, often dangerous, and invariably uncertain. To compensate for its uncertainties, half the group gathered – berries, roots, tubers, birds' eggs, insects, whatever crop could be harvested from the wild. If the hunters failed, as they often

22

did, the gatherers could provide the protein the group needed.

The discoveries of the Neolithic Era, the 'new' Stone Age, changed everything. Suddenly man was no longer dependent on hunting-gathering for his survival as he had been from the very beginning. He discovered instead that he could support himself much more efficiently by farming and herding, by agriculture and pastoralism. It was the greatest single revolution in his entire history, more far-reaching in its effects than any later advance, including the development of industrial machinery and the space probes of the last twenty years. Man ceased to be a prisoner of the natural resources available from the landscape, at the whim of the season and weather. He was able to take control of his destiny, settle down, and plan to manipulate the future in a way no creature in the planet's history had ever been able to conceive, let alone begin to put into practice.

The new technology of farming and herding came relatively late to African man. In about 5000 BC it reached the Nile Valley from the Jordan Valley, and moved inland to the Sudan. From there it spread across the Sahel corridor, the belt of grassland running along the southern border of the Sahara, over to West Africa. Meanwhile, the Egyptians were learning to use the Nile's seasonal flooding to increase their crops, and by 3000 BC Egypt had become the most densely-populated area on earth. When King Menes united Upper and Lower Egypt and proclaimed himself Pharaoh, Africa became the home of the world's first nation-state. Further south, the neolithic revolution was still rippling forward. The West Africans embraced it as agriculturalists, while the eastern tribes became nomadic pastoralists.

By 1000 BC Egyptian power was waning. The Egyptians were succeeded in turn by the Nubians, the Assyrians, and the Persians. Between 334 and 325 BC the Persians gave way to the Macedonian Greek, Alexander the Great. On his death Ptolemy, one of Alexander's generals, proclaimed himself king of Egypt and set about mapping as much of the continent as he could. The results, a combination of travellers' tales and hearsay, deeply influenced western civilisation's view of Africa for many centuries. In spite of all the obstacles he faced in his pioneering cartographic efforts, Ptolemy proved to be surprisingly accurate in his guesses about the Nile's source, a question that became an obsession with Europeans much later.

146 BC saw the Romans in control of North Africa after the fall of Carthage. To the south, at about the same time and largely unnoticed, the most important event in Africa's human history was taking place. Agriculture had provided the West African tribes with a stable source of

23

food. Dependable food supplies invariably lead to an increase in population, and often to overcrowding. It happened in West Africa. The tribes began to flood out in waves of mass migration across the continent. They reached and settled the great lakes system of the rift valleys, opening up equatorial and central Africa. Then they began to spread south, pushing the little San Bushmen ever deeper into the great Kalahari desert, a barrier which was to prove almost as impassable as the Sahara.

The migrations continued during the first two centuries AD as the Bantu pressed home the advantages given them by their knowledge of iron-working, farming, and cattle-herding. (Bantu is the name of one of the six dialects of the ancient Niger–Congo group of languages. Over the centuries it has evolved into a general description of most of the black African races. Although their expansion was not strictly a migration, which means a regular seasonal movement between one point and another, the word is normally used now for the great tribal irruptions of the time.) They moved out across the east and south, and probably down the River Zaire. The Pygmies managed to learn Bantu and co-exist with the new arrivals. The San people remained apart, retreating as the Bantu tribes advanced and retaining both their racial identity and their strange click language.

As Rome collapsed in the fifth century AD the Bantu were moving into Madagascar, until then only colonised by a few itinerant Polynesians. Then in 622 the Prophet Mohammed began his apocalyptic ministry; eighteen years later his followers had conquered Egypt and most of Arabia. In 711 the Moslem advance reached Spain. By then the Sanhaja Berbers of Morocco had bowed to Islam, a force that was to be the strongest religious and political influence throughout Africa, except in the far south, for centuries. The Sanhaja, using camels introduced into Egypt from India by the Persians in the sixth century BC, had discovered how to cross the Sahara and had opened up trading routes to the gold-mines of Ghana. These routes were now used to carry the Prophet's message to central and western Africa.

By the time the word of Islam arrived, organised Negro kingdoms had already come into existence in Mali and Ghana, at Songay on the Niger, and at Kanem to the east of Lake Chad. The first full-scale conversion of an African state happened in the tenth century, when the Tokolar Negroes of Senegal adopted Mohammedanism. During the next two centuries more followed them, including Somalia, central Sudan, and the tribes of the Horn of Africa. Not long afterwards, almost every large and permanent African settlement acknowledged the Prophet. The exception was Abyssinia (modern Ethiopia), which remained a Christian kingdom and probably gave birth to the legend of Prester John.

It was not until the fifteenth century that Europeans made their first tentative approaches to the continent. Using a new and more advanced generation of ships, notably the Portuguese-designed caravels, they began to probe the west coast. The first problem they met was at Cape Bojadar, opposite the Canary Islands, where the constant north wind blew so fiercely that no ship's master believed he could sail back against it. Then in 1434 a Portuguese captain rounded Cape Bojadar, stood thirty leagues out to sea on the return journey, and managed to tack home. In 1492 Columbus landed in the Americas, and Portugal became determined to win control of the other great unknown continent to the

Nyala bull in Mkuzi Game Reserve, Natal, South Africa

east to match the prize Columbus had won for his partners and pay-masters, the Catholic monarchs of Spain. Five years later, Vasco da Gama rounded the Cape of Good Hope. Soon the Portuguese were making settle-ments on Africa's eastern seaboard, to match those they had already made on the west coast, and supporting Christian Abyssinia against attacks from the Arab Muslims. Three centuries later, when James 'Ethiopian' Bruce – the great Scottish explorer – fell in love with the Abyssinian Princess Esther, he described her as a pale Portuguese beauty. Weapons, it seems, were not Portugal's only gift to the Princess' ancestors.

For hundreds of years the slave markets of Arabia had been supplied from Africa. The usual trading route was via Zanzibar, where buyers and sellers were often financed by Indian merchants. On the west coast the Portuguese, finding a new market for slaves in the early American colonies, took over the trade in a commodity which was almost as valu-able as gold. The monopoly they created in merchandising slaves, a monopoly approved by the Pope, lasted until the end of the seventeenth century, when they were displaced by the more aggressive and better-equipped Dutch. The next hundred years was a period of prosperity for all Europe. The slave trade profited everyone, from the African entrepreneurs with their appetite for European goods, to the Arab mid-dlemen, to the Europeans themselves who needed cheap labour in the plantations of the New World.

In West Africa the French explored the Senegal River, while the British arrived in Gambia and the Gold Coast. In East Africa the first major Bantu kingdom, Buganda, was formed on the shores of Lake Victoria. To the south the Boers, who had landed at the Cape in 1652, moved inland and conquered the land of the Hottentots, a race of mixed San and Bantu blood. Then in 1795 the British appeared and seized the colony as a reprisal for the Dutch alliance with France during the Napoleonic wars. The Boers regained it briefly, but lost it again in 1806.

As the migrations, both black and white, slowed, southern Africa's human population began to grow. By 1800 it consisted of at least two million Bantu and some 16,000 Boers. North of them, the whole central belt of Africa was still unmapped and virtually unknown to Europeans. The history of its exploration is largely a long catalogue of illness and death – mainly from the 'fever' (malaria). The white man was simply unable to stay alive for any length of time on shore, and the slave trade had to be conducted through native intermediaries. Apart from the Sene-gal River, all of Africa's major rivers were virtually unnavigable, being punctuated along their length by cataracts and rapids. The native Muslim kingdoms were hostile to infidels, and it was against the interests of their merchants to allow the white buyers of slaves direct access to the raw materials of the trade in the interior. The dark continent had daunting natural and human defenders of its secrets.

In London in 1788, Sir Joseph Banks, President of the Royal Society, formed a dining club to promote exploration in Africa. Named the African Association, the club eventually became the Royal Geographical Society. It gave formal backing and funds to many of the early expeditions, the first three of which ended quickly with the death of their leaders. Then in 1795 Mungo Park, a tall, difficult, and impatient Scot, accepted the club's sponsorship and succeeded in making his way from Gambia to the source of the Niger at Segu. A second journey took him a thousand miles downstream to the Bussa rapids, where he and the survivors of his forty companions were killed by local Africans who mistook them for marauding Muslims.

1807 marked the beginning of the end of slaving, when Britain outlawed the trade and pressed the rest of Europe to follow suit. The determination to see it finally abolished was a major motive behind later expeditions, although many of the explorers travelled with the slave traders and often depended on them for their lives. The African trading nations were far from happy to see slavery go. A large part of their trading stock became worthless and their economies were crippled. In the south the Boers, under their British governors, were even more hostile. Although they interbred freely with the Bantu, they did not consider any native African – Bantu, Hottentot, or Bushman – to be more than an inferior being without a soul whose role in creation was to serve a white master. Between 1835 and 1840, in part to register their disgust with the anti-slavery movement, they made the Great Trek across the Orange River, moving themselves and all their possessions up into the High Veld and over into Natal, thus securing access to the sea.

By the middle of the nineteenth century, the European explorers were becoming more successful. Mortality was still chillingly high, but the Lander brothers managed to finish Mungo Park's exploration of the Niger, and the German, Heinrich Barth, solved the riddle of the river's main tributary, the Benue. To the south, the greatest and strangest explorer of all had embarked on his extraordinary journeys. The Scottish missionary, David Livingstone, had crossed the 'Great Thirst' of the supposedly impassable Kalahari Desert, and turned his formidable willpower to the exploration of the Zambesi. After mapping Lake Nyasa he moved up towards Lake Tanganyika. Then he vanished for five years, only reappearing when he was found at Ujiji by the resourceful and well-equipped American journalist, Henry Morton Stanley. The two men charted Lake

Tanganyika together, but Livingstone's next journey was his last. He died in 1872, kneeling by his bed, near the present Zambia–Zaire border.

With Livingstone's death the great era of the solitary exploration of Africa came to an end. Stanley typified the new breed of explorer. Carefully-provisioned, properly-funded and well-armed, supported by large trains of porters and protected against the 'fever' by a daily dose of the newly-discovered quinine, Stanley completed Livingstone's explorations by dragging a steel-hulled boat up to the East African lakes. He sailed round Lake Victoria in 1875, navigated Lake Tanganyika the following year, and then set off to battle the dangers of the Lualaba. The journey was perhaps the most remarkable feat of navigation in the chronicles of African exploration. Stanley established that the source of the Nile was in Lake Victoria, and the Lualaba ran into the Congo River. The whole fertile Congo basin was now open to settlement by Europeans. The age of the white colonist in central Africa had arrived.

Stanley returned to Europe with the good news. When the British showed a marked lack of interest, he took his discovery to Belgium. The King, Leopold, was fascinated by the American's account and when the Belgian government refused to back his ideas for colonisation, Leopold decided to shoulder the financial burden himself. As a result the area became known as Leopold's Congo. By 1900 most of the rest of Africa had been divided between the European powers. The French added to their already significant presence by taking over Madagascar and the Comoros Islands. The Italians took control in Eritrea and Somalia. The Germans claimed modern Tanzania and part of Cameroon and Namibia. The British captured Sudan, overran Zimbabwe at the enthusiastic prodding of Cecil Rhodes, and by 1902 at the end of the Boer War had the rich Rand goldfields of South Africa back in their hands. Even Leopold managed to extend his territory to the shores of the East African lakes.

Victory by the allies in the First World War meant that German Africa became available for redistribution. The British acquired South West and German East Africa; the Belgians took Burundi and Rwanda; while the French were given German Cameroon, leaving most of West Africa from Algeria through the Sahara down to the Bight of Benin in French hands. France's empire in Africa was now only exceeded by Britain's, which reached from Cairo to the Cape. In 1935 Mussolini invaded Abyssinia. The British were forced out of Somalia and at the start of the Second World War the Italians occupied the whole of the Horn of Africa.

The Italian triumph was brief. By the end of the war they had been thrown out not only of the Horn, but also from their formerly well-entrenched position in Libya. The victors were the British, whose power and influence in Africa reached its peak in 1945. At the same moment the famous winds of change began to blow across the continent from the east. Nationalism was throwing up new leaders all over the globe, and India quickly proved too difficult for the heirs of the Queen-Empress to hold. India was returned to its peoples and so too was Egypt. In South Africa, the recalcitrant Boers were also creating trouble again. This time they used the ballot-box rather than their rifles. In the elections of 1948 the Boer-sponsored Nationalist Party was elected with an overall majority. Its victory allowed South Africa to leave the Commonwealth and follow the policy of *apartheid* (separateness), a policy designed to prevent the country's black majority from ever becoming a serious political or economic force.

In 1951 the British withdrew from Libya and five years later from the Sudan. Almost immediately all the colonial powers were in retreat. The last to leave were the Portuguese who, under the dictator Salazar, held on to their possessions until 1974. Then with Salazar's overthrow Angola, Guinea Bissau, and Mozambique gained their independence. White rule in Rhodesia was prolonged by the settlers there until 1980; when the country emerged as the black African state of Zimbabwe. By 1985, only the Republic of South Africa remained under the control of 'foreign' settlers – settlers who, as they defiantly point out, colonised the land at the same time as the migrating Bantu tribes.

Post-colonial Africa had, and still has, a host of apparently intractable problems to solve. The colonial powers left a legacy of arbitrary boundaries drawn by remote civil servants on a map. The boundaries suited the needs of the colonists, but often took no account of the realities of tribal groupings or Africa's geographical features. Many of independent Africa's subsequent civil wars, like the Ibos' struggle to create their own state in Biafra, had their roots in this random process of division. Democracy and parliamentary rule, as understood in the West, have had an equally difficult and turbulent passage. Many countries which instituted elections on independence have produced a 'strong man' who took power and then stayed on as the head of a one-party state. Yet a number of these tribal father-figures – as their fellow citizens often regard them – men like Kenyatta, Nyerere, Kaunda, Hastings Banda, and Seretse Khama, have proved remarkably cautious and temperate leaders.

For those of Africa's inhabitants who were there long before man, it is just as well they have done so. Africa's wilderness depends for survival today far more on the wisdom of the continent's independent black nations than it ever did on their temporary white rulers.

Two
The Beginnings of Conservation

Once upon a time, humans, animals, plants and the wind, sun and stars were able to talk together. God changed this, but we are still a part of a wider community. We have the right to live, as do the plants, animals, wind, sun and stars; but we have no right to jeopardise their existence.

Beliefs of the San Bushmen.

Conservation of the wild and its animals is often thought of as exclusively a requirement and concern of the twentieth century. In fact, conservation has been practised by human societies very much as it is now for thousands of years. King Cyrus of Persia established a number of well-stocked and carefully-wardened game parks in the middle of the sixth century BC, while four hundred years earlier the Assyrians were already breeding lions in captivity for return to the wild, anticipating today's reintroduction programmes by three millennia. There was, of course, a major difference in motive between the conservationists of early civilisations and those of modern times: the animals then were protected for the chase.

Hunting is almost certainly the very earliest of all organised human activities, an inextricable part of man's evolution and survival for hundreds of thousands of years. Long before man emerged his ancestors, the *Australopithicenes*, had been hunters too – as is shown by the piles of fossil bones of prey animals unearthed near the sites where their remains have been found. Both early and more recent man lived in groups and both also foraged in the bush to support themselves. Each of the two activities was an insurance policy against a failure by the other. If the hunters were unsuccessful, the gatherers provided the group's food, and vice-versa.

As every hunter knows, from a falcon to a lion to a man, the chase often fails. The prey, whether a bird or an animal, is usually wary and well capable of defending itself. If it lacks the commoner and more obvious defences like speed, horns, or talons, it will have developed others. The porcupines, for example, have a formidable shield in their barbed quills. If an attacker like a lion snags a barbed porcupine quill in its side, the barbs can gradually draw the quill by the action of the lion's muscles into its heart or lungs – eventually killing the lion. Not surprisingly, with generations of accumulated experience behind them, lions have learned to tackle porcupines only with the greatest care. Caterpillars, butterflies and moths, the favourite prey of many birds, have evolved a whole spectrum of defensive techniques. They range from mimicking other dangerous creatures to storing poisons in their bodies which are harmless to them but deadly to their predators.

It is impossible to tell what proportion of his time and energy early man devoted to hunting and what to gathering, or even which members of the group practised which activity. Studies of the San Bushmen in the Kalahari suggest that the two techniques were fairly evenly balanced, with the men concentrating on the hunt and the women on the wild harvest. Given the uncertainties of hunting, gathering might seem a surer way to acquire the group's protein but the fruits of the wild harvest vary with the season, and even at their most abundant they have to be cropped in the face of strong competition. A host of small animals, birds and insects are intent on raiding the same larder. Many of them can do it more efficiently than man, burrowing with less effort beneath the ground or using their wings almost effortlessly to plunder the tree-tops.

Whichever system was the more productive, and so the more favoured, the human users of both had an overwhelming common preoccupation – the other creatures of the grasslands, savannas and forests where man grew up. As prey to the hunters or competitors to the gatherers, animals defined and controlled man's life. He lived among them and off them in a delicate but resilient equilibrium of rivalry and companionship. They were as powerful and vital a presence as the sun or rain. They were also, like the sun and rain, precious beyond measure. If the animals vanished, so would man. Even gathering was only possible in a world where the plants and trees were fertilised, pollinated, distributed, and brought to maturity with the animals' help. Once the animals had gone there would be no wild harvest left to collect.

Seen from that perspective there was no real difference between man and the animals. They were simply members of different nations who shared a common home. They communicated in different ways, they had different habits and requirements, they lived by certain different rhythms. Yet they were all neighbours in the same community and contributed to each other's welfare. A man might take a gazelle as prey. When the man died his body would be left out for the scavengers to feed off, for the jackals and hyenas which rank with him in the food chain. The scavengers would return his energy to the earth where it would help nourish plants to rear another generation of gazelles, to the ultimate benefit of all four users of the planet's energy.

Sometimes the partnership between man and the animals was even closer. Early man, probably to make good a deficiency in his diet, developed a passion for honey. After generations of watching him a group of African birds known as the honey-guides discovered this, and learned to take advantage of it. The birds had no use for the honey. They wanted the grubs and larvae in the hive. The hives, however, were well-protected by the hard mud walls constructed by their bees, a defence

Lion with zebra, South Africa

the birds were unable to penetrate. The honey-guides learned to dip down over a hunter-gatherer man, lead him to the hives with a clattering zig-zagging flight through the trees, and take the grubs and larvae after he'd used his much greater strength to break open the hive walls and remove the honey. There was no competition between the two; each wanted different parts of the hive. But without co-operating neither would have survived as healthily – and in the case of certain individuals, men or birds, possibly would not have survived at all.

What was absolutely vital to early man was that animals remained abundant. That meant keeping in balance with them just as all the animal nations, of which he was one ranking equally with the rest, had to stay in equilibrium with each other. If man had been able to tip the scales and increase his numbers dramatically, his demands on the antelope herds for food would have soared. As a result the herds would either have dwindled to the point of extinction, or hunting pressures would have driven them from the range in search of safer pastures. In either case the consequences for man would have been disastrous. Dependent on water and unable to travel beyond his home territory without it, he would have been faced first with local starvation. Starvation would have led to a crash in the human population and the community's size at the end could well have been smaller than the nucleus on which its unnatural growth had been built. The catastrophe might not even have ended there. When animal populations are slaughtered out of an area, it can be years before they return. By then man himself might well have become locally extinct.

It never happened because early man lacked the technology to dominate his fellow nations in the wild. He was governed instead by the same natural laws as they were, like them increasing his numbers in the feast years of good rains and contracting them in the famine cycles of drought, but always maintaining the balance between himself and his physical environment. Nor was the traffic between him and the wilderness in any sense one-way. The animals were a crucial regulating mechanism of his own life; equally he was one of theirs. From very early on man, as a group hunter, had a significant role in controlling the population sizes of several of Africa's largest creatures, notably elephant, rhino, hippo, giraffe, and the bigger antelope. Providing far more protein for the same investment of energy required in the hunt for a small gazelle, these animals inevitably became his favourite prey.

Later, with his discovery of the use of fire, man's impact on the African landscape and the other creatures which inhabited it became even more striking. Quite when, let alone how, man first learnt to ignite and manipulate fires on the continent's grassplains will almost certainly never be known. The best guesses range from 50,000 to 350,000 to one million years ago. Whenever it began the consequences were dramatic. Random natural fires, started by lightning, had always been a factor in the shaping of the countryside and its vegetation mantle. Regular and systematic burning by man, to move game or open up his hunting territory, was something quite different. Great tracts of savanna that otherwise might have been slowly colonised over the centuries by the African forest were kept permanently open. The grasses they were allowed to produce year after year fed the 'plains game' animals – the antelopes, zebra and buffalo – and in turn their predators – lion, leopard, cheetah, hyena, jackal and hunting dog. If the tree canopy had been able to creep forward, in many places most or all of them would have disappeared. Instead the grazing and browsing herds, and all the myriad forms of life associated with them, flourished as never before.

The exact nature and extent of early or 'ecological' man's influence on the evolution of the African wilderness is likely to remain as much a mystery as the dating of his discovery of how to use weapons and fire. All that can be said with any certainty is that his impact was ancient, far-reaching in its effects, and yet capable of being absorbed by the wild-life communities on which he continued to depend, and used by these communities for their own benefit. The discovery of farming and herding as alternative and more efficient ways of acquiring food altered the entire equation. Afterwards man was no longer a tightly-fitting piece in the jig-saw mosaic of the natural world, as integral a part of its symmetry as the soil, rain, sun and plants. He stood apart, triumphant but troubled, both master of his destiny and at the same time still inextricably enmeshed in webs of blood, bone and muscle, of hunger, fear and lust, of all the impulses and instincts he had shared for more than a million years with his relatives and companions on the planet, the birds and animals.

In the time-scale of human existence farming and herding are very recent developments. They originated barely 12,000 years ago. By then man, or his recognisable ancestors, had been on earth and in the business of living for at least one million years. Like any living creature, man starts off as a product of his past. His shape, size and weight, his physical skills, his eyesight, hearing and sense of smell, his brain and instincts and much of his behaviour, arrive imprinted on him as a package at conception. Modified where necessary very slowly over immense periods of time, they are the result of adaptations to the stresses and demands of survival by generation after generation of forebears, passed on through

34

the tiny programmed biological data-banks called genes.

For today's man the long corridor of human evolution means that only 1% of our genetic inheritance comes from the short period since our modern ancestors became farmers, herders and, as one result, city-dwellers. On the other hand, no less than 99% of what forms and shapes us is inherited from a past when we were hunter-gatherers. To illustrate it in a different way one might take a dark-suited merchant banker reading the *Wall Street Journal* as he rides in a chauffeur-driven Rolls Royce to his office in a Manhattan skyscraper. Only his left foot, encased in a smart leather shoe, owes its design and making to the era of civilisation – of cities. Everything else, his legs, hips, trunk, shoulders, arms, neck and head, his eyes, nose and mouth, even the pump of his heart and the bellows of his lungs, was engineered and tooled for the requirements of living among the lions and antelopes of the central African grasslands.

Of course such an assertion needs some explanation and qualification. Genetics is still far from an exact science. While the basic principles of how a creature like man is shaped and acquires his identity are generally understood and accepted, there are still whole areas of genetic inheritance to be explored. Under conditions of rapid and turbulent flux and stress, an organism may be able to adapt itself – and pass on the adaptations to its progeny – far more quickly than is conventionally assumed. The banker therefore may not owe merely his left foot to the 12,000 years of his civilised past, but his right one too and one of his arms as well. On the other hand, analysis of the molars and their enamel covering in the recovered jawbones of the *Australopithecines* show them to be virtually identical to the teeth of modern man. Teeth in every species evolve for a very specific function – to break down the favoured foods of their owner so they can be digested and converted into energy. Taken together with what we know of *Australopithecine*'s diet and our own, the almost irresistible inference is that we inherited our teeth from him.

Vast puzzles need solving, but overwhelmingly the evidence available supports the view that the mould which stamped us out was carved far back in our past and long before we turned to farming and herding. It was a past that lasted one million years. For 4,000 human generations, even as we measure them now in what would until recently have been considered unnaturally long spans of twenty-five years (by modern reckoning less than eighty generations have passed since the birth of Christ), man's life was dominated, encircled, almost measured by animals. They shared the planet as his equals. He lived cheek-by-jowl with them as neighbours. They were the first objects he saw when he woke and the

35

last before he slept. Their behaviour warned him of changes in the weather, of the arrival of predators which might attack him, of the revolution of the seasons. He watched their children being born as they did his. Sometimes he took in and reared one of their orphaned infants. The animals did the same with his own.

The relationship between them was so deep and intimate it is not surprising that when man began to develop self-consciousness – an awareness of passing time, of the past and the present and the future with all the vast perplexing questions the ideas posed – he looked at his fellow members of the animal world for answers. Many of the very earliest excavated human settlements have yielded vivid evidence of how he tried to grapple with the concept of eternity through the animals. When the archaeologist Emil Baëchler dug into the floor of the Drachenloch Cave in the Swiss Alps in the 1920s, he unearthed a stone chest. Lifting the chest's lid he discovered the skulls of seven bears, all neatly packed and facing towards the cave's entrance. Beside them, equally carefully arranged, were a number of the bears' bones. Digging deeper, Baëchler came on other chests with similar meticulously-stored contents.

For an archaeologist the discovery was immensely exciting. From other findings the site was known to have been used by Neanderthal man. The chests Baëchler gouged out of the ground were the oldest stone constructions ever found. More than that, they showed that by at least 60000 BC man had invested animals with ritual or magical significance. The evidence is even more vivid in the prehistoric cave paintings at places like Altamira and Lascaux. Over 80% of all Palaeolithic or old Stone Age rock art is devoted to birds and animals. Quite what magic was involved can only be guessed at. Much of it almost certainly had to do with ensuring the animals' fertility. Other rites which the paintings record seem clearly designed to bring success to the hunters. Some, where the large and dangerous predators like lion are shown, probably involved protective magic to keep man safe from their attacks. Others, much more puzzling to modern man, appear to deal with rites of expiation.

Early man was a hunter. To eat it was necessary to kill. The problem was that those he had to kill were his fellow citizens, the animal members of the other nations which surrounded him. He not only had a close friendship with them, they were his relations. Killing a relative, however natural and necessary for a predator, was never something to be undertaken lightly. Unless it was done with proper ceremony and the proper respects were paid to the dead animal afterwards, all sorts of misfortunes might befall the hunter. Its spirit might demand vengeance. The other members of its herd might be offended and leave the range. In an uncer-

Thomson's gazelle, Kenya

tain world, where every cloud that darkened the sun might be a portent, almost anything was possible. So the hunter took great care to honour his prey and cleanse himself of the shedding of its blood. By the time of King Cyrus and the Persian Empire, the need to kill wild animals as a fundamental requirement of human existence had long since vanished. Agriculture and herds of domestic stock supplied all the food man needed. Theoretically, hunting should have withered away and disappeared in the buried middens of prehistory, together with Stone Age

37

man's flint axes and bone arrows. In practice, no such thing happened. On the contrary, as Cyrus' game parks and the Assyrians' lion-breeding programmes show, hunting flourished. It developed, of course, into a very different activity from that practised for the previous million years. It was largely shorn of its taboos and magic rituals, although codes of 'fair' hunting gradually emerged later in various societies, notably in Britain and Europe. It became an organised sport which was both a test and, practised successfully, a proof of the right to kingship. The Egyptian Pharaohs had their triumphs in the chase recorded on carved stone friezes and displayed to the public as evidence of their authority. Following the lead of the kings, hunting was taken up by the nobility in many countries and jealously guarded as a symbol of wealth and power. Between the tenth and twelfth centuries, countless European farmers were forbidden to hunt their land, which remained the right of the feudal overlord. By the fifteenth century, they were allowed to scare off game from their crops, but the penalties for even mildly wounding a beast of the chase remained brutal.

The basic nature of hunting has never changed. From the start it has demanded patience, laboriously-acquired skills, exposure to heat, cold, rain and sometimes danger, including the risk of death. As often as not a hunt ends in frustration, with nothing to show at the end for all the hardship and expenditure of energy and money involved. Before the emergence of farming and the growth of human settlements, first as villages and then cities, hunting was unavoidable. It was the chief, and sometimes the only, means of supporting life. But for the past 12,000 years it has been obsolete. From well before the time of King Cyrus up until today a hunting expedition means leaving a warm permanent shelter, venturing into the open wilderness, and confronting a multitude of hazards – from the elements, to the weapons of one's fellow hunters, to the assaults of the intended prey. And the reward for all this expenditure, this risk, this physical and mental punishment? In measurable terms – nothing. The most successful modern hunt cannot yield the protein available at a fraction of the cost at the simplest village shop.

The only convincing explanation for what would otherwise be inexplicable, man's continuing fascination with hunting late into the twentieth century, thousands of years after it has ceased to be of any practical use, is that the habit has been bred into him. It permeates his blood and bones and latent thought processes. It is as natural and instinctive as the reaction of a domestic cat to a trapped mouse. The cat seems to 'play' with the mouse sadistically. In reality, the cat is not playing at all and certainly not with sadism, a characteristic unknown in the animal

38

world. It is simply testing itself, honing its reactions, obeying the instructions of genetic messages encoded in its body at a time when its survival depended on speed and skill. It is like an athlete unconsciously asked to go through a cycle of training. In responding to the chance to hunt, man is doing the same.

An understanding of *why* modern man still hunts can in no way be taken as condoning *how* he hunts today. His ancestors tracked and killed animals to survive. They studied them with fascination. They looked on them as their brothers and sisters. They hunted only when it was absolutely necessary. They killed the bare minimum and made their peace afterwards with the prey's spirit through elaborate rituals. The idea of hunting for something called 'sport' would have been bizarre, odious and insane to them. Even worse, if that were possible, it would have invited fearful retribution. The guiding spirits of the herds and of the sun, moon, stars, wind and rain which embraced them all, would have struck back ferociously. Witnessing a contemporary fox or otter hunt, or a shoot of driven pheasants, they would have watched fascinated and appalled : fascinated by the technology harnessed to crop the protein, appalled by the mindless waste and cruelty.

Hunting survives and thrives as a powerful atavistic impulse, almost as urgent in its need for satisfaction as hunger or sex. Yet while the instinct to hunt remains as strong as ever, deprived of its real function and purpose most forms of hunting became debauched and corrupted long ago. Examples of its perversions run through all of recorded history. Some of the worst excesses inevitably followed the invention of firearms. In a single afternoon in the early eighteenth century, for example, the German Bishop of Würzburg killed forty-three red deer stags, ninety-four hinds, thirty-two newly-born fawns, two roe deer, and ten wild boar. The animals, gathered in pens from the forest over the past week by his huntsmen, were driven along fenced corridors to a raised pavilion where the Bishop was entertaining his friends. As each terrified animal passed below him, the Bishop leant down, rested the muzzle of his gun against its head, and blew out its brains. Afterwards, he noted with satisfaction, his admiring guests congratulated him on his skill and bravery.

Yet paradoxically from the very start of civilisation hunting, even at its most debased, was the wild animals' staunchest and most effective protector. The reason was straightforward. For hunting to continue there had to be adequate wild animal stocks. Wild animals, as the earliest modern man rapidly discovered, competed with him for the land's resources. They ate the crops on his farms, they consumed the pasture intended for his cattle and sheep. Understandably, whenever possible he began to kill them not for food but as pests. If it had not been for the draconian hunting laws in existence from before the Middle Ages prohibiting the taking of game, Europe would almost certainly have lost all its larger mammals. Astonishingly, in what for centuries was the most densely-populated area of the globe, only one full species and three sub-species have vanished: the auroch (a massive wild ox), the Caucasian bison, the Portuguese ibex, and the wild horse. The last may well have been a natural casualty. A creature of open plains, the wild horse came under pressure when Europe's forests expanded soon after the Ice Age, and probably finally disappeared through interbreeding with the ancestors of the domestic horse of today.

The other three were unquestionably victims of human predation — the Caucasian bison vanished in a frenzy of slaughter, only partly for food, as recently as the time of the Russian Revolution. Conservationists look on the loss of even three species of large animal as grievous enough. What the toll would have been if the early hunting laws had not been passed and enforced is almost impossible to imagine. With one exception, for 3,000 years and perhaps longer (certainly from the time of King Cyrus until the middle of the last century), those laws and a handful of folklore taboos — it was 'unlucky' to harm certain creatures and, conversely, looking after others brought good fortune — remained the wild's only real protection. The exception was the creation in 1548 by the Mayor of the Swiss Canton of Glarus, Magistrate Joachim Baldi, of the Kärpf Game Sanctuary. Within the sanctuary, Baldi decreed, all the birds and animals were to be left in peace. Quite what prompted him to take this then-extraordinary step (it happened only fifty-six years after Columbus landed in America and forty years before the Spanish Armada set sail) is far from clear. Whatever it was, the Kärpf sanctuary stands out as a shining beacon in the general darkness and degradation of human attitudes to the wild at the time. Happily it still exists today, preserved as Baldi intended.

A further two and a half centuries were to pass before the next tentative step towards the creation of a natural reserve, as the term is understood now. In 1806 an expedition commanded by two American military officers, Captain Lewis and Captain Clark, made its way back across the Rocky Mountains after wintering at the mouth of the Columbia River. Having agreed to split their forces to cover more territory on their return journey, Clark took his half of the party up the Gallatin River and then across to the Yellowstone River. Running short of supplies he was forced to turn back before he could explore its source. With him on the expedi-

40

Defassa waterbuck, Uganda

tion was a former hunter and trapper named John Colter. The following year Colter discharged himself from the army, returned to the Yellowstone, and followed it upwards. He found the river emerged from a lake surrounded by an extraordinary landscape filled with bubbling mud pools, hot springs, and soaring geysers hurling steam and boiling water high into the air.

Colter, an excellent self-taught cartographer, made a careful map of the area, which he passed on to his former commanding officer, Captain Clark. For years the map, which Clark incorporated in his own meticulous survey of the American west, was derided as yet another example of the tall stories for which the early frontiersmen had become fabled. In saloon jokes the Yellowstone became known as 'Colter's Hell'. Then, in 1870, another and much more respectable expedition climbed up the course of the river. Its members included a US federal judge named Cornelius Hedges. Studying with astonishment the landscape charted by the maligned Colter, whose description proved to be no fanciful invention but sober and accurate, a remarkable idea came to Hedges. The area was unique, a miracle of nature. The whole American west, as Hedges knew well, was being stormed by the pioneers. Sooner or later Yellowstone would fall to their assaults like everywhere else. Tracks first, then roads, then railways, would pit and scar the countryside. After them would come the urban sprawl of towns, factories and mines with dust and smoke and industrial clamour.

The size of the recently-united states, Hedges reflected, was immense. There was an urgent need for land for human settlement, but the sheer scale of the country allowed room for something else too – for the preservation of untouched islands of the original landscape. In 1872, less than two years after Hedges' visit, President Grant signed a Bill which created the Yellowstone National Park. The speed with which it happened was extraordinary and a tribute to the energy and vision not only of Hedges and his supporters, but also of the President and the US Congress. Even more extraordinary was that it happened at all. The late nineteenth century, particularly in America, is commonly regarded as the most materialistic period in history, when the industrial revolution had finally completed man's domination of the natural world and he was able to use, or more often abuse, its resources at will. Yet in the proclamation of Yellowstone, America, to its eternal credit, gave the world its first National Park.

At the time men like Hedges, able to see beyond the short-term advantages of plundering the earth to the disasters which would inexorably follow, were rare but not unique. By 1870 the USA already had the beginnings of a conservation movement. New, fragile, and vilified by the majority, it had been pioneered by observers and thinkers like the Creole-born painter, John James Audubon, and the emigré Scot, John Muir. The fame of the wonders of Yellowstone, the movement's first tangible achievement, spread rapidly and the idea of Parks, almost as national status symbols, was soon adopted by other countries. In 1886 Canada created the Glacier and the Banff National Parks. New Zealand came next in 1894, when the hot springs and geyser region of Tongariro was protected. Australia's Mount Buffalo National Park was founded in 1898. Europe moved more slowly but in 1909 Sweden gave national protection to several areas, and from then on the pace accelerated.

At the start and almost without exception Parks were proclaimed for their scenic beauty. Beauty in the prevailing view meant the bizarre, the vast, the remote, and the dramatic. The more awesome and rugged a range of mountains, the swifter a river, the more precipitous a waterfall, the darker and taller the trees of a forest, the greater were the chances that they and their surroundings would be given protection. The protection was not so much against man as against the visual evidence of his presence provided by metalled roads and buildings. The criteria were aesthetic and the aesthetics were concerned almost exclusively with the earth's 'sculpture'. The living dimension of a landscape, its communities of plants, insects, birds, and animals, were considered, as far as they were considered at all, as a pleasant but minor element of decoration. An area of flat, drab and mosquito-infested marsh like the Coto Doñana in southern Spain, regarded today as one of the most vital and fascinating reserves in the world, would barely have merited a second glance from even the most dedicated conservationist of the late nineteenth century.

Then three further developments took place. The Parks had always had their bird and animal populations. As the unprotected land round them was colonised and ravaged by man for farms, communication lines, cities, and factories, the number of the Parks' wild inhabitants was swollen by 'refugees'. The result was that the wildlife became more visible. Not only were its numbers greater, but the animals protected from hunting lost much of their fear of man. It gave the human visitors the chance to see wild living creatures in their unspoiled home environment – the bears, moose, red deer, chamois, falcons and eagles which before they had only read about in books or heard about in third-hand hunters' tales. At the same time the realisation grew that it was *only* in the Parks that they could be seen. Outside they had either disappeared altogether, were disappearing rapidly, or had been made so shy by persecution they had become virtually invisible.

43

The emphasis in people's awareness of National Parks had changed. At the start a visitor looked with awe at a towering forest-covered mountain and noticed out of the corner of his eye a bear crossing a clearing on one of its slopes. Later he began to concentrate with fascination on the bear and only vaguely noticed the mountain behind. The change in attitude is still far from universal. It will probably intensify as the wildlife outside the parks dwindles still further. On the pendulum theory of human behaviour it could reach a point where, because of their rarity, only the animals and birds are looked at and the landscape is ignored. More likely, and certainly more optimistically, an equilibrium will be reached where the two, the animals and their ranges, lock together in balance and can be observed for what they really are – matching elements in a single equation.

In Africa this shift in focus has taken, and continues to take, rather different forms. From the beginning the priorities of nineteenth century conservation in other parts of the world, landscape first and animals second, were reversed. According to the values of the nineteenth century Africa had relatively little in the way of 'landscape'. There were, of course, exceptions and Africa being what it is – vast, extreme and prodigal – the exceptions were stupendous: the tumultuous cascades of the Victoria Falls, the soaring Ethiopian Mountains of the Moon, the plunging ravine of the Rift Valley. Much more characteristic of Africa's terrain, however, are dense and featureless forests, rolling grass plains and savannas, and huge areas of thornbush. Even if they were deserted they would still have many absorbing features, but they were not and are not obviously grand, strange or dramatic. They were not of course deserted. What they held, and in places, still hold, were populations of animals and birds so huge, dense, dazzling and varied that they awed the human eye and mind just as deeply as any snow-flanked peak in the Rockies.

Protection and conservation have never been an easy matter anywhere in the world. Every one of the earth's landscapes under attack by man poses different problems and requires different solutions. Generalisations, notoriously, are difficult to make. Yet it seems reasonable to say that preserving a mountain is relatively simple. Millions of tons of rock are very hard to destroy, however ferociously assaulted. A river is much more vulnerable. It can be dammed, diverted, tapped, or even drained; but rivers have a habit of surging back and refilling their original channels, and they will continue to do so until human technology can establish control over clouds and rainfall. Even forests, more fragile still, have a certain resiliency. The most efficient mechanical saw still takes several minutes to fell a mature trunk, and even when the trees have gone, their

Bat-eared fox, South Africa

seeds can remain in the soil for years – ready to spring back into life as soon as they are given the chance.

Animals are different. They lack a mountain's mass and hardness. Unlike rivers rain will not revitalise them. It does not take a few minutes and some heavy equipment to fell them, but a split-second, a single man on foot, and a piece of cheap mass-produced technology he can lift with a finger. And they do not leave seeds in the earth from which years later they can regenerate. Once they disappear they have gone for ever.

Africa in conservation terms is not rock or water or wood but warm-blooded life – its animals. Its chief glory is also its main potential tragedy. It has been so for centuries.

45

THREE
The Growth of the National Parks

When the Dutch Commander Jan van Riebeeck landed near the Cape of Good Hope in 1652 and founded the settlement of Cape Town, the countryside round Table Bay was teeming with wildlife, including elephants, lions, rhino, and huge herds of antelope. To the handful of colonists who arrived with van Riebeeck, it seemed as if they had found an inexhaustible living cornucopia which would provide them with unlimited food, trade, and sport for ever. Yet in 1656, van Riebeeck was forced to order his tiny group to observe certain restrictions on hunting. In less than four years the animals were noticeably dwindling. By 1677, still only twenty-five years after southern Africa's first white settlement, Governor van der Stel had to go further: he proclaimed a number of species of antelope fully protected. The herds were no longer just dwindling – they seemed to be on the point of vanishing.

What happened at Cape Town in the mid-seventeenth century was both the first manifestation of the frightening vulnerability of Africa's animals to the white man and his guns, and the first European attempt to do something about it. The initiatives of van Riebeeck and van der Stel proved largely ineffective. The early settlers, like their descendants, did not take kindly to authority of any sort. In any event, as they spread out inland they moved beyond the range of enforceable controls. There was yet another problem: everyone agreed that some animals – for instance lions, leopards, and hyenas – were naturally bad and harmful, and bounties were paid for their destruction. It made little sense to the settlers that the 'good' animals like the antelope, which in their terms were good only as a source of food and hides, should not be killed too. The well-intentioned attempt to preserve certain species at the expense of others proved as counter-productive then as it was to again and again in different ways later.

The pioneering farmers were only one of the hazards to the Cape's wildlife and, as far as their hunting activities were concerned, a relatively minor one. By and large they were too busy with their new landholdings to do more than kill predators and shoot the occasional buck for the table. Far more of a menace were the adventurers and professional hunters who followed them, drawn to the colony by stories of its vast numbers of big game. They slaughtered animals by the thousand and the hundred thousand. By 1702 they had exterminated all the elephants in the immediate region of the Cape. Fifty years later, with the colony well established and its population growing rapidly, new legislation was introduced to protect hippo, rhino, buffalo, and eland. It met with the same lack of success as van der Stel's measures had almost a century earlier. The colonists were too scattered, too ruggedly individualistic, too convinced of their innate superiority over the animal kingdom. The beasts had been put there by God for man's use. No human government was going to regulate how the settlers dealt with them. Their authority to kill came from the Holy Bible and they were answerable only to the Lord.

Not all of the colony's inhabitants were as stubborn as the farmers or as greedy as the hunters. Two Swedes, Sparrmann and Thunberg, who were employed as doctors by the United East India Company, became fascinated by the area's fauna and flora, and set out to study it. They were the first of a whole series of eminent eighteenth-century naturalist visitors to the Cape, men like Andersson, Wahlberg and Burchell who are best-remembered now for the birds and animals which carry their names. Their interest, efforts, and warnings were not enough to save several magnificent creatures. By 1800 the bluebuck, or blaauwbok in Afrikaans, a sable-like antelope with a shining velvet blue coat, had been shot to extinction. In 1835 the Great Trek opened up the modern Orange Free State and the Transvaal, and exposed their huge concentrations of game to the trekkers' guns. Not long afterwards, the true zebra or quagga, the 'wild horse' of the old colonists and known to zoology as *Equus quagga quagga*, disappeared, slaughtered so its hide could be used for grain sacks. Somehow the great Cape lion, *Felis leo melanochaitus*, held on until near the end of the nineteenth century. Then it too joined the tragic catalogue of Africa's lost animal nations.

By then the Free State Authorities and the parliament of the Transvaal, the Volksrad, had begun to be troubled by what was happening. On every side the animals were retreating. Life, even if it was only animal life, was ebbing from the land. The once quick and throbbing bush was becoming bloodstained and silent. The bloodstains were washed away by the rains but the silence remained. The effect was eerie and puzzling, and without knowing exactly why, a number of colonists become disturbed. As early as 1837 the Free State passed a series of strict game laws. The Volksrad followed in 1846. Offenders were liable not only to have their guns and ammunition confiscated but to lose their waggons too. In a pioneering culture where a man's waggon was everything from his home to his store to his fortress, the threat should have been more than enough to deter poachers. Yet once again the laws turned out to be toothless. The authorities simply found themselves powerless to enforce them and the massacres continued.

One person who was particularly worried by the devastation was 'Ohm' Paul Kruger, the affectionately-named 'Old Uncle Paul' who had become President of the Transvaal Republic. A legendary hunter in his youth, Kruger had undergone the conversion which has been experienced by many of today's best and most experienced game wardens. After being obsessed by hunting for years, Kruger eventually sickened of it. He realised that the power of his gun removed any element of skill or 'sport' from the chase, and that in any event its invariable outcome, the death of the animal, was purposeless. He had no need of the protein and each time he fired a creature died for nothing except to satisfy his own vanity. Even worse, he saw he was contributing to the disappearance of entire species. In 1884, barely a year after being made President, he put to the Volksrad a proposal to create wildlife sanctuaries.

In late nineteenth century Africa the idea of wildlife sanctuaries was virtually unknown. The assembly to which Kruger presented it consisted of dour, pragmatic farmers. They believed in the Bible, in the family, in money, and in agriculture. If they thought of Africa's wildlife at all, they thought of it as vermin. Kruger's proposal was shocking, offensive, and heretical. Shocking because it came from one of their own kind; offensive in that he also happened to be their chosen leader and so, of all people, should have known better; and heretical because it was a clear repudiation of God's word. Kruger was not only suggesting the lowest forms of life should be protected, he was also arguing for precious land to be put aside for them to infest. It was nothing short of defying the Almighty and denying food to His own children.

Predictably, what followed was a bitter and protracted battle. Those opposed to Kruger were many and passionate in their convictions. He had his allies but even with their support and his own imposing presence and authority, it was a full ten years before he won even a modest victory. In 1894, and still in the face of virulent hostility, he managed to get an area round the Pongola River proclaimed as the Pongola Reserve. (It was sadly de-proclaimed in 1921.) In 1897, Natal established the Hluhluwe area of Zululand as a reserve. Meanwhile, Kruger continued to fight for another and much larger game park in the Transvaal in the Lowveld countryside. In 1898 he gained his last success when the Sabie Reserve was created. Soon afterwards he was forced to leave South Africa during the Anglo-Boer war, and he died exiled from the veld he had loved for so long and so deeply.

Sabie's early years were bleak. Although its wildlife populations had some degree of natural protection from the presence of tsetse fly, the area had been regularly raided for a long time by hunters during its cool dry winters. Throughout the Anglo-Boer conflict, it suffered from attacks by hunting commandos on both sides, who slaughtered its game to provide meat for their respective forces. By the end of the war the area was little more than a wasteland. Then, on the signing of the peace

Bushbuck, Kenya

treaty of Vereeniging, the victorious British re-proclaimed Sabie a reserve. In July 1902 its first game warden was appointed. The man given the job was a British army officer named Colonel James Stevenson-Hamilton. He envisaged a brief policing role that would last for perhaps eighteen months before he returned to his regiment and his career. As it turned out he had taken on a lifetime's work. Stevenson-Hamilton eventually retired in 1946. By then Sabie, enlarged and renamed the Kruger National Park, had become one of the wonders not only of Africa, but of the world.

Although the Kruger, as it is usually known today, was protected from 1898 onwards, for its first twenty-eight years it remained a reserve, only acquiring the status of a National Park in 1926. The terms Park and reserve are often used interchangeably. In fact there is an important distinction between them. The International Union for the Conservation of Nature has identified eight different categories of protected land. The categories, which are gradually being accepted as a basis for the conservation planning in many parts of the world, range from areas preserved in a natural state of 'deep freeze' for scientific study and where visitors are strictly excluded, to others where all the normal modern human activities are carried on and perhaps just a single species is protected. Two of them, generally abbreviated to 'Parks' and 'reserves', describe what most people visualise when thinking of a game sanctuary – natural areas, safeguarded from human development, where the interests of the wild and its creatures are paramount. The difference is in the degree of protection each is given.

A reserve can be created by a district council, a corporation, or even an individual. Its future is often decided by short-term changes in local conditions. The council may want the land for housing, a corporation may go into liquidation, an individual may die and his heirs decide to sell their inheritance for development. A National Park, on the other hand, is protected by the highest authority in the country, normally by a statute of its parliament. As such it is an expression of the wishes of the whole nation. For a National Park to be de-proclaimed, the spectre that haunts all conservationists, a new law would need to be passed overriding the old. Theoretically, National Park status confers protection for ever. In practice, of course, in a world of soaring human populations, social flux and conflict, and increasingly violent competition for natural resources, such an idea is no more than wishful thinking. Yet so far no National Park has been de-proclaimed anywhere in the world, although some Parks have had the size of their proclaimed areas reduced.

Early as it was by African standards, the Kruger was not the continent's first National Park. That honour belongs to the Albert National Park in the eastern Congo. In 1902 a German officer, Oskar von Beringe, who was exploring the border regions of Uganda, the Congo, and modern Tanzania, killed two large apes on Mount Sabino. He fired thinking he was shooting at chimpanzees. When he examined their bodies he discovered they were gorillas, creatures only known until then from Cameroon and Gabon in distant West Africa. Von Beringe's victims, which he slaughtered in their mountain home, were slightly different from their lowland relatives to the west. For a long time they were believed to belong to a new and different species, although contemporary zoologists now treat them as a sub-species of the lowland gorilla.

When news of von Beringe's discovery spread out museums in Europe and America immediately became keen to acquire specimens of this 'new' great ape to add to their collections. A number of expeditions were sent to the Congo, including one in 1921 led by an American naturalist and taxidermist named Carl Akeley. Akeley returned with five bodies which, preserved, stuffed and mounted, were placed in the American Museum of Natural History where they still remain. During his expedition Akeley also managed to make a brief study of the gorillas alive in their natural surroundings, and even took some film of them. He realised their numbers were small and if the demand for specimens continued, as seemed inevitable, they would rapidly disappear. When he got back Akeley drew up plans for a gorilla sanctuary in the area. The plans were brought to the attention of King Albert of Belgium. In Albert, Akeley found an enthusiastic supporter. The king had become fascinated by conservation since visiting the Yellowstone and Yosemite National Parks, and in 1925 the Albert National Park in the then Belgian-administered Congo was proclaimed by royal decree.

At the same time far to the south the fledgling conservation movement, in no small part the child of Kruger's vision, was beginning to make progress. The work of the courageous, determined, and incorruptible Stevenson-Hamilton, a man who as well as living by an inflexible code of honour and duty was also a shrewd and effective politician, was transforming the Kruger in people's minds from at best an eccentricity, at worst an evil perversion, into a source of national pride and pleasure. The problems he faced at the start, and in many ways continued to face until his retirement, were daunting. Large areas of the original Sabie had been shot out during the war and several species had vanished. Hunters and poachers, white and black, bitterly resented the reserve and continued to raid the wildlife that was left. Stevenson-Hamilton's resources of men, money and supplies were tiny. The reserve had virtually no

Springbok ram, ewes, and juveniles in Nxai Pan National Park, Botswana

roads and even less in the way of accommodation for visitors. He had been entrusted with the stewardship of a kingdom the size of Wales or Massachussetts but with the equipment to defend, conserve and exhibit a country garden.

Stevenson-Hamilton battled on. He was a soldier brought up in the iron belief that good soldiers never acknowledge defeat. His style of leadership was neither aggressive nor flamboyant. It was prudent, considered, almost painfully quiet and stolid; it was also implacable. Slowly the marauding hunters learned to stay away from his domain: retribution might be long-delayed but when it came it was remorseless. Slowly the lost animals returned as their pastures and woods became havens again. Slowly tracks began to link the different sectors of the landscape, rivers were bridged, primitive lodges built, and people began to visit the reserve. What they saw, the bright and shining communities of wildlife that almost everywhere else had been reduced to thin and frightened shadows on the veld, enthralled them. They went home, they talked excitedly about the Park, and others set out to make the same pilgrimage.

In 1931, building on the success of the Kruger, the conservationists managed to get a huge space of red sand dune, scrub-floored valleys, and dry watercourses in the northern ranges of South Africa, proclaimed the Kalahari Gemsbok National Park. The early Dutch settlers had the habit of naming Africa's new and unfamiliar creatures after their real or imagined resemblance to animals they knew at home. Wildebeest, for example, was a simple and convenient way of identifying a creature that looked a little like a wild version of the domestic cow. Bok, or buck, was the general term for the various species of European deer. Springbok, understandably in view of the animal's characteristic behaviour, was the deer that jumped. Gemsbok, the great long-horned oryx, was more puzzlingly named after the chamois.

The Kalahari Gemsbok National Park also represented an achievement of a different sort. Animals have their territories and ranges but naturally take no account of man-made political boundaries. The lines drawn on the map of Africa by the colonial powers not only arbitrarily divided its human tribes; they also sliced at random through the infinitely more ancient homelands of its wildlife. When reserves began to be created there were many places where natural logic dictated they should span a national border. The landscape, after all, was real while the line was imaginary. All too often human rivalries and jealousies meant the reality was ignored in favour of the fantasy. Reserves ended abruptly at some meaningless point on the ground commonly marked by an iron fence, through which the animals could only gaze in bewilderment at what

53

for millions of years had perhaps been their winter feeding grounds beyond.

In the case of the Kalahari Gemsbok National Park, sanity for once prevailed. The natural range of the gemsbok and the other animals of the area stretched from South Africa into the neighbouring country of Bechuanaland. The authorities of both countries agreed the border between the two should be left open and the Park should occupy the land on either side. In 1948 South Africa left the Commonwealth to become an independent republic. Twelve years later Bechuanaland, now called Botswana, also gained its independence and joined the coalition of its black neighbours in their struggle to topple the white regime to the south. On almost every prediction, the shared Park was to be one of the first casualties of the new alignment. Happily, the pessimists were confounded and the run of good sense continued. In spite of their governments' profound disagreement on almost every other issue, the two countries continued to share the Park and the border remained open.

1931 in South Africa also saw the creation of two other National Parks. One embraced the Addo Bush not far from Port Elizabeth, where the last elephants in the eastern Cape Province were struggling for survival. The other, the Bontebok National Park, was established to try to save the antelope whose name it bears. Early South African explorers and hunters described finding herds of bontebok so huge they were unable even to guess their numbers. When the original Park was proclaimed near Bredasdorp, only seventeen bontebok could be found to put in it. With the addition over the years of occasional individuals found elsewhere, the tiny group just managed to hold on. Then, in 1960, the Park was moved to a new site near Swellendam where the grazing was richer. Since then the herd has grown to about 300, and there are now perhaps another 500 bontebok in other South African reserves.

A few years later, in 1937, a further National Park was proclaimed near Cradock in the Cape Province's Great Karroo to protect the Cape mountain zebra. Zebras, members of the horse family, are much more usually associated with flat plains and grasslands. However, in the Cape, a race of zebra had managed to adapt to living on steep mountain slopes and almost sheer ravines in a landscape normally colonised by wild sheep and goats. For a long time the attempt to save them seemed to have come too late and by 1964 there were only twenty-five mountain zebra left alive. Then their breeding slowly started to become more successful and today the Park supports over two hundred.

When the maturing Paul Kruger began to abandon hunting and develop his vision of wildlife sanctuaries instead, South Africa was

54

almost exactly two hundreds years 'old' in terms of its experience of
the white man and his guns. East Africa, in contrast, was virtually
untouched. Ironically, at the very moment when the idea for the Sabie
reserve took shape in Kruger's mind, two thousand miles to the north
the first wave of explorers and hunters was flooding over the virgin
East African plains and grasslands. They found the same vast concentrations of animals Kruger's ancestors had discovered in the south, and they
set about annihilating them with the same manic gusto. Fortunately for
the wild, a few lessons had been learned in the two centuries since van
Riebeeck landed at the Cape. Numberless as the herds of Africa's animals
seemed to be, they were not, it was now acknowledged by at least some
colonists, infinite. If uncontrolled hunting was allowed, the herds would
vanish. It had happened in the south and there was no reason why the
pattern should not be repeated in the equally game-rich east.

Whether that mattered, or why it might matter, were still open questions. No one had any very clear answers. There was still little more
than a vague sense of disquiet, the same troubled awareness of blood
wastefully staining the bush and life somehow draining from the clean
fresh land that had disturbed the members of Transvaal's Volksrad. However unfocussed, the anxiety was enough to ensure that in the early twentieth century, after the imperial powers – Britain, France, Germany,
Belgium, and Portugal – had largely finished slicing up what was left
of the new continent, large areas of their colonies were at least tokenly
declared reserves. The impetus towards conservation was given a
vigorous push forward by a congress which opened in London on 8
November 1933 called the International Conference for the Protection
of African Fauna and Flora.

The conclusions of the conference were admirable and, on the surface,
unexceptionable. Every African country without a reserve network was
strongly urged to create one. Wherever possible the reserves should be
given the status of National Parks. Particularly threatened species were
identified and their 'host' nations were encouraged to give them priority
protection. The key divisive issue only really surfaced after the conference had ended. It remains the most contentious problem, and the
one with the most far-reaching implications, in man's relationship with
the wild to this day – and the implications affect man just as vitally
as they do the wilderness and its creatures. What, finally, *is* a reserve?
What role does man have to play in it, whether as an 'owner', a manager,
or a visitor? How, in fact, does he stand in relation to the planet and
its living resources – reserves only being the planet and its life writ small?

The London conference was unable to produce even broadly-agreed answers. The Belgians, for example, came away determined on a hard-line approach. As far as possible their African reserves would be sacrosanct, rigorously cordoned off from man. A few approved visitors would be tolerated, although certainly not encouraged, in some restricted areas like parts of the Albert National Park. From other and more sensitive areas of the same Park they would be banned. Only scientists would be admitted and even their movements would be carefully monitored and controlled. The South Africans, in contrast, decided to actively encourage mass tourism by developing facilities in places like the heart of the Kruger – even to the extent of building chalets, swimming-pools, and children's playgrounds within the Park. Britain, then the largest of the continent's 'land owners', decided on a typically prudent and bureaucratic compromise. Britain would protect its colonial reserves as best it could and determine the most satisfactory future course of action in the light of experience.

More than forty years later it should be simple to assess the merits and flaws of the three approaches – and of course there were gradations between them – and with hindsight apportion praise or blame. It is not. The issues and the problems remain just as complex and intractable as they ever were. Theoretically, and certainly to the purists, the Belgian approach was not merely the best but the only logical one. If the purpose of a reserve was to protect the landscape and its wildlife from man, then man had to be kept out. The trouble was that the creation and preservation of reserves everywhere was, and still is, a political act: conservation depends on the will of the people, the voters, and the money they provide as taxpayers. People by and large are unwilling to vote and pay for the upkeep of places from which they derive no obvious benefit, and which they are not even allowed to visit.

From that perspective, the perspective of political 'realism', the South African attitude was much more sensible and constructive. By encouraging visitors and showing them the splendours of the wilderness, they would build up a base of support and goodwill to ensure their reserves' survival. Unfortunately, it did not prove quite that simple. The South Africans did indeed win a large measure of public support, but in the view of the purists the wild paid a horrifying price for it. The very appearance of modern man and his technology in a wilderness area unquestionably alters its character, balance and patterns, When his presence is accompanied by roads, cars, buildings, even 'planes, all of which are part of life in many contemporary Parks, the impact on the landscape and the natural life of its inhabitants can be devastating, even if it develops in ways the normal visitor is seldom aware of.

56

Cheetah, Kenya

TOP *San rock painting in Giant's Castle Reserve, Natal, South Africa*
BOTTOM *Buffalo, Kenya*

Wildebeest on migration, East Africa
INSET *Wildebeest in Nairobi National Park, Kenya*

TOP *Gerenuk browsing, East Africa*
BOTTOM *Topi with young in Masai Mara National Park, Kenya*

Leopard, Kenya

Lion, Kenya

Zebra in Ngorongoro Conservation Area, Tanzania

Marabou storks, South Africa

In one conscientiously-administered reserve a decision was taken to build a lodge for visitors not far from a fine stand of forest trees which sheltered a rich community of African wildlife. The lodge, carefully designed to blend into the landscape, was erected and quickly became very popular. From its balconies and viewing platforms visitors could watch a whole range of birds and animals at close quarters. Unfortunately any settlement of modern man invariably generates waste. A group of marabou storks discovered a food source in the lodge's rubbish dump. The storks settled nearby and began to breed, using the trees as roosts at night. Before anyone realised what was happening the trees began to die, their branches breaking under the birds' weight and their roots poisoned by the acid in the birds' droppings. Soon the patch of forest vanished and so did the birds and animals it had supported for centuries, leaving the lodge isolated in a wasteland.

57

According to strict environmentalists, such incidents are the inevitable result of attempting to cater for tourist visitors. In their view, the reserves which do so are nothing more than debased open-air zoos, where the animals' behaviour is as artificial as that of any performing bear penned in a cage as a curiosity in the nineteenth century. The arguments, which had started even before the 1933 London conference, continue to be debated just as fiercely today. Meanwhile the British compromise, apparently so bland and unimaginative, proved after all to be probably the best option available at the time. Or, more accurately, it would have been if the policy had been followed as intended, and if the turmoil of world events had not intervened.

Well before the London conference, Britain had gained Tanganyika – modern Tanzania – as part of the spoils of war following the allied victory over Germany. Amongst Tanganyika's chief glories were the Serengeti plains and the huge concentrations of game they supported. When the motor car reached East Africa and the British colonial authorities started to build a network of roads, Serengeti became a magnet for tourists and, more sinisterly, for hunters – both trophy hunters and straightforward killer-traders. Very soon they were massacring the animal populations. During the twenties, one small party on a brief visit slaughtered sixty-seven male lions, and left cursing the lack of luck and time which had prevented the tally from reaching three figures. In 1929, in an attempt to halt the death toll, part of the plains was declared a reserve, but it was not until 1937 that hunting was forbidden over most of Serengeti. Three years later, the area was proclaimed a National Park, finally achieving the protection that its brave, stubborn and often-frustrated warden, Monty Moore, had been fighting for with the help of his wife for more than a decade.

By then the Second World War had broken out. Remote as its main theatre of conflict in Europe was, the war was to have terrible consequences for East Africa's wildlife. The most immediate was to reverse many of the protective measures of the previous years and accelerate the carnage. After their successful campaigns in Abyssinia, the Allies were left with thousands of enemy prisoners, many of whom were held in camps on the floor of the Rift Valley. To provide them with food, the animals of northern Kenya were killed in multitudes. When the war finally ended, much of the game had been shot out, not only in the north but also in the southern ranges of the Rift Valley too. For the wild the situation was critical, but in another sense the problems had only just started.

Staffing levels in the reserves proclaimed before the war – and without competent wardens and rangers a reserve was a meaningless concept – had plummeted. Everywhere human populations were growing with frenetic speed, and the clamour for land was becoming deafening. Bulldozers and four-wheeled vehicles had made the most remote and isolated areas of the landscape, for long inaccessible to man, open to exploitation. Post-war colonial administrators were not merely uninterested in conservation, they were actively hostile to it. Conservation simply meant trouble. Good productive land whose yield might have fed hungry local mouths was being kept in cold storage by a romantic ivory-tower élite who had lost all contact with reality. Where poaching took place on official reserves, and it was rampant throughout East Africa, authority turned a blind eye. The people had to eat. If that involved illegally cropping a few buck, so be it. Far better they should grill a wildebeest haunch

Crowned cranes, Chad

over some remote bush fire, than throng the streets of the colonial settlements in hunger riots.

Not all the colonists took the same view as their superiors. They were just as aware how powerful and dangerous a threat hunger could be to any human society, white or back equally, but they did not see any merit in such a blatantly short-term solution – especially one which could only give a general official sanction to lawlessness. What would happen when the antelope and wildebeest had completely disappeared, as they certainly would, and yet there were even more human mouths to feed? A handful of settlers set out to challenge their masters. In many places they acted mainly from instinct, on the same deep-rooted but unspecific impulse which had galvanised the early South African conservationists. Like them, they were often ranchers and farmers, shrewd, hard-headed and pragmatic. Like them too, they were not always sure exactly what they were trying to preserve, but they had the same sense of something vital seeping from the landscape – and the same conviction that irreparable harm was being done to Africa.

In Kenya one of their most forceful leaders was a man named Colonel Mervyn Cowie. In 1946 he persuaded a deeply reluctant administration to turn part of the Athi Plains near the capital into the Nairobi National Park. A few years later the Tsavo National Park was established. In 1952 the Queen Elizabeth and Murchison Falls National Parks were created in neighbouring Uganda. Other reserves were proclaimed in Rhodesia (modern Zimbabwe), Gabon, Cameroon, and Senegal. The French, not a nation historically noted for vision or altruism, had surprisingly and to their credit proclaimed several important reserves in their African colonies during the 1940s, such as the Bamingui–Bangorna and the Saint Floris National Parks in Ubangi-Shari, and the Mount Nimba Reserve in Guinea.

Further south, a few reserves had been established in Tanzania before the First World War, while the country was still a German colony. In 1912 Kaiser Wilhelm gave them to his wife as an impulsive, romantic and pointless present, and they became known locally by the scornful name of *Shamba ya Bibi*, 'Wife's Land'. When the British took over the colony, they gathered the reserved areas together and in 1922 named them the Selous Game Reserve. F. C. Selous, who was killed by a German sniper in 1917 as a serving officer on active duty at the age of sixty-six, was one of Africa's greatest white hunters and naturalists who started his career as an ivory poacher. Later he organised President Theodore Roosevelt's hunting safaris and the two became firm friends. Then, like so many hunters before and after him, Selous' interest turned more and more to conservation. The immense Park was named to commemorate his efforts in the area; but its most important early guardian was one of its first chief wardens, C. J. P. Ionides.

Ionides, like Selous a Briton educated privately in England, also began his African career as an ivory hunter. By the time hunting soured on him, Ionides had become fascinated by snakes, which he studied and collected for zoos and research institutes all over the world. Known in Africa and far beyond as the 'snake man', he was autocratic, dogmatic, impatient, and, by the conventions of the time, eccentric. He was also a brilliant natural historian, an effective if sometimes arbitrary disciplinarian, and an implacable defender of the Selous wilderness. Today the Selous covers an area twice the size of Belgium, and in 1982 it was proclaimed a World Heritage Site. It is one of the splendours of Africa and an understandable source of national pride to the Tanzanians. The year after the Selous became a World Heritage Site, the city fathers of London were asked to approve a resolution by one of the city's councils to change the name of Selous Street, a tiny byway in the capital, on the grounds that it was an affront to black African sensitivities. While the request was being considered it was discovered the street was not named after F. C. Selous at all, but after a distant cousin of the hunter-naturalist who had been an artist and a local London benefactor. The discovery made no difference. The change in name was duly sanctioned for the original reason.

Now, while independent black Tanzanians celebrate the glories of what they have always known as the Selous, six thousand miles away in another continent to the north a handful of bewildered white Londoners are still searching a small renamed street for their lost mail. The incident, in its sadness, irony and muddle, is a vivid illustration of the fearful confusion that accompanied the retreat of the colonial powers from Africa – and continues to this day. As the winds of change gathered force and independence approached for many African countries, cynics predicted chaos and conservationists disaster. Once the black majorities achieved power, they believed, Africa's Parks would be swept away and the land seized for human settlement and farming. Much of the history of post-independence Africa has certainly not been happy, but to a considerable extent the pessimists have been confounded once again, not least those in the conservation movement.

There are today many more National Parks and reserves in Africa than there were in the days of colonial rule. A major part of the reason is unquestionably self-interest. On independence the new governments, particularly in the poorer countries, realised that tourism was a vital source of foreign earnings and the continent's most valuable tourist attraction was its wildlife. There was therefore every incentive to preserve it. In certain countries, allied to self-interest came a growing feeling of something more fundamental, a feeling that the wild and its creatures were an integral part of Africa's heritage and should be preserved not merely for the revenue they generated but in their own right. Once again, Tanzania was a shining example.

Shortly before Tanganyika, as it then was, achieved independence in 1964, a conference was held in Arusha. Attended by leading naturalists like Sir Julian Huxley, the conference was largely the brainchild of a German, Dr Bernhard Grzimek. A courageous and far-sighted zoologist who with his son, Michael, by then tragically dead after an aircraft accident in the field, had carried out pioneering studies of Serengeti's animals, Grzimek was determined to do what he could to safeguard the new nation's reserves. The leader of the Tanzanian independence movement was Julius Nyerere, soon to be the country's first president. Before the conference opened, Nyerere sent the delegates a message which became known as the Arusha manifesto:

> The survival of our wildlife is a matter of grave concern to all of us in Africa. These wild creatures amid the wild places they inhabit are not only important as a source of wonder and inspiration but are an integral part of our natural resources and of our future livelihood and well-being. In accepting the trusteeship of our wildlife we solemnly declare that we will do everything in our power to make sure that our children's grandchildren will be able to enjoy this rich and precious inheritance. The conservation of wildlife and wild places calls for specialist knowledge, trained manpower and money, and we look to other nations to cooperate in this important task − the success or failure of which not only affects the Continent of Africa but the rest of the world as well.

Nyerere's pledge was honoured. Of Tanzania's ten National Parks, no less than seven were created after independence; so too were over half of its game reserves. Today, about 12% of the country's land surface, some 46,000 square miles, is under protection. Further to the south in Botswana, which became independent two years later, the proportion is even higher: almost 17% of the country is National Park or reserve. Most other African nations have opted to follow the same policy, even if not on the same scale. There are now relatively few of the continent's many different landscapes, habitats and animal communities of which fragments or samples are not conserved in one or more of the thirty-eight countries (including Madagascar) ranging southwards from the Sahara to the Cape.

FOUR
Life in the African Landscape

Falling asleep at night after the first day of a first expedition to an African reserve, the visitor's mind will probably be crowded with images of sunlight, landscape, and animals.

Other impressions will jostle for space, too. The freshness of the dawn breeze at the day's start, the changing colours of the grass and trees as the sun climbed higher, the passage of clouds and the calls of strange brilliantly-plumaged birds, the scents of dust, crushed herbs, and wood-smoke from the evening fire. But the first three, the sunlight, the landscape, and the animals, will be the dominant memories. Sunlight and landscape, however dazzling and varied, are common features of the human experience. Animals, particularly Africa's animals, are different.

Seen in the wild for the first time, some species of African wildlife – like elephant, lion, zebra, and giraffe – will be instantly recognisable. Many others, particularly among the antelopes and gazelles, will be much less familiar and harder to identify. For a while they tend to blur into a single group. Then, as the days pass and the watcher's eye becomes sharper and more knowledgeable, the group separates and individual identities begin to emerge. A sable antelope becomes quite distinct from a roan, a hartebeest from a gemsbok, a puku from a lechwe. They are no longer all part of the same amorphous throng, but distinct individuals from different nations and races.

At the same time, if the safari (an African word for a journey) is long enough, the visitor will probably begin to notice other differences and make other connections. Several of the now clearly-distinguishable members of the antelope family will be seen grazing on one stretch of landscape. As the safari continues the landscape changes, and so does the composition of the herds. Some of the species in an area travelled through earlier will still be there while others will have vanished to be replaced by new ones. What becomes apparent, in fact, is a direct link between the types of landscape and the animals found there. The herds of the various species are not scattered at random, as may have seemed the case at the start. Each species is anchored to a particular sort of terrain – or more precisely, because the animals are evidently feeding, to the particular type of vegetation that covers it.

The pattern of landscape and animals changing in unison does not only apply to the African reserves' largest and most striking inhabitants;

Impala in flight, Kenya

it holds good equally, as it does everywhere else in the world, for every form of African wildlife, from mongooses to mosquitoes, wild cats to bees, puff adders to eagles. All of them, along with the hundreds of thousands of other creatures which make up the continent's wilderness community, change as the landscape and its vegetation changes. From the start to the end of their lives, every one of them depends on Africa's plants.

The plants, in turn, depend upon soil, sunlight and, crucially, water. Very broadly, the type of vegetation covering any given area of land reflects the annual amount of rainfall it gets. In an area where less than five inches fall a year, only a few highly-specialised plants are able to grow and the ground remains desert. If in the same place the rains were to rise to fifteen inches a year, they would produce grass plain and scattered bush. And if they increased even more to fifty inches annually, the rains would eventually create forest.

Of course, within that simple formula there is an almost infinite number of variations. The type of soil on which the rain falls — whether it is deep, absorbent loam or a shallow layer of earth over a rocky base — is a major factor in deciding what grows there. So too is the temperature on the ground and the rate at which the rain evaporates. Altitude plays a significant role: the same amount of rain falling on a mountain flank will produce quite different results in the valley below. Often the influences which shape the vegetation are apparently minute. The soil on the shadowed side of a boulder will absorb more water than that on the side facing the sun. Rain falling on a bush will evaporate faster on the ground beneath its edges than at the bush's cool, dark centre. In either case, a separate micro-climate is formed which will rear a different group of plants than those supported by another patch of earth only a few feet away.

The way the rain falls also profoundly affects the plant life on the ground below. Thirty inches in a few annual weeks of deluge followed by long months of drought have an entirely different effect from exactly the same amount of rainfall spread evenly over the whole year. Yet however the rain comes and whatever myriad factors affect the way the earth receives it, the result in all its extraordinarily subtle and multi-faceted expressions is the same, and the fundamental principle remains true: animals are both the creations and the prisoners of plants; plants, equally, are the products and captives of sunlight, soil, and water.

With the exception of the Ethiopian highlands and a few majestic scattered mountains, Africa has no great ranges to compare with the Himalayas, the Rockies, or the Andes. Aside from that, the continent contains almost every variety of landscape on earth. Desert, grass plain, bushy savanna, woodland, forest, jungle, marsh and swamp and delta, snow-flanked hills, volcanic bowls, torrential streams and rivers, immense lakes – virtually no fragment of the planet's physical diversity is unrepresented. In each, whether on land, underwater, or at the meeting-point between the two, the rains have created a distinct mantle of vegetation, a habitat – the word means simply a place to live. And each habitat provides food for its own range of wildlife.

In a sense, habitats are like individually furnished and stocked living-rooms. To that extent Africa can be seen as a huge mansion containing thousands of different rooms leading from attic to basement level off a maze of corridors. The majority of the mansion's wildlife inhabitants are firmly locked inside the room provisioned for them. If fire or flood sweeps over it, they remain trapped inside it and die. Even if they could escape, they would have no idea how to use the different furniture and supplies in another room further along the corridor – how its larder door opened or the plumbing worked to provide water. For them the result would be the same.

Other animals, in contrast, have learned across the centuries how to escape from their rooms when threatened by disaster. They have explored the geography of the corridors outside and discovered other rooms, provisioned almost identically to their own, into which they can move when theirs becomes temporarily uninhabitable. When the debris behind them is cleared away, the damage repaired, and the room restocked, they can return to where they came from.

Some species, across the same immense periods of time, have become even bolder and more imaginative. They have refused to accept being assigned any particular room in the mansion. Instead they use the building like gypsies, wandering the corridors as they choose, opening doors on every side and raiding whatever larder they find within. In the African reserves the last category is probably best-represented among the larger animals by the foraging baboon packs. Highly-sophisticated in their hunting-gathering way of life, they have learned to be omnivorous, eating everything from plants to meat, grubs to birds' eggs, carrion to fruit. As a technique for living it gives the baboons great flexibility. They can occupy a whole range of habitats from grass plain to woodland to mountain. Equally, if necessary, they can move between them as the food supply fluctuates seasonally from one to another.

As a result, baboons are among the most widely-distributed of all African mammals – found in more of its differently-provisioned rooms than almost any other species. To a considerable extent they have solved the problem many other animals are still forced to grapple with. The rooms they are given are not consistently stocked in the same way throughout the year. Their larders empty and fill according to the seasons. To a baboon an enforced change in diet is relatively unimportant. Whatever the month there is normally something left on the shelves, even if the stocks in winter are quite different from those in spring. But the more specialised an animal is in its feeding requirements, the more acute the problem becomes.

Fortunately for the real specialist – the animal which depends for survival on a single food source – whenever the larder empties of the chosen stores in one place it stocks up with them again in another. Africa's open-skied rooms are not tied to foundations in the ground. They are the settings for moveable feasts which follow the restless shiftings of the rains. To keep pace with them, to keep alive, many animals have to travel the corridors on migration for hundreds and often thousands of miles. In distance and sheer numbers, the largest movement is made by birds. Every year, as food supplies run down in the African winter, an estimated 5,000 million birds head north for Europe. There they fan out to breed everywhere from the shores of the Mediterranean to the rim of the Arctic. When autumn approaches and the European larder starts to become depleted, the massive aerial caravan takes flight again and returns south.

The passage of the migrating flocks is an awesome sight. On the Bosphorus and the Straits of Gibraltar, where they prefer to make the sea-crossing to Europe, the birds can blot out the stars at night and leave the daytime skies ribboned with endless cords of wing-beating travellers. Yet for every one of them which makes the journey, nineteen more remain behind. Africa's total bird population is close to 80,000 million. The rest, the residents, make their own, shorter migrations within the continent itself.

The distances they travel depend upon a number of circumstances of which the most important, again, is the type of their individual food requirement. Some barely have to move at all except in severe drought years; others make regular but short migrations. These can be horizontally across an area of the landscape, vertically upwards and downwards between hill-flanks and valleys, or a combination of the two. By and large, the more specialised a feeder a bird is, the further it may have to go. The two species of flamingo that inhabit Africa both sieve lake shallows for tiny organisms breeding in the water. The water has to have a certain alkali content and be at a certain temperature for the diatom and blue-green algae crop to ripen. It also has to be at precisely the correct depth for the flamingoes, walking on the bottom as they pump and sluice their delicately-engineered bills, to harvest it. If any element in the complex equation is out of balance, the lake becomes useless and the birds are faced with starvation. To survive they can be forced to fly thousands of miles, making a journey just as long as many of the flocks travelling between Africa and Europe, to find somewhere else where the algae are flowering at the right time and in the right conditions.

No one yet fully understands how the phenomenon of migration works. In the case of the huge flocks which make the twice-yearly journey between Africa and Europe, although the reason for their voyage seems straightforward, the means by which the birds complete their journey are more mysterious. As Africa's larder empties and Europe's fills, the flocks move from one to the other. Dealing with the flamingoes, among several other species, the puzzle becomes more complicated. For years on end a Kenyan soda-lake can provide the algae the flamingoes need. Generation after generation of birds grow up to depend on it. Then the temperature, the alkali content, or the water-level changes, and the larder's shelves become bare.

Addax, Chad

Faced with the catastrophe of famine, the flamingo flocks should wither and die. They do not. One night they will lift from the sterile water, take to the air, and fly south apparently without the experience of any navigators to guide them. Their destination will be somewhere like the flooded Makgadikgadi salt-pans of central Botswana. Many of the birds will perish on the journey; far more are likely to reach the Makgadikgadi complex safely. There they will rest and feed. Afterwards, as the Makgadikgadi pans dry out, the surviving nucleus of the flock will return strong to Kenya where their home lake will be filling again.

Parallel movements to those airborne migrations are constantly taking place all over Africa on the ground, although on nothing like the same scale as happened in the recent past. The toll of hunting, human colonisation, and land clearance has dramatically reduced the numbers of animals which rolled in vast waves backwards and forwards across the continent for hundreds of thousands of years. Today, even where the diminished herds manage to cling on outside the protection of the reserves, their natural journeys in the wake of the rains are increasingly blocked by cattle quarantine fences and other man-made obstacles. Yet a few mass movements still take place. The most spectacular is the migration of the Kenyan–Tanzanian wildebeest herds between Serengeti and the Masai Mara, when up to a million animals can be on the move at the same time.

As with the birds, the more specialised a feeder an animal is, the more it will have to depend on seasonal travels to survive. To overcome this dependence, some plant-eating species have developed techniques to use their habitat's larders almost as effectively as the baboons. One example is the springbok. A browser and grazer, its method of feeding as the year changes and passes traces an upright semi-circle through the surrounding vegetation. At the start, after the annual rains, it lives off the new leaves several feet above the ground. Then, as summer advances and the plants begin to die back, it progressively lowers its head and feeds on whatever remains, moving closer and closer to the earth as the dry months pass. By winter it is feeding underground, digging for roots and tubers almost as far below the surface as months earlier it had foraged above ground. Finally the rains return, the grasses begin to shoot, and the springbok starts to work up the other side of the larder's shelves until it reaches leaf-level again.

As they feed, many animals will travel considerable distances in loops, whorls, and zig-zags across a plain. The ground they cover may add up to hundreds or even thousands of miles annually. Yet they are not, in the conventional sense of the term, migrating. They stay year-round within the room assigned to them, their home range, and find whatever they need from its own resources. Other species, travelling much shorter distances, are often called 'true migrants', because they regularly change one habitat for another. By that measure, an insect which crawls down from a tree canopy as the leaves fall in autumn to a different environment on the trunk only a few feet below is considered a true migrant.

Like all sciences, natural science is based on the framing of laws and demands exact definitions. The problem with definitions is that they can all too easily become labels to be pasted over pigeon-holes. African wildlife does not fit easily into pigeon-holes. Migration, however defined and whether it involves birds, mammals, or insects, is a constant and fundamental feature of the African reserves. For the visitor, the best solution is probably not to become entangled with the niceties of how a scientist would try to categorise animal movements in the wilderness; better to look at the reserves as they are – spaces of landscape filled with a ceaseless ebb and flow of wildlife. Nothing is constant. The patterns rearrange themselves as in a kaleidoscope minute by minute, day by day, month by month – and finally year by year. Whatever happens, all that is sure is that the balance is preserved. And, once again, the arm which supports the scales is made from plants.

Blending elements in soil and water, plants use the process of photosynthesis, the technique of 'making with light', to extract energy from the sun. As they do they grow and spread out. The energy is for their own use. It is their very life. But once it has been created and stored in the plants' bodies it can be plundered by every other creature in the reserve – providing they can overcome the defences developed by the plants to protect it. If they can, if they succeed in raiding the plants and acquiring it, the energy is transferred to themselves. They then become its custodians and in turn make themselves vulnerable to attacks by others equally hungry for the precious commodity. If the attacks are successful the energy is passed on once more.

The passage or transfer of energy takes place through feeding. The plants produce and bank the stuff of life – every other creature robs them of it. The majority, from elephants to ants, do so directly, taking their nourishment straight from the vegetation mantle. Others stand back. They wait until energy has been passed from plants to animals – and then thieve it from its new guardians. They are the predators like lions and leopards on the ground, eagles and insect-eating swallows in the air. Others still are even more patient. They, among them the scavengers and vultures, wait until the second tier of energy consumers

70

Oribi in Gorongosa National Park, Mozambique

weaken and then plunder their energy stocks.

The sequence builds up in a series of interlocking pyramids. At the bottom, always, spreading out on a wide green base, are the plants. In a narrower band above them come the grass and vegetation eaters. Higher and narrower still is the next band, the predators. Finally, above them and narrowing even further, come the carrion feeders, which in effect live off all the three previous levels – the vegetation, the vegetation eaters, and the flesh eaters. At that stage the energy cannot be passed on any longer; no creatures have yet evolved techniques to acquire and use it. When that point is reached species like beetles, feeding off a vulture's decomposing body, return the energy to the earth. There it is absorbed by a new generation of plants and the cycle starts again.

In the African reserves the transfer of energy along the food chain does not, of course, always take place in an orderly progression. Energy can circulate for a time at the same level before being passed on to the next. An ageing lion, for instance, can be pulled down and devoured by a pack of hyenas. An unwary member of the hyena pack may then be caught and eaten by a pride of hunting lion. The pride may have an injured and therefore vulnerable member. The next night another pack of hyenas may run down the injured lion and feed off him. The pattern could be repeated almost indefinitely and all the while the energy would be circulating at the level of the predators. But the end result is always the same. Energy passes up the pyramid, returns to earth when it reaches the apex, and then starts on its journey once more. And even when it appears trapped for a time at a certain level, not all of it will, in fact, remain there. Predators do not consume all of their prey. Some parts, and so some of the energy, are left behind in the discarded bones, gristle, and hide. Other species feed off them and their gatherings from the energy bank will complete the cycle more quickly.

Equally, energy is spent by every living organism in the process of daily life, when it is lost to the living pyramid and returned to space in the form of heat – so making it necessary for the plants to be constantly at work retrieving it. The key to any animal's survival is to acquire as much, or more, energy every day as it spends. If it goes into debt on its energy balance, its life support systems start to break down. A hunting cheetah can run at speeds of up to seventy miles an hour, allowing it to catch up on a fleeing gazelle at eight yards a second. But it can only maintain its top speed for about half a mile. Beyond that, and taking into account the fact that a large proportion of a cheetah's hunting attacks are unsuccessful anyway, long experience has taught the animal it will spend more than it will gain. So cheetahs very rarely launch a chase if the intended gazelle target is more than two hundred yards away. A combination of instinctive stop-watch and calculator has taught them that with every yard they race further they will, literally, be running deeper and deeper into debt. The same holds true for every other wildlife species. Energy must not only be available for survival – it must be available at, or below, the cost of survival.

If plants are the creators of the energy which animals need to live, then it would seem logical that the more plantlife there is in any given reserve, the more animals there will be in the reserve too. To a considerable extent, this is true. As deserts give way to scrubland and then to wooded plain, the numbers of species and the size of their populations rise. But there are qualifications to the general rule. Tropical or rainforests are the greatest areas of plant productivity on earth. A single small forest tree can weigh more than the ten or twelve tons of grass produced annually on an acre of open savanna. Yet the vast majority of the tree's weight is made up of inedible hardwood and the parts which can be eaten, where the energy transfer might take place, are out of reach of the creatures which would be able to use them. As a result, there are fewer animals in Africa's forests than on its savannas.

Savanna, originally a North American term, describes an area of grass plain with scattered bush and trees. After the rainforests, the African savannas are the continent's most fertile landscapes. Unlike the forests, the vegetation they produce is close to the ground and accessible. In consequence, the savannas harbour huge animal populations. Numbers alone, the counting of visible heads, have long since proved an inadequate measurement of a reserve's wildlife populations. However rich and fertile any space of landscape is, it can only raise a finite amount of plants – and so create a finite amount of energy to support its animals. As different species tap into its energy in many different ways and on many different levels, the concept of animal biomass has come into existence instead.

The animal biomass is the total weight of all the living creatures which a landscape can support. For the purposes of reaching it all the animals there, from elephants to mice to ants, are hypothetically loaded into the same bowl on the scales and then weighed. It is clearly not an easy exercise. The weight of the larger species, which can be counted individually, is relatively simple to calculate. For instance the exact number of elephants in a herd can be obtained and a remarkably accurate estimate of their combined tonnage worked out, which even reflects the different sizes of the males, females, and young. As the species grow smaller, counting and estimating become more and more difficult. By the time a biol-

Honeybadger, East Africa

ogist is dealing with, say, different varieties of rats and mice, let alone the grazing ants, it turns into a matter of informed guesswork based on samples taken from a tiny fraction of a landscape's surface.

The problem is compounded by the fact that, pound for equal pound, different species feeding off the same vegetation layer need to take different amounts of energy from it. In general terms, the smaller an animal the more energy it requires to go about its business. Five tons of mice in a reserve will eat more plant matter than a five-ton elephant. Despite these difficulties, calculating the biomass remains the best way yet devised of measuring a reserve's animal communities. The landscape can only produce so much plant-derived energy; the biomass is the living population that energy can support.

In some particularly fertile savannas, the biomass can be almost as heavy as fifty living tons on every square mile. The reason for the huge weight of animals is not only the richness of the well-watered soil that produces the thick vegetation, but the different ways in which the many creatures that make up the biomass crop the plants and each other as they use it. A visitor watching herds of animals grazing a plain in a reserve might understandably assume they must all be feeding from the same plants in the same way. The plain's grass covering looks the same,

74

so does the slow drifting movement of the herds' passage across it. The truth is quite different.

The grass layer is not made up of one species but many – all as distinct from each other, in spite of their seasonally common spring-green or summer-gold colours, as the animals are themselves. Some of the herds will be feeding exclusively on one group of grasses, other herds just as exclusively on another. Other herds still will be sharing the same grasses but eating them at slightly different stages of their growth. Zebra, wildebeest, and hartebeest, can all crop the same pasture sown with the same plants at the same season of the year without ever intruding on each other. They all have separate requirements which the landscape can meet without strain.

The landscape will not only be mantled with grasses. It will have shrubs, bushes, and trees too. Further species, the browsers, will be feeding off them, taking shoots, leaves, and twigs often at considerable distances above the ground. Some animals, the combined browsers and grazers, have learned how to use the two techniques: they can crop the plain both at grass and undergrowth levels. Whatever system an animal uses to tap the plants' energy, and each one has evolved over millions of years, it will not compete with a neighbour's. Competition in that sense is wasteful and destructive. Instead, the subtly different feeding techniques have developed to complement each other. Across the millenia, the natural impetus has been to see that every area of landscape supports the largest possible biomass.

Although a reserve's wildlife is totally dependent on the plants there, the traffic between animals and vegetation is far from being entirely one-way. As with every facet of wilderness dynamics, reliances are mutual. Many plants depend on animal life, whether in the form of mammals, birds or insects, to fertilise them through pollination; others use animals to help distribute their seeds. Hooked to an animal's hide or carried undigested in its stomach the seeds can be deposited to germinate miles from where they were grown. If a disaster then took place in the original habitat, the plant would still survive somewhere else.

Some animals protect the plants' general health. Topi antelope feed off the dried-up stalks of several grasses which most of the other grazing animals find unpalatable. As they do they help prevent a build-up of dead vegetation and so limit the effects of subsequent lightning-caused fires. Without the topi the fires, feeding on an accumulated blanket of combustible matter, would blaze like furnaces and incinerate the fallen seeds and root systems beneath. Instead, they sweep quickly and lightly over the surface, cleaning the ground rather than baking it. Elephants, in contrast, can change the very character of a landscape's vegetation. Uprooting trees as they feed they can convert woodland into open grass plain. Once the mature trees are felled by the elephants, their timber dries out and burns when fire strikes next. The seedlings in the earth are too small to survive the flames and gradually grasses, with their faster life-cycles, take over from the trees.

In the case of the elephants one group of plants benefits at the expense of another, though the benefit is only temporary. Elephants have large bones and tusks which require substantial amounts of calcium, and the principal source of their calcium is very likely tree-bark. Without calcium and therefore without trees, the elephants would die. So a natural control mechanism comes into play. When elephants have cleared most of the trees within a certain range and created grass plain instead, the size of the elephant herds dwindles: there is simply not enough bark any longer to supply the needs of the original numbers. As the numbers fall the trees begin to return.

First bush and scrub spread out from the rims of the remaining woodland areas, and the grasses retreat – unable to flourish in the scrub's shade. Among the new undergrowth, tree seedlings take root. Before, the seedlings would have been destroyed by the annual fires. Now, screened by the bush and scrub which halt the passage of the fires, they survive. The seedlings grow into trees, the grasses and bush draw back, and the woodland advances. Eventually it will recolonise its former territory. When that happens the elephant herds, provided with ample supplies of tree-bark once more, will start to expand, and another of the wilderness cycles will begin again.

The process is immensely slow and the time-span for its completion huge, to be measured in hundreds or even thousands of years. It is not a single phenomenon, an isolated event taking place in one part of Africa at a given moment, but one of millions of overlapping and interlocking revolutions continuously taking place all over the continent at the same time. Some revolutions complete a full cycle; others come to a halt at some point round the circle and branch off in another direction; others still dry up and peter out. Desert becomes grassland and wildlife moves in; the grassland evolves into forest and the animal communities alter; then the rainfall pattern changes, the forest withers away, the desert rolls forward once more, and the animals retire.

The African landscape is never static. Nor, of course – because they are only the landscape in miniature – are the continent's reserves. Volatile and dynamic, they are each, individually and as a network, bound together in a constant state of change. No visitor to an African reserve

Serval cat, Kenya

will ever see quite the same as the visitor the day before or the day after. During the night before a visit, a tiny shower of rain may have fallen. By the following evening the amount of available moonlight will have changed fractionally. Both, and an almost limitless number of other events, will have affected the wildlife on the ground below. The antelope herds will have arranged themselves in different patterns, the lions and leopards selected new hunting angles across their ranges, the owls chosen new flight paths, the bird-eating snakes new trees to raid.

They are all involved in an immensely elaborate series of manoeuvres not only to acquire the day's energy requirements from the landscape, but to make sure they control their layer of the energy source so it can support them in the future. While there is no direct competition for food between different species, there is inevitably intense competition between members of the same species. With a finite amount of energy available at every level, only a given number of animals of each type can survive. If its numbers rise uncontrollably a species will exhaust its segment of a landscape's energy supplies, wipe out their source, and at the same time destroy itself. To prevent this happening, every animal has had to develop mechanisms to regulate the size of its population.

77

Wildlife species have done this by dividing the landscape into an intricate tapestry of territories and ranges. A territory is essentially the most important space in an animal's world – its breeding-ground, the place where it perpetuates itself. As such it is a fortress and inviolable. It is defended by its owner until death, or until defeat in battle by an invader forces the owner to give it up. A range, which encompasses the area where an animal feeds, is occupied more loosely. Several members of the same species can share a common range, while only one individual, or a group of individuals where a species functions in groups, can hold a territory. In certain animals there is no distinction between the two. To hyenas, a group animal, they are indivisible. A hyena pack needs the same amount of land to provide its food as it does to breed – and it guards its dual-purpose sector of the landscape against any intruder of its own kind.

Hyenas defend their room in the African mansion in compact well-organised packs led by the females – larger and more aggressive than the males. Lions, another group animal, have adopted a different technique. The female, the lioness, is smaller than the male lion. Unlike hyenas, where both sexes congregate and work together, lions and lionesses lead separate lives, although sharing the same territory. If a foreign lioness attempts to move into the group's territory, the females will drive her off; the male lions will do the same if a strange male appears. But both will tolerate the appearance of a member of the opposite sex. The reason almost certainly is to create a genetic mix for future generations. A stranger's arrival, at the right time, under the right circumstances, and at the right level of the pride's hierarchy, introduces new blood to the group and is therefore accepted.

Some species hold the same territory for most or all of their lives. In others the length of time varies widely, depending on factors like the changing patterns of available food over the year and the pressures of fighting during the mating season. A waterbuck will keep its territory for several years. On the other hand, its near relative, the kob, can only hold on to a territory for ten days or so before being forced to find a new one. During the rut, wildebeest may hold their territories for as little as a few hours. Then, because the females have moved on, the males – among the ungulates only males defend territories – have to abandon their ground and move on too.

In the last two cases the area of a territory is tiny and its purpose almost entirely symbolic. But whether tiny and symbolic or large and practical, encompassing a feeding range as well, territories play a vital role in the existence of all forms of wildlife. They limit the size of each animal population to what the landscape can support without being over-used. And through the competition required to obtain them, they ensure that only the strongest and healthiest members of every species survive.

With territories so important to wildlife, it is not surprising that they are marked out by the wilderness equivalent of walls and fences. In the wild, walls and fences take three main forms – sound, sight, and smell, although each is used for other purposes too. Sound is a matter of calling: a roaring lion, a barking deer, a singing bird, will all be laying claim to their particular sector of the landscape and warning off intruders. Visual defence consists of display: an antelope will climb on top of a termite mound and show himself off to the surrounding plain, inhibiting a rival from approaching his ground by the image of his physical presence. Marking territory by smell is achieved by using glands and excreta: antelope encircle their territory with scent smears discharged from glands in front of their eyes, hyenas by smears from their anal glands, hippo and white rhino through deposits of dung and urine.

Soil, sun, and rain, interacting to create plants. The canopy of green, charged with energy, rippling out across the landscape. Bands of animals tapping into the energy for life and then passing it between themselves at rising levels, until it is eventually returned to the earth to start its travels again. The change in the animal communities with each change in the habitat. Movement and migration as the year turns. The shifting tapestry of range and territory. The different strategies worked out by the different species to organise themselves, survive, and breed. The slide-rule accuracy in the rise and fall of the animal biomass as the wildlife maintains its equilibrium with the vegetation, expanding in the years of plenty and contracting in the years of want.

These rhythms are the same all over Africa. Gradually, to the watchful visitor, they will become apparent in its reserves. Each is like a living algebraic equation of almost unimaginable complexity but which, worked through, always balances, always proves itself. Nothing is missing, nothing is out of place. There is not one living organism, from a lily to a sparrow to a rhinoceros, too few or too many.

Africa's Parks and reserves have been called the last fragments of the Garden of Eden. Their creation over the past century was the first essential step to saving what remained of the African wilderness, but it was still only a beginning. Once protected, the biotic communities of their wildlife, the complex natural associations of birds, animals and plants which made the reserves live and breathe, had to be cared for.

The process, it increasingly became apparent, required a new science – the science of wilderness management.

FIVE
Managing the Wilderness

In the shimmering midday heat a white rhino cow with a calf trotting behind ambles up through the acacia trees to a water-hole. Massive and implacable, they both look like creatures from some infinitely remote past, from a lost world of dinosaurs and pterodactyls. The other animals already drinking, a majestic greater kudu bull, a pair of glossy-coated sable antelope, a group of slender impala, prudently part to give them shore space. On the bank above, an old male baboon, the leader of a foraging pack, makes a desultory attempt to couple with a young female, abandons it, scratches himself, and digs out a grub from a tree-root. In the shallows a purple heron stands staring frozen and intent at the dark opaque surface. High overhead the silhouette of a hunting eagle circles the sky.

Apart from the occasional scuff of a hoof in the sand at the water's edge, the grunt of a warthog edging forward, the little splash caused by a lowered mouth, the drowsy air is quiet. Then, on the grass plain beyond, a grazing zebra lifts its head, skitters nervously, and whinnies. The zebra has spotted two crouching lionesses half-hidden in the long grass. At the alarm call the rest of the zebra herd whirls round, gallops a short way across the plain, hoofs drumming in a cloud of dust, and then turns to study the lionesses warily from a safer distance. At the pool the rhino cow and its calf trudge back into the trees, and the antelope fan out round the shore again. Silence returns and the constant passage of animals to and from the water continues.

The scene, or ones very like it, will be familiar to anyone who has ever been to an African reserve. Watching the animals in the heat and stillness of the vast and remote African landscape, a visitor can get the impression he is seeing the world as it was at the beginning – untouched and uncontaminated by man. This is what the planet would be like if man had never mixed his greed, technology, philosophies and weapons

Nyala in Lengwe Game Reserve, Malawi

in its affairs. The feeling is understandable, and in a sense it is also true. The African reserves are living fragments of the ancient landscape, of a lost and different world. But even in the immensity of the Serengeti or in Tanzania's vast and lonely Selous National Park, the idea that modern man is absent is incorrect. Generally unknown to the visitor, out of his sight although often close to the very spot where he is standing in the wilderness, a whole array of human attitudes, plans and support-systems are busily at work. Known collectively as 'reserve management', sometimes styled 'management by intervention', they are largely responsible for the fact he sees a wilderness at all — or at least for the sort of wilderness he sees.

The apparently paradoxical concept of managing a wilderness inevitably has an even shorter history than the contemporary idea of a reserve.

81

When the first modern reserves were established, it was generally assumed the wild would have enough protection if hunting, farming, and human settlement were forbidden. Free from those lethal pressures, it was thought, the animals in any given area would be safe. Within the protected enclaves they would breed and multiply, and the life of the natural world would continue in microcosm as it had done on a much larger scale before man's invasion. Some small adjustments might, of course, be needed. Faced with the virtual disappearance of several species of antelope from the Sabie area, Stevenson-Hamilton, the Kruger's first warden, decided to 'control' several of the Park's large predators such as lion, leopard, and cheetah. As a policy decision it seemed not only sensible but obvious. The predators took the antelope; the antelope had almost vanished; if the predators were reduced, the antelope would return.

So, in the Kruger's case, it proved. Once the antelope populations had been re-established, Stevenson-Hamilton ordered his rangers to stop shooting the animals which preyed on them. From then on, he decided, nature would be allowed to take its course – always given that man and his technology would be waiting in the wings to intervene again if nature ran off the rails. The painstaking and resourceful Stevenson-Hamilton was among the best friends and allies Africa's wildlife has had. But he also made his judgements in the light of the prevailing wisdom of his time, and he applied them on his own ground – a piece of ground that was unique. The Kruger was not only one of the earliest protected areas in Africa: it was, and for long remained, much the largest – only Tanzania's later-established Selous National Park is bigger. Yet what worked in the early days of the Kruger, it gradually became apparent, would not axiomatically work in other smaller reserves. Even in the Kruger's vastness, Stevenson-Hamilton's policy of minimal intervention – it was all he could do given his tiny resources – and then 'hands off' soon proved inadequate.

The problem there, as elsewhere, was the nature and dynamics of what science has learnt to call an ecological unit, or eco-system. The African continent consists of a huge mosaic of different wildlife worlds, interlocking but distinct, where man-made maps and borders are meaningless. Somewhat like a constellation of planets revolving round a sun, these natural worlds differ enormously in size and character. Some, like the East African grass plains are as big as a large European country. Others, a group of coastal lagoons for instance, may cover no more than a few square miles. Each, large or small, lives by its own rules and is to a considerable extent self-contained and self-sufficient. When it comes to creating reserves an area of coastal lagoon poses relatively few difficulties: the entire little 'planet' can be isolated and protected, and afterwards left to continue its life in peace.

Conserving grassplains, however, raises problems and issues on quite a different scale – and scale itself is the first. By the time conservation became of concern to the continent's new human colonists, Africa's natural planetary system had been randomly sliced and apportioned. It was difficult enough to get a reserve proclaimed in just one of the artificial and supposedly homogenous 'countries', as the arbitrary segments of the living planets were now called. When logic, wisdom, history, and all the observed rhythms of life dictated that a reserve should span the border between two countries, it normally proved impossible. With few exceptions – the South African–Botswanan Kalahari Gemsbok National Park is one already mentioned – national jealousies and rivalries sabotaged co-operation. A cast-iron grid, deadly and bizarre, had been welded and hammered down into the heart and lungs of Africa. The best the early conservationists could do was battle for a few tiny and artificial planets within an already artificial constellation – and hope.

The science of ecology, the study of the planetary nature of life in all its complexities and ramifications, is comparatively recent. To men like Stevenson-Hamilton at the start of the century, it was little-known, and certainly not in all the subtle and complex variations it embraces today. He, and his contemporaries in the field, were pragmatists: they often had a hunter's or a farmer's background, and the shrewd observant eye of both. They knew certain effects had certain related causes. When they saw an imbalance in the wild (such as the virtual disappearance of antelope in the Kruger) they took appropriate action. The first necessary step was to stamp out hunting and poaching. At the same time, 'controlling' lion and leopard was as obvious a remedy as weeding to protect a grain crop. Combined with other measures their rough-and-ready approach seemed to work, at least for a while. Then other and more puzzling problems began to emerge, both in the Kruger and elsewhere in the African reserves.

By the mid-1950s, the hippo population in Uganda's Ruwenzori National Park, carefully protected like all the other animals in the Park, had increased to a level where they were flattening the riverside pastures to bare, compacted earth. Nothing could grow on the animal-created brick floor spreading out from the water, and the hippo, together with a range of other grass and bush-eating creatures, were being forced to search for food further and further away. The problem was the reverse of the one which had confronted Stevenson-Hamilton in the Kruger. For the first time, it appeared there might be too many animals in a reserve, rather than too few. The solution was proposed by two young American zoologists studying the Rwenzori on Fulbright Scholarships in 1956. They recommended the hippo should be culled to reduce their numbers. The advice was accepted, the cull took place, and the results were outstandingly successful. Erosion was halted, the land began to heal, grass

Tsessebe in the Okavango Delta, Botswana

returned to the rivers' banks, and herds of other animals, by then severely depleted as a consequence of the scorched-earth effect of the hippos' overgrazing, grew back to their former levels as they started to use the newly-green waterside meadows again.

The Rwenzori hippo cull was probably the first scientifically-suggested instance of modern human regulation of an African wilderness – of management by deliberate intervention in a natural landscape. Stevenson-Hamilton and his kind had been locals, old hands in the bush who knew its lore and operated by simple, sturdy rules-of-thumb. They did no more than tend, prune and weed according to principles handed down by their ancestors. At Rwenzori in 1956, an entirely different set of rules was adopted. Scientists, in Rwenzori's case from a remote part of the world, were allowed to determine policy. Policy consists of ideas, human ideas. Policy applied to the African reserves means choosing what to save and what to kill. The consequences of the Rwenzori decision for every reserve on the continent – and every plant, animal, bird, and insect which inhabit them – were and remain incalculable.

From the start, the idea of management in African reserves, even where it was apparently as beneficial as in the Rwenzori, has had its opponents. Management tries to stabilise a reserve, in a sense to freeze it at a given moment, ideally when the amount of energy circulating within the area is at its highest level. But the wild, the critics argue, is never stable. It is in a constant state of flux and so too are its animal populations. They and the landscape should be left to regulate themselves. In reply, the supporters of intervention point out what can happen when they are. One of the most vivid illustrations of non-intervention took place in Kenya's Tsavo National Park in the early 1960s. By then, some twelve years after the Park's creation, its protected elephant population had increased to a size far larger than the Park could support. Desperate for food, the great herds stripped the Park bare of its vegetation and turned Tsavo into a wasteland. Then the elephants began to starve, and in the end more than six thousand died. For a time Tsavo was effectively destroyed as a reserve.

All other considerations aside, Kenya was and remains heavily dependent on tourism for foreign earnings. With its elephants gone Tsavo had lost its major tourist attraction, and the local economy was dealt a severe blow. Not surprisingly, from then on Kenya, in common with virtually every other African country, has opted for reserve management. The main aims in managing reserves were formulated by the Bourlière Committee during the first World Conference on National Parks held in Seattle in 1962. Since then they have been widely adopted and form the basis for most management activities today. Recognising that most of the world's Parks are not self-contained ecological islands but fragments of larger systems, and so subject to unnatural stresses and pressures, the Committee recommended that every reserve should be scientifically studied and an individual management plan drawn up to suit its particular problems and requirements.

What this means in practice varies from country to country, even from Park to Park, depending on the available resources of manpower and money, the level of the local commitment to conservation, the economic importance of a given reserve, and a number of other factors. Botswana, which in its reserves in the Kalahari and the Okavango delta has some of the richest and most rewarding wildlife areas in Africa, was also for years one of the continent's poorest and most inaccessible countries. As a result, only a minute portion of its tiny national budget was allocated to their conservation. On the other hand, the South African province of Natal, which in size would be lost in a corner of Botswana, is economically wealthy, dedicated to conservation, and richly-endowed with reserves which cover a whole spectrum of southern African landscapes, habitats and animals. Its wildlife department, the Natal Parks, Game and Fish Preservation Board, is imaginative, well-funded, vigorously-directed, and staffed by a large body of committed professional naturalists and wardens. In many ways, its activities provide a model of wilderness management by human intervention which most other nations would like to copy.

The Natal Parks Board has four separate but complementary divisions: administration, conservation, research, and interpretation. The administrative branch deals with all the many requirements of running a large, publicly-funded department, from the servicing of its four-wheel drive vehicles to the pensions of its staff. Conservation is the province of the men in the field, the resident game wardens, rangers and scouts at each of the reserves. Working closely alongside them are the scientists in the Board's research arm. Finally, the officers in interpretation – like most African wildlife bodies the Board has a military structure and all its members wear uniform – have the task of explaining to the public how the reserves are created, what they contain, and why they are important.

In charge of every reserve, the local commanding officer of its human garrison, is the warden. While he is the ultimate authority on the ground in his territory, entrusted to take life or death decisions at his own discretion, his principal task is to see the reserve is managed according to the master plan drawn up for it. The plan will have been prepared by his superiors, the senior staff officers at the Board's headquarters. In formulating it they will have been guided principally by the advice of the Board's research scientists. Before deciding how much and what sort of management any reserve needs, the scientists will have tried to guess the answer to one question which ranks in importance above any other: what is the reserve's carrying capacity?

Although an ancient and fundamental principle of all livestock-farming, the idea of 'carrying capacity' tends to be unfamiliar to modern city-dwellers. It means no more than the number of animals a given space of land can support without over-burdening its plants. If the plants are over-exploited, if they and the underlying soil are asked to provide food for too many creatures, a sequence of degradation starts. The animal biomass has to eat to live. Overloaded in weight and numbers, it starts to crop the grasses, bushes and trees down to their roots to acquire the protein it needs. Weakened by the demands the herds put on them, the plants are unable to reproduce and regenerate. Then the Tsavo effect sets in. The plants wither and die, the animal populations collapse, and all too often the ugly process of desertification sets in, when a once fertile landscape is converted into wasteland.

Working out the carrying capacity of a modern ranch in a temperate climate is relatively easy. The dairy or sheep farmer has generations of human experience to draw on. He is running together one or at the most two or three species of familiar specially-bred domestic animals. His pastures are sown with a few carefully chosen types of plant. He can eliminate many of the competitors for their crop with pesticides. And he can largely compensate for any vagaries in the weather or soil by using irrigation techniques and artificial fertilizers. In an African wilderness, the problems are infinitely more complicated. First of all, a reserve's carrying capacity is never constant, but varies year by year according to Africa's unpredictable rainfall. In good years with heavy rains, a reserve may be able to support ten times as many animals as it can during a period of drought. In several parts of Africa, droughts and rains seem to occur in cycles, but so far there is no reliable method of making long-term weather projections and very few means of compensating for climatic changes when they happen.

In addition, the reserve manager is confronted not by one or two species of animal feeding on a handful of known plants at ground level, but has to deal with perhaps fifteen different large creatures, and a multitude of smaller ones, cropping hundreds or even thousands of vegetation species at every level up to eighteen feet above ground – in the case of elephants, which can uproot even taller trees, effectively much

87

higher still. Unlike sheep or cattle, the behaviour and feeding habits of many of the animals will be almost unknown. In the case of the smaller and shyer animals which are active mainly at night, the creatures may seldom have been seen, let alone studied or counted. Yet every one of them is a consumer, an essential part of the biomass jig-saw, and has to be taken into account.

There are still more factors to be assessed. Domestic stock has no large predators: they have been eliminated by man. Antelope and the other vegetation eaters, in contrast, have a variety, including lion, leopard, cheetah, hyena, jackal and hunting dog. All of them play a part in determining the size of the herds inside a reserve, and the effect of their food requirements needs to be calculated. (Outside the reserves, under natural conditions, the herds determine the numbers of the predators, rather than the other way round.)

Carrying capacity assessment of the wild, like its parent reserve management, is a very recent discipline. Throughout Africa some fundamental 'new' principle is being discovered almost every month. In time, *if* time is allowed, it may gradually develop from a discipline into a science and eventually into a real understanding of how wilderness dynamics work. Meanwhile the best it can do, given all the variables and intangibles, is try to estimate what any given reserve can support at its optimum – in the 100% year falling midway through a cycle of good rains when the vegetation, the herds, the predators, and all the other associated forms of life are in balance and at peak productivity. In such a year the reserve may, for example, be able to support 2,000 elephants, 800 giraffe, 4,000 zebra, 15,000 wildebeest, 10,000 impala, 200 lions, and so on, without overtaxing the plant communities on whose health and vigour they all ultimately depend.

The 100% year, the 'Eden' year, is the exception and not the rule, as the wilderness manager knows all too well. What it provides him with is a golden top line from which to work down to the realities of the average. Past records and his own informed guesswork may indicate that only one in eight years is an Eden year, and that for the rest of the time the reserve normally realises perhaps 65% of its energy potential. That percentage should therefore determine its 'stocking level', the numbers of the various animals it can support in the average years. If management policies are cautious, and more and more are becoming so in the light of experience, even the average figure will be cut back to allow for contingencies, for an unexpected drought or an uncontrollable bush fire.

The carrying capacity assessment, and the prudent stocking level it recommends, is the most fundamental of all wilderness management tools and provides the basis for every reserve's master plan. Translated into the lives and realities of the animals it means, in the hypothetical reserve described, the Eden year population of 2,000 elephants is always kept at 1,200, giraffe at 480, zebra at 2,400, and in the same ratio for every other species. 'Culling' or 'cropping' the different species so they do not exceed the population levels set for them to safeguard the reserve's overall health is a task that falls to conservation. It is carried out only at certain times of the year, usually during the African winter, and is designed to cause the minimum distress to the herds or groups involved – no cull, for instance, takes place during the breeding season or just after the female antelope have given birth to their young.

Different species require different culling techniques. Wherever a country's wildlife department has sufficient money, the smaller herd animals like impala are more and more often shot by the warden, or one of his rangers, from helicopters. The right animals, bucks or does depending on which is in surplus and in what proportion, are more easily identified from the air; death from an expertly-fired shotgun is usually immediate; and trucks on the ground can be directed by radio to pick up the carcasses. The collected meat can then be sold, often at low and heavily-subsidised prices, to the villagers in the surrounding communities. Other larger animals pose different problems. In the case of lion, a surplus of young females is often absorbed without noticeable difficulty by the local prides. These 'extra' lionesses fail to breed, act as companions and nurses to the young of the pride's productive females, and then seem to wither away. Young male lions are very different. Truculent and assertive, they normally turn from the prides, driven out by the dominant male, and start to raid the farms neighbouring a reserve. In consequence, they tend to be stalked and shot by the reserve staff, using light-intensifying night lenses, before they can become a nuisance.

A much happier alternative to culling is 'translocation', moving the surplus individuals in a reserve's population of a certain species to another area where the species has either disappeared or its stock is below what the landscape can support. The technique of translocation was largely pioneered in Natal and resulted in the triumphantly successful 'Operation White Rhino'. By the early 1960s the African white rhino, once distributed over much of Africa, was on the verge of extinction. Hunted and poached throughout its range for its meat and horn (the latter not, as is often thought, in demand as an aphrodisiac, but as an Asian cold and fever cure and in the Arab world as a dagger-handle), the species had been reduced to no more than perhaps fifty individuals. This last handful precariously clung on to life in Natal's Hluhluwe and

Umfolozi game reserves. Even there the tiny population was under threat, but at the eleventh hour, with rigorous round-the-clock protection from the Board, the decline in its numbers was halted.

Like many animals, given peace, protection and stable surroundings, the white rhino is remarkably resilient. Within a few years its numbers had started to rise. Soon there were more animals than the reserves could support. The orthodox solution, culling the surplus individuals to keep the population at a level Hluhluwe's and Umfolozi's plant life could tolerate, was deeply distasteful to the Board. Culling might be a necessary management activity for a species widespread and well-established elsewhere. In the case of the white rhino, which had been exterminated in its traditional ranges throughout the rest of Africa but where pastures, now protected, still existed which were capable of supporting the animals, there had to be another answer. That answer was translocation.

The saga of how Natal's surplus white rhino were eventually redistributed round virtually the entire globe – and saga is the only word to describe what happened – is long and well-documented. At the start, only a handful of men were involved, among them John Geddes-Page, who later became the Board's director, the Hluhluwe reserve's warden Ian Player, and a Kenya-based veterinary zoologist named Dr A. M. Harthoorn. The problems they faced were daunting. Somehow a swift, wary and dangerous wild animal weighing over two tons had to be immobilised, crated into a truck, transported for hundreds or even thousands of miles, and then brought back to life – all without the inevitable trauma of the experience damaging or at worst killing the creature.

In Kenya, Dr Harthoorn had developed a prototype anaesthetising dart with a hypodermic needle at its tip. Fired from a gun at short range, the impact of the needle in the rhino's hide caused a capsule containing the anaesthetic to rupture, discharging the liquid into the animal's bloodstream. A few minutes later the rhino collapsed. It was then resuscitated by a hand-injected antidote and, while still only half-conscious, roped and guided into a special container. The container was hauled out of the bush, loaded on to a truck, and despatched to its destination, where the captured rhino was released. That was the intention, but often in the early stages there were dismaying problems and setbacks. Calculating the right dosage of both anaesthetic and antidote – the correct amount varied according to the animal's age and weight – was immensely difficult. Sometimes too much was given and the animal died of shock. On several occasions the darted rhino disappeared in the thick bush and could not be found before the anaesthetic had worn off. From time to time the antidote proved too fast in its effects and the handlers were

Red lechwe, Zimbabwe

suddenly confronted at a distance of a few feet not by a drowsy amenable creature, but by two tons of enraged pachyderm.

The translocation team – at the start the term 'translocation' to describe a wilderness management activity had not even been minted – stubbornly persevered. Over the years their techniques became more and more sophisticated, and the results more and more successful. Today, for instance, rhino are darted from helicopters, rather than after a laborious, hazardous and often fruitless stalk on foot, and virtually no anaesthetised animals are lost. The guns, needles and drugs used in every phase of the capture programme have been constantly modified and improved, so have the container crates and even the transporter trucks. By October 1970, a total of 730 of Natal's white rhino had been moved

– alive and well – to other areas, mainly in southern Africa. By 1981, twenty years after the operation started, the figure had climbed to well over 2,500. Groups of white rhino were established and breeding in reserves and zoos around the world, in countries as different as Switzerland, Taiwan and Burma. By then, the operation had been so successful that the IUCN felt able to remove the animal from its Red Data Book of endangered species.

The white rhino was not the only species to benefit from translocation and the often painful, occasionally heartbreaking lessons learned as the technique was developed. Its relative, the black rhino, has also been successfully moved to new ranges. So too have a host of other animals, ranging from lion to tiny members of the antelope family. In many instances the reason has been another wilderness management practice – 'reintroduction'. By the time the conservation movement gathered impetus in the years after the Second World War, very few parts of Africa had escaped the impact of modern man as farmer, herder or hunter. Many of the new reserves, and often the older-established ones too, had long-since lost a number of species which once inhabited them. Where possible, as part of the policy of trying to restore the landscape to its original state, today's wilderness managers try to bring these animals back.

The first target is to establish that a missing species was indeed there originally. A particular area may, for example, appear to be typical cheetah country. There may be cheetah in almost identical habitat on either side and therefore the animal, absent from the reserve, should be returned. For the conscientious reserve manager, informed guesswork based on appearances is not enough. There may equally well be an unknown natural reason to explain why cheetah are absent from that particular piece of land, and furthermore why they were never there. Accordingly he looks for harder evidence. One source is in the oral lore and traditions of the local tribes. Free of any dependence on a written culture, the information handed down in tribal story, fable and chronicle is often remarkably detailed and accurate. Another source is the journals of the nineteenth century European explorers, missionaries and hunters. A third, the oldest and best of all, is in the Bushman cave paintings, the rock art of the San peoples.

Even when the evidence is overwhelming that a lost animal was once a natural inhabitant of the reserve, it is not always possible to bring it back. Sometimes the reason is straightforward. A reserve that used to carry elephant may now be too small to support them. In other places there may be different problems, many of them still understood only partially, if at all. In an area that for hundreds of thousands of years unquestionably carried wildebeest, a reintroduced herd of healthy breeding animals may puzzlingly decline and die. Possibly the original herds used the reserve for nine months of the year but depended on another area of land with slightly different vegetation, now inaccessible because of the reserve's boundary fences, to supply an essential ingredient in their diet during the other three months. Alternatively their failure may be due to some disruption of the complex mechanisms governing their breeding habits. They may perhaps need a whole series of neighbouring herds with which they can exchange partners.

Some animals, in contrast, create difficulties after reintroduction because of their very success. The swift and elegant cheetah is, quite properly, categorised as 'vulnerable' in the Red Data Book list of endangered species. Throughout Africa, the cheetah is rare and dwindling. But where the animal is returned to a reserve with adequate protection, it breeds, in the words of one despairing warden, 'faster than rabbits'. The cheetah's natural prey includes antelope. Inevitably, several reserves have found their stocks of antelope, among them herds of species as rare and vulnerable as the cheetah, reduced to the point of local extinction following the animal's reappearance in their territory.

The brown hyena provides yet another illustration of the still-unresolved problems and hazards of reintroduction. Of Africa's two hyenas, the brown and the spotted, the wary nocturnal brown hyena – named the 'beach wolf' by early Afrikaans settlers from its habit of scavenging along the shoreline – is the rarer and more threatened. Like several other lost species, it too was once resident in several southern African reserves from which it has now gone. Quite recently in Natal, an attempt was made to return it to a suitable area under the Board's administration. As the wild stock was too small, evasive and scattered to be gathered and redistributed by darting, it was decided to breed from the few hyenas already in captivity and turn the young loose. Breeding captive brown hyenas, even in large and remote 'natural' compounds inside a reserve, proved difficult and frustrating. The early litters were consistently killed and eaten by their parents within twenty-four hours of birth. Finally, a group of young was successfully reared and released.

The young hyenas' contact with man had been minimal. To all intents and purposes they had grown up naturally in the same wild landscape which was now their home. Yet within days of their release, all of them had established themselves round the reserve's two hutted camps for visitors. Quite contrary to the mistaken popular view of hyenas as cowardly scavengers, they are brave, powerful and resourceful predators, capable of driving even lion from their prey. The released hyenas

93

Spotted hyenas in Nairobi National Park, Kenya

clustered round the camps because they had learned to associate food with man. They raided garbage cans, broke into store-rooms, and even attacked visitors carrying dishes across the few brightly-lit yards of concrete path between the camps' kitchens and the huts. Very quickly, and happily before any visitors had been injured, a decision was made to destroy them, and the rest of the programme was abandoned. A well-intentioned experiment, launched and directed by wildlife experts, had ended in failure.

Even more important than reintroduction as a management activity is its reverse, the elimination of what should not be in the reserve. Here the problem, which is particularly acute in southern Africa, is not animals but plants. Soon after the first Dutch settlers colonised the Cape they started importing and planting a whole range of 'useful' trees, bushes and shrubs, such as the South American prickly pear for hedging, in which they thought the local flora was deficient. During the eighteenth and nineteenth centuries the desire to change the natural African vegetation became almost obsessive, and new plants poured into Africa from

94

all over the world. In many places the consequences, totally unforeseen at the time, were and continue to be catastrophic.

The introduced plants, usually referred to now as 'aliens' or 'exotics', were largely immune from the natural checks which had evolved over millions of years to keep Africa's indigenous plant communities in balance. Equally, they were released from the similar constraints, like disease and cropping by insects and animals, which played the same role in their own home environments. The newcomers did not merely thrive, they expanded at an explosive rate, crowding out the African natives. Huge, ancient pastures vanished, rivers were choked and forced to change course, rich, many-faceted forests were replaced by grim and silent stands of foreign eucalyptus or fir.

Not all of modern man's activities are axiomatically damaging to the wild. Some advanced forms of life, notably among the birds, can adapt with astonishing speed to take advantage even of the manufactured litter which accompanies an urban culture. It has taken barely thirty years for the little European tit to discover that glass milk bottles with foil lids are an excellent food source, and to incorporate the cream at the bottle's top into its 'natural' diet. In parts of Africa, electricity pylons have provided nesting-sites where none existed for millennia, and certain birds of prey, having discovered how to use them, have been able to extend their range and increase their numbers. In Britain, the red fox, a quintessential animal of wild open country, has suddenly learned to colonise cities. But the tits, the falcons and the foxes tend to be the exceptions. In general, the landscape, its plants and its creatures have evolved together very slowly over immense periods of time, and further vast periods would be needed for any element in the interlocking pattern to adapt to significant changes in another.

When a space of African grassplain or forest is invaded and displaced by plant strangers, the original bird and animal communities normally have no idea what to do with the newcomers. Their patterns of life, their digestive systems and their breeding habits are all adapted to quite different areas of sun and shade, leaf and berries, bush and branches. A weaver bird is unable to build a nest from foliage it cannot stitch together. A browsing antelope cannot feed if the green canopy is suddenly raised above its reach, even if its stomach could process an Australian leaf. A leopard cannot hunt if the cover of the undergrowth is removed. Inevitably the birds and animals are driven out along with the native plants with whose lives their own are inextricably tangled.

Generally the process of alien plant invasion is relatively slow and the wilderness manager has at least a chance to fight back. A considerable part of many reserve budgets has to be spent year after year on trying to control the newcomers – eradication is virtually impossible. The campaign is labour-intensive and expensive. Spraying of modern chemical compounds is usually ruled out, mainly because of the unknown effect of their toxins on other forms of life. At the moment the best that can be done is to slash, prune and weed by hand. Sometimes the threat lies outside the reserve and even that defence is unavailable.

One important South African reserve is threaded by two rivers. Before reaching the reserve the rivers pass through large and recent commercial plantations of New Zealand spruce. Every year the maturing trees drop hundreds of millions of seeds in the water. So far the rivers have carried the seeds through the reserve and deposited them harmlessly in the sea to the south. But periodically the rivers flood and briefly cover miles of the reserve's plain where the soil is particularly rich. If a flood coincided with a seed-fall, when the water retreated the plain would be left sown with millions of alien spruce. Hardier and faster-growing than the native bush, the spruce would quickly start to take over. Theoretically the new trees could be removed, at vast cost, but only by repeatedly clearing all the vegetation over the huge inundated area. As that would create a dust-bowl, in practice all the warden could do would be to watch as the heart of the reserve, together with its teeming bird and animal communities, withered away in front of his eyes and an empty alien forest took its place.

Under natural conditions, of course, the floods that follow good rains are usually welcomed by reserve managers. All over Africa the supplies of water available to the wild dwindle every year as more and more is taken for human use. As a result, careful water management has become as important as any other management tool. There are two main ways in which a reserve's water can be manipulated: by conserving the naturally-available supplies, and by adding to them. Conserving water is normally done by providing a reserve's major rivers with a system of weirs and sluices. This allows the torrents of the wet season to be husbanded and spread out over the year, producing at least some flow even during the driest summer months. It can protect unique water-dwelling forms of life, which might otherwise become extinct in summer, and it checks the natural tendency of the larger animals to crowd round the few permanent water-holes and degrade the surrounding pastures by over-grazing. In the well-funded and well-managed large National Parks, like the Kruger, water conservation can be carried even further by the building of dams. These can give a reserve and its wildlife populations a measure of protection against a sequence of drought years. Sup-

East African montane rainforest at Mount Rungue, Tanzania

TOP *Highveld in Giant's Castle Reserve, Natal, South Africa*
BOTTOM *Sunset over the Linyanti River in Chobe National Park, Botswana*
OPPOSITE TOP *Volcano National Park, Rwanda*
OPPOSITE BOTTOM *Simien Mountains National Park, Ethiopia*

Mount Kilimanjaro, Tanzania

plementing a reserve's water is a matter of tapping underground supplies, where they are available, through boreholes and pumping the water to the surface.

Parallel to the management of water, and just as significant, is the management of fire. Long before the appearance of man, let alone modern man, natural fires caused by lightning were a constant and fundamental factor in sculpting the African landscape and the lives of its creatures. After the rains the grasses lifted green and succulent. Drying out after flowering they fell back to form a mat over the soil. Each year the dead canopy became thicker. Left alone it would soon have prevented the sun from reaching the earth beneath and triggering a new season's growth. Lightning, aided later by early man, ensured it was not left alone. A discharge from an electrical storm ignited the combustible dead grass, the entire suffocating layer was consumed by fire, and the plants grew up again.

In theory, leaving aside the almost unknown effects of early man's impact on the African landscape through his use of fire, the vegetation in today's reserves should be left to the natural modifications still imposed on them by lightning-caused fires. Whatever a human manager does, electrical storms still flare, lightning still ignites dry grass, and dry pastures are still set ablaze. Experience, however, has shown a natural phenomenon only works properly under natural conditions. Today's protected fragments of Africa are not natural spaces – they are much too small. A spark from the skies no longer necessarily promotes, or even regulates, a reserve's plant growth – it can devastate it for years, or even centuries. A fierce savanna fire will eat into the rim of a neighbouring forest. Once, the forest would have gradually expanded to reinhabit its lost territory. Now, deprived of the needed space encircling its trees, it tends to shrivel and contract. With each successive blaze the forest's territory becomes smaller and smaller, until eventually the last of its trees has gone.

To prevent this, and for a variety of other reasons affecting the health of his wilderness, the reserve manager takes over the role of the random lightning strike. Dead grass-matter is never allowed to build up to a level where an accidental blaze might incinerate anything the prevailing wind drove it towards. Instead the reserve's pastures are carefully burned on a rotating pattern which echoes the medieval usage of agricultural land. It means that throughout the year at least some part of the reserve has grass for its grazing animals. In the larger, unfenced reserves controlled burns have a further use. As animals naturally gather on areas of new grass, poachers set fire to pastures just outside the reserve's borders and slaughter the game when it leaves its sanctuary to feed. When that happens, the warden can entice them back to safety by fires that stimulate growth inside the reserve.

Poaching is, of course, a major problem throughout Africa, and even in the best-staffed Parks preventing it occupies a considerable part of the warden's time. It varies from subsistence killing, where a local tribesman enters a Park on foot in search of an animal for food, to wholesale commercial slaughter of entire herds by gangs equipped with trucks and automatic weapons. Although the subsistence poachers usually have relatively little effect on a reserve's wildlife, they have to be pursued as vigorously as the gangs to prevent a manageable problem from becoming an epidemic. The effect of the organised gangs, on the other hand, particularly on populations of elephant and rhino, is always devastating. The wardens do their best to contain the menace – they do not have the means to defeat it – but the task is invariably difficult, dangerous, and frustrating. The gangs have as little compunction about murdering humans as they do about slaughtering the animals of the wild. Many Parks are vast and their management budgets tiny. The manpower and resources necessary for effective counter-measures are seldom available. Often a warden only knows the gangs have raided his reserve when he finds the hideously mutilated bodies of animals left to die in agony.

The best short-term hope of checking the massacres probably lies in wider and more firmly-enforced international agreements prohibiting trade in wildlife products. The obstacles to achieving even that limited target are daunting. In a number of African countries there has undoubtedly been involvement at high political levels in the poaching business and the rewards it brings. The same has been true in some of the consuming nations, which import ivory, rhino horns or leopard skins and sell them on the retail market. Even where agreements are made with the best intentions, the difficulties of policing them and giving them teeth remain huge. A rhino horn or a piece of raw ivory is an easily recognisable object, but the poacher's poisoned net is now cast much wider and catches the living as well as the dead. Unless he has an advanced degree in zoology, the most conscientious customs officer is unlikely to be able to tell the difference between two small and apparently identical parrots, one of which happens to be common and the other so rare that trade in the species is forbidden by a treaty he is paid to enforce. When it comes to plants, just as vital ingredients of the natural landscape as its birds or animals and often just as threatened, the problems appear to be almost insurmountable.

The only real answer is a fundamental change in attitude by today's

Reticulated giraffe, East Africa

consumers of the carcasses of the wild. When the modern banker has finally learned the obscenity of buying his wife or mistress a leopard-skin coat, and the wife or mistress the obscenity of wearing it; when the rich young Arab, insecure about his sexuality, turns in disgust from buying a dagger with a rhino horn mount to advertise his maleness; when 'collectors' all over the world abandon in shame the idea of adding further pieces of carved ivory to their shelves: then, and only then, will the market vanish and the slaughter cease. Meanwhile, reserve wardens all over Africa will continue to lie awake at night listening for the sound of distant gunfire, and set out sick at heart next day to search for the blood seeping into the earth.

SIX
The Problems and Possibilities of the Future

The achievements of the Natal Parks Board, and there are bodies similar to it all over Africa, have been remarkable. They have shown that with research, resources, and commitment even a pocket of the natural landscape, a little splinter shaved off an original eco-system, can be conserved in health and stability. Using imagination and modern technology they have saved species like the white rhino from extinction. They have fought back against the lethal assaults of poachers, answering guns with law and good sense. They have not merely preserved vignettes of original Africa, they have restored vandalised areas of the wild, removed their alien invaders, repopulated them with their original inhabitants, and nursed them back to health.

Yet the science of wilderness management, still barely a generation old, is already starting to raise almost as many disturbing questions as it seems to answer. Virtually none of its practices, even those which appear on the surface the most sensible and innocuous, have turned out to be quite as straightforward in their effects as those who pioneered them once believed. For example, in a world where man is increasingly greedy for water, drilling boreholes to supplement a reserve's supplies seems a logical and constructive solution. Animals which would otherwise die will now survive. The reality is proving subtly but perhaps crucially different.

Even among similar and closely-related species of grazing antelope, studies are revealing marked differences in their diet. One species may feed off a variety of grasses; another may be dependent on just a few which also happen to belong to the spectrum of plants used by its relative. When an artificial water-hole is created, both species congregate round it. Over the years that follow the 'broad-spectrum' feeder progressively gains an advantage over its 'narrow-band' cousin. When the narrow band of grasses, used by both, is grazed out, the broad-spectrum antelope simply turns to other plants. The narrow-band feeder has no such choice: it must forage further and further from the water-hole to find the few types of grass on which it depends.

Eventually the narrow-band or specialist feeder can be forced so far away that it can no longer make the double journey from the water-hole to its grazing grounds and back again. Distance, measured in miles, is not the only limitation. A reserve boundary fence can perform exactly the same function. In either case when the narrow-band feeder's grasses have gone, it dies out, and after its disappearance the pastures are left to its broad-spectrum relative. The relative may be smaller and swifter, a difficult prey for predators. As a result, the lion, leopard, cheetah, hyena and jackal populations may decline. With a reduction in their numbers, the populations of the smaller scavengers decline too; so do the numbers of birds like vultures. At the same time the insect life of the reserve will be changing to reflect the altered composition of its vegetation. In the end the entire ecology of the area will have been altered.

Impala, Botswana

Again, while culling is now widely-accepted as an essential management activity, its consequences may prove to be rather different from the ones intended. Much modern culling, as in the case of the common and widely-distributed impala, is carried out from a helicopter. The herds are flushed from the bush in front of the helicopter, and the chosen animals killed from the air by shotgun. Given the need for culling in the first place the technique is probably the most humane and efficient available. The problem is that while ninety-nine out of every hundred impala will take flight at the sound of a helicopter's blades, one may lie up in the bush and refuse to move. Some warp in the animal's make-up will have made it a maverick, a freak in the herd.

Under natural conditions the warp would almost certainly have made the impala more vulnerable than its companions to lion or hyena, and so its garbled genetic message would have been eliminated from the stock. In the artificial conditions of a reserve, where the most efficient 'predator' is a helicopter, to be a freak can be a considerable advantage. The freak survives while the normal animal dies. Next year, having bred, the freak may have transmitted its strange behaviour pattern to its young. Within a few years there may be a dozen animals which refuse to run before a helicopter's blades. Meanwhile, the rest of the herd is being culled as before. Ultimately the original herd of 'normal' impala may vanish altogether, and be replaced by an entire population of mavericks. In that case, certainly as far as the landscape, the vegetation and the reserve's other animals are concerned, virtually a new species – as alien as the helicopter itself – will have been introduced into the reserve. The aberrant race of 'impala' may survive, but the reserve will never be the same again.

The problem, or more accurately the difficulties in recognising the problem, is partly a matter of naming – of the use of words. 'Culling', in spite of its long and familiar history as a term to describe what man intends to be a constructive intervention in the animal world, is in reality a euphemism, comforting but misleading. True culling in the wild is a natural process created by delicate natural selective pressures where the old, the weak, the diseased and the deviants are eliminated in the greater interests of the health of the herd. So far man, in the form of the wilderness manager, has little understanding of how those delicate pressures work. Even with the highest motives and after the most thorough research the best he can now do is to 'kill' what appear to him to be surplus individuals in a given animal population. Whether the ones he chooses to get rid of are those the wild would eliminate of its own accord is quite beyond him to measure. Recognising this, a number of zoologists have courageously started to insist that 'honest' language is used to describe the operation. To them, the annual cull has become the annual kill.

Other management policies, seemingly quite uncontroversial on any level, may have totally unforeseen consequences. In the relatively early days of the Kruger, as later in many other reserves, it was decided to put in a network of roads to allow visitors to see the game from vehicles. As petrol or diesel-powered cars provided the transport for the vast majority of visitors and as the visitors (as voting citizens) were the ultimate authority over the Park's existence, it seemed a sensible, almost essential, decision. The roads were built. In the first year they received an enthusiastic welcome. Then the winter rains came. The water ran off the roads' surface and drenched the soil deep on either side. Inevitably the African bushes and grasses found and colonised the verges as an extraordinarily fertile breeding ground. Within a few years the vegetation was so dense and high that the very reverse of the wilderness managers' intentions had been achieved. The roadside corridors were almost the only places in the reserve where it was impossible for the visitors to see animals – the game was hidden by the plants. That was not all. The waves of rainfall from the roads began to cause erosion in the surrounding earth; at the same time the behaviour of the reserve's lions started to change. For the first time in the evolution of the species it had been provided with absolutely clear and straight sight-lines bordered by thick belts of cover. Co-operative hunting in groups was no longer a necessity: the lions could take their prey individually.

Measures were quickly taken to restore the situation. The roadside grass was cut, where possible the roads were re-sited in less vulnerable parts of the reserve, and drainage trenches were dug to carry the rainwater away. As a solution it proved largely successful. Erosion was checked, the antelope dispersed naturally, and the lions reverted to their original hunting habits. The problem was, and remains in almost every African reserve where roads have been built, that yet another layer of human intervention had become necessary in regulating the wilderness. Every year when the rains fall the grass has to be cut back and new steps have to be taken to deal with the constantly-changing pattern caused by rainfall draining off the roads. Both activities are labour-intensive and both make annually-increasing demands on a reserve's budget. The roadside vegetation belts progressively thicken over the course of time and the surrounding land becomes more and more fragile each year as the funnelled rainwater cascades over it.

In other areas, the fledgling science of wilderness management is starting to come up with more optimistic findings. Until very recently, the only way to determine a reserve's carrying capacity was by informed guesswork. The animals were counted, the past years' rainfall records consulted, the likely future water and vegetation resources calculated, and a rough-and-ready stocking-level estimated. The larger mammal populations were then pruned to the appropriate numbers. Now a seemingly more accurate test of what a given area can support is beginning to be studied – the parasite 'load' in a wild animal's body. While wild animals carry and can tolerate far more parasites than domestic stock, the same principle of parasite loading operates as it does in any other living organism. The number of parasites ebbs and flows like a tide depending on the organism's health.

If an animal is well-fed and in good condition, its parasite tidal level is low. If the animal begins to age, sicken or waste, the level rises as the parasites take advantage of the weakening of its natural defences. At a certain moment, when its life-support systems have broken down beyond repair, the parasites overwhelm its body and the animal dies. In the case of an animal attacked by disease the process can be very fast. More often it happens slowly taking months or even years. By monitoring the parasitic load in the animals on his reserve, a wilderness manager can assess far earlier and more accurately than by eye or rule-of-thumb what is happening to the reserve and what it can naturally support. Long before deterioration in the vegetation becomes apparent on the ground, the number of parasites, which can be calculated either from carcasses or from eggs in the animals' faeces, will tell him something is wrong. Action then can stabilise a situation that otherwise might take years to retrieve.

With a few exceptions, disease in game has not usually been considered a major management concern. The natural diseases which affect wild animals have traditionally been seen as a normal population control mechanism, like the availability of water or food. The exceptions, however, were deadly and, until quite recently, impossible to combat. In 1896–97, when an epidemic of the lethal cattle disease, rinderpest, swept south from Central Africa, buffalo, eland, kudu, and many other hoofed species, died in hundreds of thousands or even millions. As late as 1970 a disastrous outbreak of anthrax almost exterminated the elegant roan antelope, a species particularly vulnerable to infection. Since then, vaccines against anthrax have been developed and where, as in the Kruger, a reserve has adequate resources, the roan herds are immunised every year by vaccine darts fired from the air. If another rinderpest epidemic broke out, the same action would be taken with rinderpest vaccine to protect breeding groups of all the species which might be imperilled.

105

Similar measures would be put into effect against outbreaks of rabies and lung sickness.

Such steps, in the same way as culling and water provision programmes, are now widely regarded not merely as legitimate but as essential wilderness management activities. Man, it is felt, has hacked through the natural planets of the ancient eco-systems, plundered their landscapes, and destroyed their self-sufficiency. If, late in the day, he wishes to conserve a few fragments of the past, of the vanishing world of his own beginnings, then he must apply all his ingenuity and the resources of his technology to the task. The fundamental problem, which increasingly preoccupies a newer and more thoughtful generation of wilderness managers, of wardens, scientists and rangers, is that the more successful they are in conserving and restoring wilderness areas, the more dependent on man the survival of the wilderness becomes. Culling, immunisation against disease, and the translocation of endangered species all require costly and sophisticated helicopters, guns and transporter trucks. Artificial water-holes need pumps and fuel. Roadside grass belts can only effectively be cut back by specialised machines.

The cost and other continuing requirements created by human intervention are, once embarked upon, almost limitless. At the moment, at least in those reserves where adequate funds are available, the results have been triumphant. Yet the triumphs are also, in the true sense of the word, artificial. They owe at least as much to man and his intellect as they do to the buoyant resilience of the natural world. What would happen if management funds ran out? If the helicopters, culling guns and vaccine darts were withdrawn? If fuel was no longer available to supply the pumps raising water to the boreholes? If the roadside grass-cutting machines were abandoned and left to rust? Would the roan antelope, prevented by immunisation from developing its own defences against anthrax, collapse and disappear at the next onset of the disease? The buffalo, eland, and kudu vanish when rinderpest struck? The herds of impala, carefully culled for years, explode in numbers and then wither into nothingness as, unprepared and subject to no control, artificial or otherwise, they exhausted the vegetation? Would the lion populations, hunting the man-made belts of roadside grass, crash when their prey deserted them?

The answers are unknown. For the present, almost everyone actively involved in reserve management accepts that some form of human intervention is inevitable. Ecological man, hunter-gatherer man, was just as natural a factor in shaping and regulating the ancient landscape as the elephant or the leopard. With his disappearance modern man has to take

106

on a comparable, if much more extensive, role. At the same time, more and more concerned wardens and scientists are starting to search for ways to cut down the degree of human intervention and return the regulation of the wild to the wild. The planets of Africa's eco-systems may have been scythed apart by man, but perhaps their inhabitants, the animals, birds and plants, can learn how to exist under the new conditions of their own accord. Perhaps culling is not as essential as is now believed. Perhaps the supply of water can after all be left to the unpredictable rains. Perhaps roan and buffalo have the capacity to develop their own immunisation to anthrax and rinderpest. If man gradually withdraws the technology which now maintains a wilderness in the state he has decided suits it, the African reserves may go through profound changes – but possibly they may emerge better and more naturally-equipped for survival in the longer term.

The key is research – research above all into the intricate relationships, forged over millions of years, between the soil, the plants and the larger consumers of the vegetation mantle, the antelope, buffalo, rhino and zebra. On their backs, under natural conditions, ride almost every other form of African wildlife, from scavenging vultures to the great predators like lion, leopard, and hyena. If and when those delicate and self-adjusting interactions are understood, it may prove possible for man to retreat and leave the wild to a much greater extent alone to follow its own rhythms. Meanwhile, managed or not, wilderness reserves continue to pose questions that insistently demand answers from those who act as temporary stewards over them.

Why, in a world where the human population is soaring and starvation has reached epidemic proportions, should spaces of potentially productive earth be frozen, barricaded, and set aside for mere animals? Why should the northern colonist – in black African eyes still often viewed as an invader of the ancient homelands – still be allowed to cultivate the 'White Man's Gardens', as the reserves are sometimes named? Why should the animal protein they create not be taken and distributed to Africa's indigenous peoples? Why, whether black or white administered, should the reserves not be open without restriction for hunting, visiting or general recreation at the choice of those who own them – the citizens of the countries in which the reserves are set?

The arguments against conservation, particularly in the poorer African countries without a tourist industry, can sometimes appear overwhelming. In fact they are fallacious on every count. The commonest and most bitter charge is that productive land is being withheld from people who, in consequence, are at best forced to live at bare subsistence level, and at worst are dying for lack of food. Break up the reserves, the critics urge, distribute the land as farms, and whole belts of poverty would be eliminated almost overnight. The real results would be utterly and catastrophically different.

In a recent study an area of rural southern Africa was divided into five categories of land-use in an exercise to see which produced the highest yield of protein per acre. The categories were highly mechanised, large, European-style farms; small, traditional, European-style farms; 'poor white' farms; Bantu farms; and the untouched natural bush. Although the study is still unfinished, its findings are already beginning to prove in hard fact and figure what many wilderness managers have long suspected. With the exception of the highly mechanised farm, the natural bush out-performs every category on the list. It produces more animals and natural cereals more consistently than even the traditional European farmer can achieve. Taking into account the fact that he, like his even more intensively-assisted peer, has to rely on expensive machinery, fuel and artificial fertilisers to help him obtain his yield, the discrepancy becomes still more remarkable.

The bush, left alone, is not only a more efficient provider of food than man. It does its work without any help from aids like the oil which powers the farmer's tractors – an ever more costly commodity whose supplies in any event are finite. When it comes to the other two categories, the poor white and the Bantu farmers, there is simply no competition. In other words, to break up and distribute reserve land as farms would either result in its yield plunging suddenly and dramatically, very probably (on the basis of all past experience) with the eventual consequence of complete degradation, leaving the land unable to support either man or animal; or alternatively, given the availability of large amounts of money, machinery, fuel, fertiliser and expertise, maintaining its yield at the previous level or perhaps for a short time even fractionally improving on it. Sophisticated technology and large sums of money tend to be rare commodities in rural Africa. Even if they were common, the sheer absurdity of such a decision should be obvious to even the most dogmatic agricultural entrepreneur.

Unfortunately, there are a number of man-made obstacles to the logical alternative – leaving the bush to do its work and harvesting its crop. The most serious are cultural and psychological. When an area of natural bush is claimed and cleared by man, the most common replacement for its former wild grazers and browsers is domestic cattle. Cattle are true aliens in Africa. They can eat only a fraction of its grasses, making them appallingly wasteful and destructive feeders; they have few defences against its diseases or its predators; they are so dependent on water that the pastureland round rivers and boreholes is normally reduced to a dust-bowl under the constant impact of their hoofs; finally, they yield no more protein pound for pound than the animals they displace. Yet cattle are manageable: they can be owned, counted, herded, and traded. They are a tangible symbol of status and wealth – and the taste of their meat is familiar.

Offered a choice between efficient reality and wasteful fantasy, the efficiency of the animals of the bush and the waste of the foreign cattle, the African, just like his northern contemporary, has been conditioned to opt for the fantasy. He may know pragmatically that the roasted haunch of an antelope is just as nutritious as a cut of beef, generally even more so, but wild antelope cannot be corralled and bartered as a daughter's dowry. He therefore devotes his life to acquiring cattle,

Sable, Angola

regardless of the fearsome cost to himself, his children, and the space of land on which they all ultimately depend for survival.

There are other less obvious but even more intractable problems in the face of making a rational use of the natural riches of the bush. The African wildernesses are indivisible. They cannot be segmented, plotted and apportioned as individually-owned tracts of land, any more than their wild inhabitants can be assigned to a single human owner. The animals move seasonally across the entire landscape according to a host of factors that change year by year. They do not belong to any particular sector of their physical environment. They have it all as their home and their range – forest, mountain, plain and river. In cropping them man can only reflect their own patterns of behaviour. The decisions and the distribution of the crop have to be arrived at communally. Communal decisions, like the availability of unlimited money and technology, are as rare in Africa as anywhere else in the world.

In spite of all the difficulties, some of the lessons of the wild are not only being learned but slowly applied. While it will take years to unlock the obsessive grip of cattle on the human mind, farmers are beginning to realise that cattle and wild animals need not be mutually exclusive. In most areas of Africa, both can be run together on the same stretch of land without either competing with the other for food. Cattle will graze certain of the plants that make up the vegetation cover, and the indigenous species of antelope will crop others, including bushes and trees that domestic stock would never touch. Mixed ranching of game and cattle is already becoming a significant factor in the economies of a number of countries. In some, game ranching on its own is starting to become established.

Not long ago 3,700 square kilometres in the Matetsi area of Zimbabwe were designated as a wildlife utilisation zone. For many years before, the land had been farmed to raise cattle and crops. Neither had proved economically viable and the landscape was progressively deteriorating. In 1963, one ranch-owner decided to abandon conventional agriculture and stock-rearing altogether, and harvest the wildlife instead. Within a few years, by cropping hides and meat and selling safari hunting rights, the ranch was showing a clear financial profit for the first time in its history. At the same time, the health of the land and its vegetation began to improve. In a later and more closely-monitored exercise in Kenya, the results were even more remarkable. A ranch previously used for cattle was given back to the wild. Very soon it was recolonised by its original animals, including some ten species of gazelle. The gazelle turned out to produce fourteen times as much lean meat as the cattle had done. The costs of running the ranch dropped from 66% of its income to only 20%. Net revenue rose almost five-fold, and once again the cattle-damaged landscape quickly started to heal.

Almost all such discoveries had their origins in research carried out in the African Parks and reserves. In that sense, the reserves are great natural laboratories which are being used to explore the mysteries of the most vital of all modern life sciences – the science of food production. Showing both local and national communities how they can tangibly benefit from the findings of a reserve's research programme provides one of the most convincing defences a wilderness manager can mount against those who would de-proclaim the wilderness. Nationally it can help governments decide how best to use their countries' most basic resource – land. Locally it can help improve the life of even the most rural and unlettered black African. A well-managed reserve is not only a laboratory but a practical workshop.

Often, unknown to the visitor watching game at a water-hole from a hide, half a mile away a group of tribal chiefs will be studying and discussing an erosion scar with the reserve's interpretation officer. Next week another group may be examining the effects of over-grazing by wildebeest. A week later a third group will be looking at an impala range where good bush cover has meant the grasses have hardly been touched. In time, back in their tribal homelands, the chiefs may decide to break with some of the traditions inherited from the past and put to work the lessons learned in the reserve. As over three-quarters of most of southern Africa's remaining wild animals live not in reserves but on private or tribal lands, the scope and potential for benefits from working with the natural landscape and its creatures, rather than against them, are immense.

There are other and even more concrete ways in which the reserves try to show they are assets rather than liabilities to the communities round their boundaries. By selling meat from the animal culls locally and at subsidised prices, they demonstrate that a reserve is not so much a barren enclave as a larder, a larder, furthermore, which when properly looked after can sustain its yield indefinitely. Cattle are a monoculture with all the vulnerability of a single crop. In a year where cattle fail through disease or drought, the land can offer nothing to replace them. The wild, in contrast, is a rainbow of different bands of animals. Many do not even need surface water. Species like springbok, gemsbok, hartebeest and eland can get all the moisture they require from the vegetation or from night-feeding to exploit the dew. If one of even half-a-

111

dozen species fail in any given year, as many more will survive in abundance – all equal and often richer in their protein yield to the most selectively-bred domestic stock.

Even the little springhare, as the ancient San peoples of the Kalahari discovered thousands of years ago, is a superb and consistently reliable food source. As recently as 1973 the springhares in Botswana provided 2.2 million kilos of meat for the country's inhabitants – as much as a herd of 20,000 cattle. Unlike cattle, springhares are almost invulnerable to disease or drought, and rather than degrading the landscape their presence not only enriches its vegetation but helps support a wide range of other animals. As well as meat, the reserves can offer the local communities other staples from their natural resources, such as wood for fires and cane for thatching. Outside the reserve, supplies of both may be scarce or non-existent as a result of constant over-exploitation. Inside the reserve's boundaries, the trees and reeds will have been husbanded as carefully as its animals. In consequence, given the prodigality of the natural world, there will often be a surplus available for distribution.

In the case of a reserve's wildlife, the surplus animals which have to be culled can be exploited to yield more than protein alone. Their by-products, the hides and furs, the horns and ivory, can also be sold and the revenue applied either to the reserve's funds or to the budgets of the nearby human communities. A few reserves are exploiting the economic potential of culling programmes even further. Whatever their motives, however dark and atavistic, a number of people continue to be obsessed with confronting and killing the great wild creatures of the African landscape. To secure a trophy many hunters are prepared to pay almost any price. Faced with an over-population of a certain species a reserve manager has two choices: he can instruct a ranger to carry out the necessary cull, inevitably draining the reserve's resources in the process; or he can sell the killing rights to a trophy-hunting sportsman.

In either instance the animal dies, its meat is cropped and sold, and the end result is the same. But where in the first case the reserve's money and manpower resources are depleted, in the second they can be substantially increased. The fees paid by a trophy-hunter eager to claim a lion, for example, may cover the wages of a game ranger for a month and still leave enough for the maintenance of a borehole pump. The issue of whether trophy-hunting should be allowed at all in the African reserves is comparatively recent and still extremely contentious. So far, only a handful of reserve managers have dared face up to it. Their critics charge that it offends against every cannon of responsible conservation and legitimises the mindless slaughter practised by past generations.

Ostriches, Kenya

TOP LEFT *Sacred ibis, East Africa*
TOP CENTRE *Waterbuck and pelicans, Kenya*
TOP RIGHT *Great white egret*
BOTTOM *Lesser flamingoes on Kalahari salt pans, Botswana*

TOP LEFT *Carmine bee-eater, Botswana*
TOP RIGHT *Black and white kingfisher*
BOTTOM *Saddle-billed stork*

Ethically, too, they argue, it runs counter to all the positions that concerned humanity has slowly and painfully adopted in its dealings with the wild.

The larger and rarer the animal, the more acute the dilemma becomes. Twenty-five years ago, the white rhino was one of the most threatened creatures in the world. Since then the success of Natal's translocation programme, coupled with the rhino's own breeding success in its new homes, has meant the demand for the animal has virtually dried up. Zoos and Parks all over the world can now replace rhino from their own stock. Although the animal remains endangered, very soon there will be nowhere for Natal's surplus rhino to go. They will then have to be culled. To a rich safari hunter, the prospect of killing a white rhino, a trophy unavailable legally for more than a generation, will be irresistible. Should the surplus animals be shot by reserve wardens? Or should they be sold as trophies, generating perhaps thousands of dollars which can be spent on vitally-needed conservation programmes?

For the time being, Natal has firmly set its face against permitting trophy-hunting, believing it incompatible with the nature of a wildlife reserve. The Natal Parks Board is fortunate in being, by African standards, well-funded. In other southern African reserves, other wilderness managers, just as thoughtful and conscientious, have taken the opposite decision. Surplus animals, in their view, are just another of the reserve's resources and can legitimately be cropped. An area of the reserve is temporarily zoned off and the chosen animal is shot by the client under the supervision of a ranger, who performs the same role as a professional hunter in the hunting concession areas outside. Part of the revenue is then handed over to the local tribes, to emphasise yet again that the reserve is not a wasteful enclave for an elite, but a source of benefit to the whole community.

In addition to the lessons they can teach about food and land use, and the crops they yield and the revenue they generate through tourism, there is an even more compelling practical reason for safeguarding Africa's Parks and reserves: they represent the largest and richest reservoirs of wildlife in the world. Behind their present-day inhabitants, the animals, birds, plants, and insects, lie millions of years of evolution, of priceless research and development. During that time they, like the planet's other wildlife communities, have solved almost all the problems that bedevil modern man's existence and his prospects for the future.

The whales in the seas off the African coast, for instance, have resolved the problem of friction and therefore of energy. Their bodies are so engineered that in spite of their immense size they can propel themselves through water with a tiny fraction of the energy needed to move an infinitely smaller man-made object. If the principles of a whale's design and structure could be applied to automobiles, and with time and research there is no reason why they should not, a heavy truck could cross Europe on a tiny fraction of the gasolene it currently requires. The oleander moth, in both its caterpillar and winged stages, protects itself from predators by storing poisons from its food plant in its body. These toxins, so powerful they can cause acute illness in a man who merely eats food cooked over a fire of oleander branches, attack and destroy cells. The moth can hold and manipulate them in its body without being harmed. If man can discover how to isolate, store and use them as the moth does, he may well have made a major advance in the search for a cure for cancer. The trees of the coastal African swamps and lagoons hold high concentrations of the so-called 'defensive chemicals' like saponins and cardiac glycosides. If their function can be understood and the chemicals applied in curative medicine, large steps forward may be possible in treating the greatest killer of all in contemporary society, heart disease.

The catalogue of possibilities is endless. The reserves are not only laboratories and workshops, but immense libraries and archives of stored knowledge, all of it directly or indirectly applicable to modern man's needs. Penicillin and powered flight only exist because of careful human observation of the growth of a primitive plant and the movement of air across the upper side of a bird's wings. What else he can learn from studying the wild is literally inestimable. Certainly to dispose of the Parks and reserves and the working manuals of blunt, pragmatic and hard-won learning they contain would, at this point of man's evolution, be an act of self-destructive madness without parallel in human history. If there is ever a stage at which the burning of books can be justified, it can only be after their contents have been committed to memory. In the African reserves, man has not even started to read the words on the first page – he is still searching for the index.

Tourist revenue, food production studies, research into the best use of land, distribution of local natural resources, a wider human self-interest across a whole spectrum of scientific and technological riddles – all are strong and demonstrable reasons for conserving the wilderness. Yet the care of the wild has another dimension, much less easy to quantify or rationalise. It applies to any wilderness area throughout the world, but perhaps above all to those of the African continent. Africa was man's birthplace, the cradle that rocked him, the nursery he fumblingly explored with a child's uncertain fingers. On the African grass plains

114

Lechwe in the Okavango Delta, Botswana

he stood up and took the first tentative steps on a journey that was to lead him across the earth, seeding it with his descendants stage by stage as he walked.

Today man has colonised the entire planet from the high slopes of the Himalayas to the shores of the Arctic, from the deserts of Australia to the rainforests of South America. He has even made his first moves towards colonising different worlds. Within a century it seems likely he will be settled on other revolving planetary islands in the solar system or beyond. If and when he does, his arrival there will only establish another station on the journey. A journey does not always have an end, but it always has a beginning. For man, the beginning was African and Africa will always be his home.

For years many many people visiting Africa for the first time have spoken or written about a sharp and curious sense of recognition. The landscape may be vast, alien and fearful, its large and abundant creatures threatening, but both are puzzlingly familiar. The sounds, smells and images, the call of a hunting jackal, the swirling scent of a fever tree in flower, the play of the setting sun's light over a crimson plain of trimedra grass, the beating wings of a flight of duck lifting from a lake, the grumbling night roar of a lion proclaiming its territory, the scream of elephants and the clear belling song of the palm thrush, all belong to a time until then half-forgotten. In Africa these sensations can suddenly come back like vivid and fragmentary memories of distant childhood.

Those who go there tend to be drawn back again and again. 'He who has drunk at Africa's wells,' runs the old Masai proverb, 'will always return to drink again.' In Africa man, whether black or white, is surrounded by the ancient furniture and companions of his original hearth. In looking at its landscape and animals he is looking at his first dwelling-place, at the other nations of the wilderness who witnessed his birth and grew up beside him. He may have changed. The home acres and the animals have not. The animals, in the sounds they make, the scents they give off, the spaces they fill and define, the rhythms they obey, the shadows and intricate patterns they trace on the plains through sunlight and cloud, are the same as they always were, comfortable, familiar and reassuring. So too is the land itself, however bruised and scarred by centuries of abuse.

From the very earliest recorded times, the home and hearth have been considered sacred. To desecrate them, to kill beneath the family roof, has always ranked among the worst crimes man can commit. What has held true throughout the centuries in man-made dwellings is just as true on a majestic scale in Africa today. The reserves came into being because of the carnage inflicted on the wilderness by man, both black and white. Fortunately the wild is both forgiving and resilient. Treated with care and respect it has an extraordinary capacity to heal itself and regenerate. Many of the stewards responsible for exhibiting that care now are Africa's newly-independent black nations. The task is costly and demanding and not one they should be expected to shoulder alone. The white nations of the West bear an even greater share of the blame for the damage done to Africa. They must play their part in repairing and tending the wounded landscape. The reserves will only survive in health through a partnership between the two human races.

Yet ultimately the African reserves belong to neither. They belong to all mankind, just as all mankind belongs to them. They are among the world's greatest and most vibrant glories, and every country must share the responsibility of seeing they survive for future generations of man and of their own animal nations. 'We do not inherit the earth from our parents,' in the words of the International Union for the Conservation of Nature, 'we borrow it from our children.'

The reserves are part of life's and the earth's dwindling capital. As every economist and prudent housekeeper knows, to live off and then exhaust capital is a certain recipe for misery, famine and disaster. On the other hand capital, saved and conserved, generates interest. In the African forests and grass plains the interest is returned as food, medicine, technology, health, and loveliness. That, and not bankruptcy, should be the legacy bequeathed to both the human and wilderness generations to come.

PART II

The National Parks

INTRODUCTION

The following section of the book lists the 161 National Parks in thirty-seven African countries south of the Sahara, together with those on the island of Madagascar, as they exist in 1985. (The other four African nations south of the Sahara, Burundi, Djibouti, Equatorial Guinea, and Guinea Bissau, either have no National Parks or none on which information is available.)

Here a further word of explanation is needed about the present system of classifying and naming reserves.

As outlined earlier, the International Union for the Conservation of Nature and Natural Resources has drawn up a list classifying eight basic types of protected landscape. The categories reflect in part the degree of protection given to them, and in part the reason for which they have been conserved.

Category I on the IUCN schedule covers the Scientific Reserves. These, as their name suggests, are areas conserved as far as possible in their natural state exclusively for the purpose of scientific study. Category II embraces the world's National Parks. These have much the same conservation aims as the Scientific Reserves but with two important differences. They specifically cater for visitors, for 'recreation and tourism', and they have the highest level of protection their countries can give them. Both factors working together provide them, in a way paradoxically, with better safeguards against human interference than those available to the strict Scientific Reserves. The other categories range from National Monuments, Nature Conservation Reserves, and Protected Landscapes, to Resource Reserves, Anthropological Reserves, and Multiple-Use Management Areas.

A few reserves have the additional designation Biosphere Reserve or World Heritage Site. These titles are conferred not by the IUCN but by UNESCO. A Biosphere Reserve is an area where every element, including man and his activities, is considered to be of outstanding conservation importance. A World Heritage Site describes a site of international natural history or cultural interest – for instance Auschwitz, Easter Island, the Great Barrier Reef, and the Ngorongoro Crater.

As constraints of space clearly made it impossible to cover all the African reserves in all the eight IUCN categories, a decision was taken initially to describe only those with National Park (Category II) status. These are by definition landscape and wildlife enclaves of major importance. They are also both open to visitors, and at the same time stringently protected. However, as information began to be assembled from all over the continent, problems in the chosen approach started to emerge.

In some countries a reserve which meets all the requirements of a National Park and is widely-known as such, for instance the Masai-Mara in Kenya, may turn out to be technically something different – the decree which protects the Masai-Mara names it as a National Reserve, consigning it theoretically to a different category. In other countries a so-called 'National Park' may in fact be a provincially-protected and administered reserve, which has been given the grander-sounding title locally and then over the years become mistakenly accepted as having genuine National Park status.

For the urgent business of establishing priorities and allocating wilderness conservation funds and resources sensibly and productively, a system of classifying the world's reserves is obviously essential. The IUCN schedule is a valiant and much-needed attempt to provide one. As far as possible, under its Category II definition, it has been followed here. But anomalies and contradictions, either real or apparent, inevitably remain: the IUCN itself is constantly forced to re-classify the reserves as new and more accurate information comes in, or political circumstances change. Given the nature of wilderness and the widely-differing interpretations of 'protection', 'purpose' and 'management' in the many and disparate African countries, the problems are likely to continue indefinitely.

Meanwhile, for the ordinary visitor, and even for the working scientist, it cannot be stressed too often or too strongly that categorisation in no sense reflects the inherent degree of value or interest of any particular area. Categorisation, especially when applied to the living and changing landscapes of the wild, can never be more than a rough-and-ready filing system, a convenient method of classifying what in the ends defies any real classification. Many of Africa's finest wildlife reserves can slip through the best-cast net altogether. The South African province of Natal, for instance, administers some fifty-three reserves. Several of

122

them, Umfolozi, Hluhluwe, Mkuzi, and Ndumu, to name only a handful, are for any visitor and by any criteria among the most rewarding wilderness sites not merely in Africa but in the world. Yet Natal is a province, not a country, and its reserves are in provincial and not national custody – and so disqualify themselves for inclusion here.

Indeed, it is more than possible that a visit to one of the many small and privately-owned reserves, which appear on no list and under no category at all, will produce something to equal all the wonders of a Serengeti, a Kruger, or an Etosha Pan. That, happily, is one of the wild's greatest attractions and most constant sources of excitement.

The system broadly adopted in this book is probably the most useful available at the moment. It still gives rise to certain anomalies and contradictions, either real or apparent. In some countries a reserve with National Park protection may not be called such but referred to by an older and more traditional name. In others a so-called 'National Park' may in fact be a provincially-administered and protected reserve, which has been given the grander-sounding title locally and then become known by it. As far as possible the names and titles have been disentangled, and the protected wildernesses put into their 'correct' category.

When it comes to describing what a reserve contains, its 'noteworthy' animals, birds and plants, the problems of choice become almost insuperable. A reserve is an entity. Every element within it is inextricably locked together. It can only, for example, produce so much grass. The grass-eating insects compete for its pastures with the elephants and the antelope. If the populations of the grazing ants rise, over a period of time those of the elephant and the antelope will decline because there will not be enough food to support them all. The issue is not decided by an animal's size, but its efficiency in harvesting a limited amount of food. If the ants are more efficient, as under certain conditions they may be, they will drive out a creature like an elephant one million times their weight.

Logically, and certainly according to the wild's immutable laws, any list of a reserve's natural inhabitants should include its species of ant and grass ranked equally with its elephant and lion. One day perhaps, given a deeper understanding of wilderness, it will. Meanwhile the visitor understandably remains fascinated above all by what he can most easily see and respond to – the large, the strange, the colourful, and the 'dangerous'. Acknowledging this the species listed for the Parks have been restricted to the ones which have traditionally met those criteria, notably the 'big five' of game-viewing, elephant, lion, leopard, rhino, and buffalo; to the commoner large mammals of an area; and to those

123

which due to man's impact on the African landscape have become increasingly rare. The same general criteria have been applied to birds, plants, reptiles, and other forms of life.

The Parks are grouped under the countries, listed alphabetically, responsible for them. Visitors to contemporary Africa are often bewildered by the number of unfamiliar nations it contains. To identify them and provide their reserves with some form of context, a few brief introductory notes have been given for each country. Given the volatility of modern African politics any such summary risks being out-dated by events which take place weeks or even days after it is prepared. In spite of all the uncertainties the notes seem worth providing, if only to under-line the fragility of the reserves' own existence and their vulnerability to the consequence of upheaval in the human societies which have become their stewards.

The amount of information available on the African Parks varies enor-mously from country to country, and even from Park to Park within the same country. In the case of a nation like Kenya, with a major economic reliance on wildlife-related tourist revenue, or South Africa, a rich country with a long tradition in conservation, the Parks – or at least some of them – have been the subjects of careful studies over consid-erable periods of time, and the findings are relatively accessible. In other instances, particularly among the poorer and more remote countries, even the most basic facts about the Parks are often either unrecorded or hard to come by. While the same general treatment has been applied to every Park, the discrepancies and omissions are almost always explained not by choice but by what is currently known.

Even where information is to hand, the problems may still not be over. Several species of animal, for instance, are known by different names in different parts of the continent – in spite of the fact that a common language is used to identify them. In English-speaking Africa the small widespread monkey, *Cercopithecus aethiops*, is known in some places as the green monkey and in others as the vervet monkey. Quite apart from the fact that it may not be a single species at all but several closely-related ones, the question arises of whether to adopt a single name for it and call it, say, the vervet monkey wherever it occurs – or whether to follow traditional local usage and list it as a green monkey in one country and a vervet in another. (Generally, because it has more practical use for the visitor, tradition has been followed and the local name given – there is little point in asking a game scout to point out a green monkey if he only knows it as a vervet.)

For the moment no system, except one involving laborious repetition

124

punctuated by an almost endless series of question-marks, can deal with all the difficulties. So a knife, or perhaps an axe, has been taken to the Gordian knot of the African Parks' landscapes and the enmeshed webs of their wildlife communities. Here, in short word-pictures, are where they are, what they are, and which principal animal nations inhabit them.

As a general guide for anyone planning a trip to the National Parks, the best months to visit have been given in the margin beside each Park's entry. 'Best' has been used in the sense of the traditionally-favoured game-viewing months, normally during the African winter (although this can be punctuated with periods of short rains), when the ground is dry, access is relatively easy, and many animals tend to be concentrated close to the remaining water supplies, making them easy to see. However, more and more people are choosing to visit the Parks at other seasons – for instance, just after the rains, when a different and perhaps more interesting spectrum of wildlife can be observed. The choice lies with the individual visitor, although it should always be remembered that in many parts of Africa the Parks are normally closed during the months of heaviest rainfall whether the rains come in any given year or not. Opening and closing dates for individual Parks are given in annual publications put out by most African countries.

The Parks have also been graded according to the facilities they provide for visitors. For obvious reasons, the range of these can change at short notice. In one country, internal conflict can cause its Parks to be closed overnight and all their services to be withdrawn. In another, an intensive programme of work can result in the provision of tracks, hutted camps, and ranger-guides equipped with four-wheel drive vehicles – all within the space of a single dry season, transforming what was formerly an unapproachable wilderness into an accessible reserve. Again, the best advice for the visitor is to consult one of the annual publications.

A comprehensive guide to *all* of Africa's protected landscapes – not merely its National Parks – and covering their vegetation and wildlife communities as well as their facilities for the ordinary visitor, is badly needed. Meanwhile, what follows is an indication of what the visitor can expect by way of approach and services from the Parks treated in this book.

A	First-class facilities in every respect
A/B	Roofed accommodation and good general facilities
B	Camp sites and a ranger service available
B/C	Problematical access and few local services
C	Access very difficult and almost no facilities

125

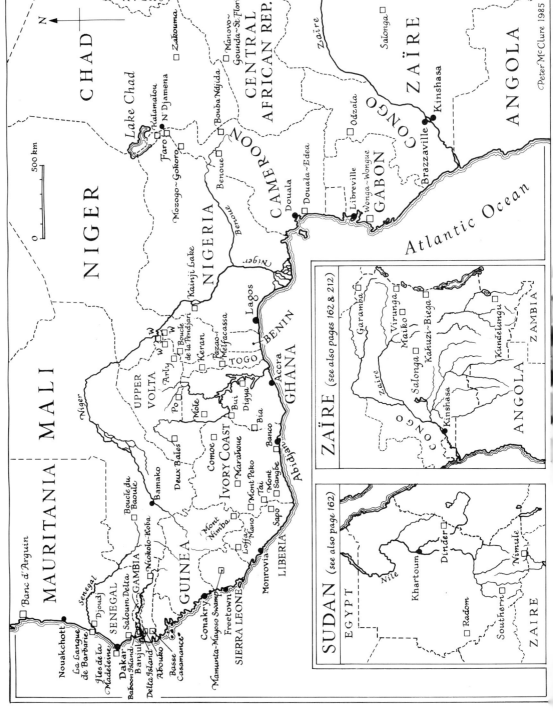

© Peter McClure 1985

WEST AFRICA

Both the physical and human geography of West Africa is dominated by its two great river systems: the Niger, 4,200 kilometres long, and the Zaire, formerly the Congo, 4,700 kilometres long. The region's climate tends to be damp and humid, with a long wet summer season, which can last for nine months, and a short dry winter. During the summer travel to the parks, particularly the remoter ones, is often difficult, and the only access in several areas is by river. At an average of 25°C, the year-round temperature is high, notably in the Congo basin which receives two metres of rainfall annually in the form of violent daily cloud-bursts during the wet months. The Gulf of Guinea, by contrast, has a pattern of four seasons, with rain from March to April and again from September to November, and dry spells in the intervening months.

West Africa is unquestionably 'Explorer's Africa'. Away from their increasingly-developed beaches, the coastal West African countries have only limited facilities for tourism. The huge inland tracts of equatorial forest contain large populations of birds, which generally flit rather than fly because of the heavy forest cover, and many butterflies, snakes, reptiles, and rodents. The larger mammals are scarcer both in species and numbers than in many other parts of the continent, and are often found living well above ground level, although the forest elephant takes advantage of the lack of undergrowth created by the dense tree canopy. Africa's equatorial forests are normally less thick than the jungles of Brazil, and are interspersed both with clearings, and with higher ground where the vegetation mantle is lighter.

As a whole the region's human population density is low and settlements are largely concentrated round the waterways. In the sixteenth century Ghana and Mali were rich and powerful independent Muslim kingdoms, but after the arrival of the Europeans the entire coast was reduced to a source for the raw materials of slavery and the other com-

127

modities demanded by the trading nations of the west. The West African countries which exist today were variously colonised and plundered by Portugal, Britain, France, and Belgium. One legacy of colonial rule survives in the countries' official languages – Ghana, Nigeria, Sierra Leone, Liberia, Gambia, and Cameroon, for example, are all officially English-speaking. Senegal, Ivory Coast, Nigeria, Ghana and Cameroon have gradually expanding facilities for those interested in Africa's wildlife, although it has to be said that no country in the region yet values its National Parks, or caters for visitors to them, as do most other nations in the east and south of the continent.

BENIN

Benin, which should not be confused with the city of Benin in Nigeria, was for five centuries the ancient and powerful kingdom of Dahomey. Conquered by the French in 1899, it then became a colonial territory in French West Africa and later an overseas department of France, finally achieving independence again in 1960. The country's climate is equatorial and humid in the south, and tropical in the north.

'W' National Park (568,000 ha.) Altitude: 250 m. Location: in the north of the country where it forms the Benin section of the international Park which extends into Upper Volta and Niger.   B/C JAN–APR, AUG

'W' National Park was established in 1954, although earlier the area had Hunting Reserve status. The Park contains a wide range of habitats including dry savanna woodland, a system of lakes and marshes, rivers, and wide grassy plains.

Most of the West African savanna species are present, including the most important savanna elephant population in West Africa. The big cats are represented by leopard, lion, and cheetah. Among the herbivores are topi, roan, hippo, bushbuck, kob, Bohar reedbuck, western hartebeest, duiker, oribi, buffalo, possibly red-fronted gazelle, red-flanked and Grimm's duiker and warthog. Also vervet and patas monkey, and Anubis baboon. Giant eland and giraffe are absent. The Park is surrounded by buffer zones managed for hunting.

128

Boucle de la Pendjari National Park (275,500 ha.) Altitude: up to
200 m. Location: in Atakora Province of northwest Benin, matching with
Arly National Park in Upper Volta.

Boucle de la Pendjari was originally a hunting zone created in 1954.
It became a reserve in 1955 and was declared a National Park in 1961.
The Park lies within the Volta depression where there is much seasonally
waterlogged soil. The quartzite cliffs of the Atakora Mountains are particularly interesting.

Pendjari's dry savanna woodland is punctuated by marsh and grassy
plain and there are some areas of previously cultivated woodland. The
Park is the largest employer of unskilled labour in the province, the work
being mainly upkeep of the roads for visitors.

The mammal population includes most of the West African species,
the main exceptions being giraffe and giant eland. Anubis baboon, vervet
and patas monkey can be found, as can leopard and lion. Elephant, hippo,
and buffalo supply the bulk. Topi, roan, waterbuck, kob, Bohar reedbuck, western hartebeest, red-fronted gazelle, bushbuck, red-flanked
duiker, Grimm's duiker, and oribi represent the buck.

CAMEROON

Cameroon is a spectacularly beautiful and varied country on the Atlantic
seaboard south of Nigeria. The north is largely semi-desert. The central
plateau consists of the huge Maroua plain, rich in minerals, filled with
game, and watered by the Benue River on its way to the Niger. South
and west lie upland savanna, where the cool hilly landscape is temperate
enough to support tea plantations. The coast is bordered by tropical
forests with high rainfall and lush vegetation. The country's wildlife,
particularly in the almost-inaccessible tropical forest zones, is rich and
diverse.

Benue National Park (180,000 ha.) Altitude: 400 m approx. with mountain blocks reaching 800 to 1,000 m. Location: in northern Cameroon
adjoining the Benue River and bordered on the west by part of the
national highway between Ngaoundere and Garoua.

Benue was established as a Faunal Reserve in 1932. It was proclaimed
a National Park in 1968, and named a Biosphere Reserve in 1981. The
terrain is very rugged with ranges of hills rising to the 1,100 m peak
of Mount Garoua. Over 800 mm of annual rainfall is recorded, and there

is a dry season between November and May.

Notable among Benue's mammals is the increasingly rare black rhino with a population in 1980 of fifteen to twenty. Leopard, lion and caracal represent the cats. Among other mammals the Park contains elephant, hippo, hartebeest, oribi, bushbuck, red-flanked duiker, common duiker, warthog, roan, Bohar reedbuck, kob, Defassa waterbuck, giant eland, buffalo, crocodile, hyena, and various monkeys.

The area is of considerable ornithological interest.

Bouba Ndjida National Park (220,000 ha.) Altitude: average 350 m with peaks to 900 m. Location: in northern Cameroon on the border with Chad.
A/B
NOV–MAY

Bouba Ndjida was established in 1947 as a Forest and Faunal Reserve under the French–British UN Mandate which followed the Second World War. It was declared a National Park in 1968, after independence (1960–61). The Park is on a large rugged plain scattered with isolated massifs composed of rocky outcrops of granites and gneisses. Numerous water-courses cross the landscape.

The vegetation is largely closed-canopy woodland and light forest, including a tree species whose oily seeds are used for making shea butter (*Butyrospermum parkii*).

The Park was established primarily to protect the black rhino and giant eland. Other species found there include elephant, cheetah, lion, hippo, buffalo, kob, Defassa waterbuck, giraffe, common duiker and red-flanked duiker. All the larger wildlife is vulnerable to poachers from neighbouring Chad.

Douala-Edea Faunal Reserve (160,000 ha.) Altitude: sea-level to 15 m. Location: in the south of the Littoral Province between Sanaga and Nyong Rivers.
C
NOV–MAY

Douala-Edea was established in 1932. It is a natural reserve bounded on three sides by rivers or ocean, and on the fourth by a rocky escarpment. The climate is semi-humid equatorial with no distinct dry season and a high annual rainfall of 3,000 mm. The reserve is drained by several black water rivers.

The vegetation consists of Congo rainforest with forty-three families of trees including various euphorbia. Mangroves occur along the coast and in the coastal lagoons. The lagoons contain West African manatee while the forest harbours many primates: black colobus monkey, red colobus, de Brazza's and the greater white-nosed monkeys, white-collared and grey-cheeked mangabeys, mandrill, gorilla, and

Buffon's kob in Bouba Ndjida National Park, Cameroon

chimpanzee. Elephant and hippo are present, so too are sitatunga, blue duiker, the giant and the tree pangolin, and the African civet cat. The birdlife is rich and abundant.

Faro National Park (330,000 ha.) Altitude: 620 to 975 m. Location: northern Cameroon.

B/C
NOV–MAY

Faro was first established as a Forest Reserve in 1947 under the post-war UN trusteeship administered by the French and the British. 1980 saw it declared a National Park. It occupies a plateau with mountainous massifs and has a climate typical of the Sudanian zone with a dry season between November and May. The annual rainfall is 1,200 mm.

The vegetation is savanna and woodland which supports a dense and varied fauna. 33 species of mammal have been recorded, including cheetah, hippo, black rhino, buffalo, Defassa waterbuck, kob, giant eland, roan antelope, topi, giraffe, elephant, and warthog. Faro has much to interest the birdwatcher and there are numerous species of fish.

131

Kalamalou National Park (4,500 ha.) Altitude: 293 m. Location: in the extreme north of Cameroon, 450 kms from Garoua, 12 kms west of Kousseri, and 70 kms from Lake Chad. An international road crosses the Park.

B
OCT–MAY

Kalamalou was first established as a Forest and Fauna Reserve in 1947 and classified as a National Park in 1972. It consists of seasonally flooded flat plains at the edge of Lake Chad, which at the north limit of the Park, on the Chari floodplain, has water-holes even in dry years. South of the main road lies open woodland, while to the north is a broad belt of taller trees. The ground here is bare in the dry season, but if heavy rains fall in August the woodland floor is covered with lily ponds, grasses and herbs. The dry season lasts from October to May and average annual rainfall is 600 mm.

Elephant are present, although the Park may provide only a part of their range. Also hippo, Defassa kob, Buffon's kob, bushbuck, topi, reedbuck, common duiker, warthog, mongoose, and ground squirrel. Among the predators are genet and wildcat, spotted hyena, and sandfox.

Birdlife is especially rich including guinea fowl, long-tailed glossy starling, fish eagle, the beautiful crowned crane, marabou and saddle-billed stork, and roller. Two bee-eaters, the dazzling Carmine bee-eater and the white-fronted bee-eater, nest colonially in sandbanks.

Mozogo–Gokoro National Park (1,400 ha.) Altitude: 440 m. Location: 25 kms from Mokolo in North Cameroon.

B/C
NOV–MAY

Mozogo-Gokoro was first established as a Forest and Faunal Reserve in 1932 and became a National Park in 1968. It has been protected from bush fires for 30 years which has led to the appearance of dry forest – i.e. woodland savanna. No tourist visitors are permitted but there is accommodation available in Mokolo for scientists working in the Park. Scientific studies include a survey on the effects of fire on the vegetation. The climate is of the mountain-steppe type.

The Park lies in a shallow basin sandwiched between Mount Mandara and the massifs of Mora. Among the mammals present are vervet monkey, patas monkey and baboon. The reptile population includes the python.

CENTRAL AFRICAN REPUBLIC

The Central African Republic, a former French colony, is landlocked, thinly-populated, and extremely poor. The country's hot lowlands are humid and, from a human viewpoint, unhealthy – the mortality rate among the inhabitants is high. Wildlife, on the other hand, is abundant and one of the landscape's main attractions to its former French rulers was its prime hunting territory.

Manovo-Gounda-St Floris National Park (1,740,000 ha.) Altitude: around 400 m. Location: in the northeast of the country on the border with Chad.

C
MAR–NOV

St Floris began as part of the Parc National de l'Oubangui-Chara in 1933 and was expanded to its present area in 1979. The vegetation is mainly West African woodland savanna, and the climate is tropical and humid with annual rainfall of between 950 and 1,700 mm. Large termite mounds are a feature of the lowland areas. There is a single rainy season and the remaining months of the year are hot.

The Park harbours 2–3,000 elephant, although the population is in decline. Also present are giraffe, buffalo, giant eland, hartebeest, waterbuck, kob, roan antelope and oribi. Baboon, savanna monkey, lesser galago or bushbaby can be found, as well as lion, leopard, wildcat, and crocodile. There are around 30 black rhino. Less common are cheetah, golden cat, hippo, reedbuck, topi, red-fronted gazelle, Brazza's monkey, and yellow-backed duiker.

The Park is of great ornithological interest with large seasonal populations of pelicans in Gata-Vakaga area. The black-headed bee-eater has become much more common in recent years. Also present is the previously-unidentified crested guineafowl in the forests of Manovo and Yagounda.

The Park has plenty to offer butterfly enthusiasts.

Poaching has affected the numbers of rhino, crocodile, leopard, elephant, and giraffe in recent years, although the situation is now improving.

CHAD

The landlocked territory occupied by Chad is substantial, double the area of its former colonial ruler France, and includes half of Lake Chad, the eleventh largest lake in the world. The lake itself, whose water level varies widely according to the season, is full of papyrus and reed beds and floating islands of vegetation. It contains crocodile, hippo, many species of fish, and a wealth of birdlife, including pelicans and maribou storks. The southern part of the country, the Sahr region, is watered

133

by rivers and supports most of Chad's population. To the east and north lie three ranges of mountains whose slopes contain leopard, oryx, addax, and several species of gazelle. The central region consists of Sahel scrub and grassland which in recent years has been badly afflicted by drought.

Zakouma National Park (300,000 ha.) Altitude: 200 to 500 m. Location: in the southeast of Chad in the Salamat district.

B/C
MAR–NOV

Zakouma is a very extensive reserve occupying a wide grassy plain crossed by seasonal watercourses which provide drinking pools in the dry season. There is some forest.

Notable fauna includes elephant, buffalo, rhino, giraffe and many species of antelope, particularly in the southwest where a population of greater kudu may be found. Among the predators are lion and leopard.

The birdlife is rich and varied.

CONGO

The Congo People's Republic, formerly Middle Congo with its capital at Brazzaville, lies between the Zaire River and Gabon, and was for many years the political and economic heart of French Equatorial Africa. The area's earliest inhabitants were the pygmies.

The Congo has extensive tropical rainforests and swamps, and wide floodplains liable to annual innundation. The forest areas are virtually uninhabited. The climate is cooler on the coast, and the most comfortable season is June to September. Communications are poor and difficult to maintain, and the country has little in the way of tourism. The capital Brazzaville has maintained its position as a cultural centre and is a clean and elegant tree-lined city.

Odzala National Park (126,600 ha. as Park and 110,000 ha. as Biosphere.) Odzala forms part of a single block of 284,000 ha. of protected land, which includes the Lekoli–Pandaka and M'boko Reserves. Altitude: 400 to 600 m. Location: in the northwestern Congo, 30 kms east of the border with Gabon and 120 kms southwest of Duesso on the Cameroon border.

C
SEPT–MAY

Odzala, which was established as a National Park in 1935, consists mainly of an undulating plateau covered with dense evergreen forest. The Park contains the blue water Lake Moba and many natural salt pans.

The driest months are January and from June to August. Rain falls on average on 112 days of the year.

Particularly notable among the Park's mammals are the dwarf forest buffalo, the gorilla population, the bongo or great forest antelope, and the elusive sitatunga. There are also populations of elephant, chimpanzee, several species of monkey and duiker, great forest hog, and bushpig. Predators include lion and spotted hyena.

Uganda kob in Odzala National Park, Congo

135

GABON

Gabon is thickly forested over three-quarters of its area, and has a low population density. Recent discoveries of mineral resources, including oil, have precipitated it into the position of one of the richest countries in Africa.

The country's climate is tropical, with a rainy season from January to mid-May. The best months for visitors are those during the cooler dry season from Mid-May to September. Although Gabon's fauna is remarkable in its numbers and diversity, much of its forest is difficult to reach. Conservation is not high on the country's current list of priorities, and most foreign tourism consists of costly hunting safaris.

Wonga-Wongue National Park (358,000 ha. – of which 55,000 ha. forms the National Park proper and the rest is administered as a managed nature reserve.) Altitude: sea-level to 1,000 m rising to 1,575 m. Location: in the coastal region between Libreville and Port Gentil, 99 kms south of the equator. **B mid-MAY– SEPT**

Wonga-Wongue was established in 1967. It consists of three principal areas – the National Park itself and the two adjacent 'domaines de chasse' or hunting territories. The Park is bisected by several rivers and lakes. The vegetation varies from humid tropical forest to stunted woodland savanna. The rainforest includes ebony and other hardwoods such as the purpleheart, and various mahoganies interspersed with climbing palm and rubber vine.

The mammals present include the shy bongo and several primates, notably the western race of the gorilla, and chimpanzees. Elephant, buffalo, sitatunga, duiker, aardvark, and the extraordinary giant pangolin are also found.

Birds include the jibaru, white pelican, bustards, and various parrots. Among the reptiles are python and the Gabon viper.

The area is particularly noted for its butterflies.

GAMBIA

The tiny republic of The Gambia, only 11,000 sq kms in area, occupies a narrow stretch of territory bordering the River Gambia. The land takes the form of a long finger reaching from the Atlantic seaboard deep into the heart of Senegal.

The country is about 45 kms wide at the mouth of the River Gambia, and narrows further inland to as little as half that distance. At the coast the river is lined with mangrove swamps. Inland the landscape on either side of the river's banks is flat with bamboo forest, scrub, and ironstone hills. The Gambia has been inhabited since the Stone Age.

Abouko National Reserve. Altitude: 100 m. Location: 19 kms from Banjul, round the lagoons.

B
NOV–MAY

Notable fauna includes various monkeys, several species of antelope, and many snakes among them python. There are also crocodile and hippo. The birdlife is very rich with over 400 species recorded, including many waterfowl, spur-wing goose, guinea fowl, pigeons and sand grouse.

GHANA

Ghana, the former Gold Coast, was sparsely-populated by man until as recently as five hundred years ago. Then it was invaded by successive waves of land-hungry immigrants from the north and east. When the Europeans began to colonise West Africa, the country was used as a base for trade in gold, slaves, and ivory. In 1901 it became a British possession.

Ghana was the first African colony to achieve independence, which it was granted by Britain in 1957. Since then its political history has been troubled. None the less it has much to offer the visitor interested in African wildlife. In climatic terms the country's temperature and humidity are high, although the weather on the Atlantic coast is almost always good.

Bia National Park (7,700 ha. with a core zone of 300 ha. and a 22,800 ha. buffer zone on the southern border.) Altitude: 145 to 230 m. Location: in the western region between the Ivory Coast border and the Bia river.

B
DEC–MAR

Bia was declared a Forest Reserve in 1935, becoming a National Park in 1974. The Park protects the headwaters of the Panabo and Sukusuku Rivers which flow into the Ivory Coast, and also the Tawya River – a tributary of the Bia. Temperatures over the year range from 20.5° to 34°C. The dry season lasts from December to March, and the rainfall peaks are in June and October.

The Park's vegetation consists of virgin rainforest, unique in Ghana, and includes many valuable timber species. Palm trees and climbers are among the moist evergreen and semi-deciduous trees. Epiphytic orchids, mosses and liverworts abound.

The forest fauna is rich and unusual, and includes a herd of forest elephant. Unusual, dry-season concentrations of animals have been observed in the centre of the Park. All the mammalian species typical of unencroached Guinean high forest are found in the Bia area, among them the three species of colobus monkey, the Diana monkey, Campbell's monkey, lesser white-nosed monkey, mangabey, chimpanzee, and probably also potto and Demidoff's galago. Leopard, bongo, buffalo and giant forest hog are present, together with various buck and a variety of rodents. Bia is also the only known natural home of the newly-described lizard *Agama sylvanus*.

The avifauna is very interesting, including some forms which may be rare or of limited range such as the Ghanaian form of the lovebird, *Agapornis swinderniana*.

Bui National Park (207,253 ha. – also quoted as 154,368 ha.) Altitude: 122 to 244 m. Location: 400 kms inland on Ghana's western border with the Ivory Coast. B/C OCT–MAY

Bui is an undulating catchment of small tributaries of the Black Volta River. The long dry season is from October to July and a short wet season lasts from June to September. Temperature ranges from 10°C to 40°C. The vegetation is Guinea savanna woodland with gallery forest along the rivers.

Noteworthy fauna includes hippo, roan antelope, hartebeest, Deffasa waterbuck, Buffon's kob, bushbuck, red-flanked duiker, grey duiker, colobus monkey, and olive baboon.

The birdlife is plentiful and interesting.

Digya National Park (312,436 ha.) Altitude: 91 to 812 m. Location: a peninsula running off the west central shore of Volta Lake. B/C OCT–JAN

Digya lies in the transition zone between the single rainy season of the savanna and the two wet seasons of the forest belt. February to April are the hottest months with temperatures of 15°–40°C, and August at around 25°C the coolest. The Park's vegetation is largely savanna woodland, with some gallery forest along the river banks.

There is a good primate population including olive baboons, green

138

or vervet monkey, Mona monkey, spot-nosed or red-tailed monkey, the colobus polykomos monkey of the short-haired Abyssinian race, and patas monkey. There are also populations of elephant, hippo, buffalo, Defassa waterbuck, Buffon's kob, roan antelope, hartebeest, and oribi. The bushpig is known locally as red river hog. Crocodiles are reported as still occurring.

Mole National Park (466,200 ha.) Altitude: 180 to 360 m. Location: in the northern region west of the White Volta. | B/C OCT–FEB

Mole was declared a Game Reserve in 1961, and elevated to a National Park in 1971. The vegetation is woodland savanna with gallery forest along the rivers. The average annual rainfall is 1,000 mm. March and April are the hottest months, while the lowest temperatures occur towards the end of the rains in August.

Mammals include various primates such as Guinea baboon, vervet monkey, patas monkey, and colobus monkey. Predators feature lion and leopard, side-striped jackal, wild dog, and spotted hyena. Elephant are present, also various ungulates such as roan, oribi, buffalo, waterbuck, Buffon's kob, bushbuck, and reedbuck.

Nile crocodile, Nile monitor, Bosc's monitor, and several terrapins and river turtles inhabit the watered areas.

There is a great deal to interest the birdwatcher.

GUINEA

Guinea, a sparsely-populated country which was a French colony until 1958, is unusual in that its territory consists of a highland watershed. The temperature is highest, up to 32°C, in April before the onset of the monsoon, and the heavy rains reach their peak between July and September – the source of the great Niger River is in the country's southern uplands.

Guinea's wildlife is very rich and includes substantial populations of leopard, elephant, antelope, and several primates. Bird and butterfly species are outstanding. There are no National Parks, but the Mont Nimba Biosphere Reserve is both a Nature Reserve dating back to 1944, and a listed Biosphere Reserve from 1980. In the same year it was also declared a World Heritage Site.

Mont Nimba Biosphere Reserve (17,130 ha.) Altitude: 450 to 1,752 m. Location: in the massif of Nimba on the border between Guinea, Ivory Coast and Liberia.   **B** OCT–MAR

Three main types of vegetation cover the reserve: high altitude grassland, plains savanna, and primary forest. Among the noteworthy fauna are Dossou chimpanzee, pygmy hippo, and dwarf otter shrew. Also present are buffalo, duiker, and various monkeys. There are numerous endemic wingless insects, myriapods, and moluscs. The forests contain many amphibian species including the endangered viviparous toad in the high grasslands, and the West African toad and frog.

IVORY COAST

The Ivory Coast is an ex-French colony which maintains close ties with its former colonial ruler. Large French and Lebanese communities remained in the country after independence, and there are now four times as many resident Europeans as in colonial days. The capital, Abidjan, is modern and sophisticated, tourism is well organised although expensive, and the road system is one of the best in West Africa. Cocoa, coffee and timber are the main sources of national income and there is a tradition of beautiful wood-carving.

Banco National Park (30,000 ha.) Altitude: sea-level to 110 m. Location: north bank of the Ebrie Lagoon round the mouth of the small Banco River, about 10 kms west of Abidjan in the south of the country.   **B/C** NOV–APR

Banco was established in 1953 to encompass an area of dense rainforest. It contains an arboretum and a few plantations, particularly of teak.

The fauna is not abundant, but white-nosed mangabey, chimpanzee and black-and-white colobus are in residence. African civet and genet are among the predators. Bushbuck and Maxwell's duiker have been recorded.

Comoe National Park (1,150,000 ha.) Altitude: 119 to 658 m. Location: on the Comoe River in the northeast of the country 600 kms from Abidjan.   **B** NOV–APR

Comoe was partly protected as early as 1926. 1953 saw it established as the Bouna–Comoe Faunal Reserve, and 1968 as a National Park. A Biosphere nomination has recently been submitted to UNESCO. The Park boasts an extraordinarily wide variety of habitats, including savanna, forest, and grasslands. The climate is tropical and humid, with 1,200 mm annual rainfall and a single dry season of six months in the south and eight months in the north. The mean annual temperature is 26°C.

The Park supports populations of elephant, 21 species of pig, and a great many buck, including kob, roan, oribi, bongo, and waterbuck. Lions are rare, but there are seventeen species of other carnivore, among them the leopard. Primates include Anubis baboon, black and white colobus, and green monkey. Giant pangolin and aardvark add to the variety.

Reptiles are well represented with all three varieties of African crocodile: the Nile, slender-snouted and dwarf, all of which are listed in the IUCN Red Data Book. Snakes are sacred to some of the native human inhabitants of the area.

Birds are not particularly abundant, but include 10 species of heron, duck, raptors, plovers and francolins, four of the six West African storks, and five of the six West African vultures.

Marahoue National Park (101,000 ha.) Altitude: 90 to 320 m. Location: in the west-central Ivory Coast.

B/C
NOV–APR

Marahoue was established in 1968. One third of the Park is savanna woodland and the rest is dense deciduous forest, including some gallery forest with good timber trees such as mahogany, tali, and iroko. The climate is tropical and humid, with rains from May to October and a dry season from November to April. The average annual rainfall is 1,100 mm.

The Park has a number of dome-like hills and is well watered by rivers. The fauna includes both savanna and forest species. Anubis baboon is plentiful, white-collared mangabey, mona monkey, and red colobus are present, as is the chimpanzee, *Pan troglodytes*. Among the predators is the African linsang, a small, nocturnal, large-eared genet cat. There are hippo, buffalo, and a herd of around 50 elephant. Bongo, red-flanked, bay and black duikers, Defassa waterbuck, bubal hartebeest, kob, bushbuck and reedbuck are among the ungulates.

Mont Peko National Park (34,000 ha.) Altitude: 400 to 1,002 m. Location: in the west-central region, 120 kms south of Man.

B/C
NOV–MAR/
APR

Mont Peko was declared a National Park in 1968. It is a mountainous area in which many summits reach or exceed 1,000 m, and is drained by tributaries of the Sassandra River. A forest reserve it has a characteristically Guinean type of climate, with a mean annual rainfall of 1,700 mm falling almost entirely between May and October.

Most of the Park is covered by dense deciduous forest, composed of such species as white and large-leaved mahoganies, wild cacao and wild rubber, and African oak. The mammal population is interesting, including leopard, elephant, buffalo and hippo. Giant pangolin and water chevrotaine are present but rare. Long-tailed tree pangolin, tree hyrax, Anubis baboon and chimpanzee shelter in the trees. Ungulates include Maxwell's and red-flanked duiker.

Mont Sangbe National Park (95,000 ha.) Altitude: 500–1,000 m. Location: in the central-west Ivory Coast, on the western bank of the Sassandra River.

C
NOV–MAR/
APR

Mont Sangbe is a Forest Reserve which was established as a National Park in 1975. There is very little information available about the Park, except that it consists of an area of tree savanna and contains a number of endemic species.

The Park is situated in a mountainous zone, the Toura Mountains, with fourteen peaks reaching over 1,000 m. The fauna is abundant and varied. Mammals include elephant, kob, baboon, and patas monkey. The birdlife includes guinea fowl, hornbills, and several species of eagle.

Tai National Park (330,000 ha. plus 20,000 ha. of buffer zone.) Altitude: 80 to 396 m. Location: in the southwest of the country 200 kms south of Man.

B
DEC–FEB

Tai was originally part of a Forest Refuge defined in 1926. Then in 1956 it became part of a Fauna Reserve. It was listed as a Biosphere Reserve in 1978, and as a World Heritage Site in 1982.

The Park is the last remaining portion of the vast primary forest that once stretched across the landscape of present-day Ghana. The climate is variable with high relative humidity. Rainfall ranges from 1,700 mm in the north to 2,200 mm in the south, reaching a peak in June and followed by a shorter wet season in September. There is a marked dry season from December to February. The temperature range is small, 24°–27°C, owing to the influence of the ocean and the forests.

The humid tropical forest has over 150 endemic species of vegetation. The trees are largely tall and dense evergreens, 46 m in height, with massive trunks and large buttress or stilt roots. Ebony and palm compete for space. Large numbers of lianes and epiphytes dominate the lower reaches. Plants which had been long thought extinct, such as *Amor-*

142

phophallus staudtii, have been rediscovered there.

Almost a thousand species of vertebrate have been identified in the Park. There are 47 out of a possible 54 species of large mammal, five of which are threatened with extinction. The primates feature mona, white-nosed and Diana monkey, black-and-white, red and green colobus, sooty mangabey, and chimpanzee. There are also elephant, and the only remaining viable population of pygmy hippo. Present too are bongo, buffalo, water chevrotaine, giant forest hog, bushpig, a remarkable range of forest duikers which includes Jentick's duiker, banded or zebra antelope, together with Ogilby's, black, bay, yellow-backed, and royal antelope. Giant, tree and long-tailed pangolins grace the shade. Leopard and golden cat are among the predators.

LIBERIA

Liberia, a prosperous nation on the bulge of Africa, has the distinction of being the only African country, apart from Ethiopia, which has never been directly colonised. Its special relationship with the United States of America dates back to the beginning of the nineteenth century when liberated black slaves arrived under the auspices of the American Colonization Company. The new settlers, either former slaves or the descendants of slaves, made treaties with the local inhabitants, and the joint society they created forms the basis of modern Liberia.

Loffa-Mano National Park (230,000 ha.) Altitude: up to 800 m. Location: on the border with Sierra Leone.

B/C
JULY, JAN–
MAR

Loffa-Mano was created in 1978–79, and includes a section of Kpelle National Forest. It lies in a well watered area, drained by the Mano and the Loffa Rivers which are punctuated by rapids and waterfalls. There are patches of low bush, marsh and savanna within the predominant rainforest, most of which is probably virgin and primary. The Park area contains a third of the Liberian forest elephant population, and the pygmy hippo is still fairly common. Other mammals include giant forest hog, water chevrotaine, black duiker, the endangered zebra duiker, bushbuck, and bongo. Among the primates are red colobus, black and white colobus, chimpanzee, and sooty mangabey. Tracks of all the classic Liberian fauna have been recorded.

Sapo National Park (130,700 ha.) Altitude: approx. 400 m – Mount Putu reaches 640 m. Location: in eastern Liberia.

C
JULY, JAN–MAR

Sapo was established in May 1983 and is bounded on the west by the Sinoe River and in the north by the Putu mountain range. The vegetation is partly swamp but mainly primary evergreen rainforest, which has a very rich, although as yet little surveyed, flora.

Most of the prominent mammals unique to Liberia are present including forest elephant, pygmy hippo, zebra duiker, and Jentinck's duiker plus five other duiker species. Also found are bongo, West African forest buffalo, leopard, giant forest hog, and many species of the West African primates including chimpanzee and the threatened red colobus monkey.

The avifauna is rich and varied although little studied. Among other rarities it includes the white-breasted guinea fowl.

MALI

Mali, known during its colonial period which ended in 1960 as French Sudan, is the largest country in West Africa. Its landlocked countryside is extremely dry and includes part of the Sahel desert. Although there is considerable potential for agriculture using irrigation from the River Niger, Mali is at present one of the world's poorest nations. Owing to its position as an African crossroads its population, although small, includes representatives of all the native African peoples – Negro, Hamitic and Semitic. During the 1970s the area suffered severely from drought.

Boucle du Baoule National Park (350,000 ha.) Altitude: 300 m. Location: on the Baoule River approximately 200 kms northwest of Bamako in western Mali.

C
NOV–APR

Boucle du Baoule was protected as a reserve in 1950, and created a National Park in 1953. Adjacent to it are the Fina Faunal Reserve, the Badinko Faunal Reserve and the Koungossambougou Faunal Reserve. The Park and all three reserves were designated a Biosphere Reserve of 771,000 ha. in 1982. The Park lies on the Madingue Plateau and is watered by the Baoule River. The vegetation in the southern part is grassland with some tree cover; to the north lies the Sahel zone with little grass and spiny vegetation, while the remainder is covered by a dense canopy of riverine forest with creepers and bamboo. The average annual temperature is 29.7°C and the rainfall 950 mm.

Vervet, or green monkey, and infant in Kruger National Park, South Africa

Large mammals include elephant, leopard, lion, cheetah, hippo, giraffe, roan antelope, Defassa waterbuck, giant eland, eland (in the Fina reserve), hartebeest, and warthog. Also present are three primates: Anubis baboon, vervet monkey, and patas monkey.

The abundant birdlife includes many migratory species.

MAURITANIA

The Islamic Republic of Mauritania became independent in 1960, having been under French domination since 1903. Two thirds of the country is desert which has been advancing slowly for the past few thousand years. Only in the south round the Senegal River is agriculture possible.

Banc d'Arguin National Park (1,173,000 ha.) Altitude: from sea-level to 15 m. Location: on the West African coast.
C
SEPT–JUNE

Banc d'Arguin consists of a vast area of coastal seas and mudflats, with fourteen permanent islands. Some of the offshore islands have mangroves.

The Park is of major ornithological importance as the crossroads for multitudes of aquatic birds on migration between Europe and northern Asia, and most of Africa. Over 2 million broad-billed sandpipers have been recorded in the winter. Other migrants include hundreds of thousands of black terns, tens of thousands of flamingoes, thousands of white pelicans, and hundreds of spoonbills. Various species breed on the islands, including terns, flamingoes, herons, cormorants, spoonbills, and white herons. The Park also contains an important spawning area for fish.

The small population of monk seals is now threatened as a result of the collapse of their breeding caves in 1982.

NIGER

Although 6,000 years ago the Niger area was fertile and well watered and there are archaeological remains of a flourishing culture, the modern Republic of Niger is a country invented by colonial bureaucrats. None of its boundaries bear any relation to either geographical or population divisions. It has no seaboard, and access to foreign ports is long and difficult. The country has one permanent watercourse, the River Niger, which traverses the south west of the landscape for 500 kms and supports the majority of the five million population. Over half the country is desert with a typically hot and arid climate, although in other parts heavy rains fall during July and August. The droughts of the early 1970s took a severe toll of both human inhabitants and wildlife.

'W' National Park (220,000 ha. contiguous with 'W' in both Upper Volta and Benin.) Altitude: 180 to 338 m. Location: 125 kms southeast of Niamey on the right bank of the River Niger, and extending to the intersection of Niger, Upper Volta and Benin.
    B
    DEC–APR

'W' takes its name from the shape of the double bend in the River Niger between the points where two tributaries from the west, the Tapo and the Mekrou, flow into it. The valleys of both tributaries are deeply incised and, together with the Barou rapids, are the chief scenic attraction.

The vegetation is savanna woodland, together with gallery forest. The temperature ranges from a maximum of 36.1°C to a minimum of 21.6°C. Rainfall is unpredictable, although it averages between 700 and 800 mm a year.

The Park contains healthy numbers of carnivores, including lion, leopard, cheetah, both hyenas, jackal, serval cat, and caracal. Elephant are present, as are hippo, buffalo, Defassa waterbuck, kob, oribi, topi, roan antelope, and hartebeest. The smaller ungulates are bushbuck, red-flanked and grey duiker, reedbuck, warthog, dama gazelle and red-fronted gazelle.

There is a varied and abundant birdlife, headed by the raptor populations of fish eagle, martial eagle, harriers, vultures, and goshawk. Guineafowl, bustards, hornbills, and francolins are found throughout the Park. Migratory aquatic birds arrive from February to May and the waterbirds most frequently encountered are geese, ducks, waders, ibises, storks, herons, and egrets.

There are still some crocodiles in the river.

NIGERIA

Nigeria, a federation of states formerly under British colonial rule, is the most populous and one of the largest countries in modern Africa.

147

The climate of the coast, the Bight of Benin, was for long infamously hostile to Europeans – 'Beware, beware, the Bight of Benin, / Where one comes out though forty go in.' Malarial prophylactics and modern medicine have largely eliminated the coast's former dangers. Inland Nigeria has a great basin of tropical rainforest in the south, while savanna predominates to the north. The capital, Lagos, is hot and humid, and the long rainy season lasts from March to November. The rainfall in the south is around 2,000 mm annually, but drops sharply in the north to under 250 mm. Temperatures average 29°C in the south, and range from 43°C to below 4°C in the north.

Kainji Lake National Park, Borgu division (392,400 ha.) Altitude: 120 to 346 m. Location: west of the River Niger in Kwara State.   B/C DEC–MAR

Kainji, which embraces a central part of Lake Kainji on the River Niger, was first established as a Forest Reserve in 1961 and became a National Park in 1975. The Park's vegetation is wooded savanna with some forest. The Kainji Dam was finished in 1972.

The Park shelters around 65 species of mammal including lion, leopard, caracal, elephant, buffalo, western hartebeest, kob, hippo, giant pangolin and manatee. Cheetah have recently been observed (1979). There are also around 30 amphibians and reptiles.

350 species of bird have been recorded.

SENEGAL

The Republic of Senegal gained its independence from the French in 1958 but has maintained its links with France. Although the country's per capita income is low, the capital, Dakar, under the influence of poet–philosopher President Leopold Senghor, is the centre for arts and literature of West Africa.

The country has to depend for its living on such agriculture as is possible on its rather pool soil. Peanuts are the main cash crop, and a cotton industry is developing. Tourism is mainly French and limited to the beaches of Dakar. Elections are held regularly, and the state is multi-party.

Basse Casamance National Park (5,000 ha.) Altitude: 0 to 11 m. Location: in the southwest of Senegal, near the border with Guinea Bissau.   C NOV–APR

Established in 1970 Basse Casamance lies in a well watered area only a few kilometres from the ocean, and its water courses ebb and flow with the tide. The Park's vegetation falls into three main types: the last tropical forest in Senegal, wooded savanna and. in the west, mangrove. The climate is tropical.

The most obvious mammals are the populations of primates, among them the mona monkey, but more than 50 species have been recorded, including occasional manatee, hippo, and several antelopes in large numbers. The area also supports a great many reptiles, among them the Python de Saba and the Naja cracheur.

The Park is well known for its magnificent butterflies and the bird checklist contains more than 200 species, including a number of Palearctic migrants and Ethiopian area species.

Djoudj National Bird Sanctuary (16,000 ha.) Altitude: from near sea-level to 20 m. Location: in the extreme north of the country on the delta of the Senegal River, 15 kms north of Ross-Bethio and 60 kms northeast of Saint-Louis.

B/C
SEPT–APR

Djoudj is an outstanding bird sanctuary in the delta of the Senegal River and the Gorom Stream. The climate is Sahelian with alternate wet and dry seasons. The minimum annual rainfall is 300 mm and the mean annual temperature 27°C. In the dry season it is the only naturally green enclave in the region, while during the rains rafts of waterlilies flower in the flooded zones.

The area, one of the first sites with permanent water south of the Sahara, is one of the three key West African sanctuaries for Palearctic migrants, and some 300 species of bird have been recorded. From September to April around 3 million migrants pass through, mainly ducks and waders, among them garganey, shoveller, pintail, ruff, and black-tailed godwit. Thousands of flamingoes nest regularly as do white pelicans, white-faced tree-duck, fulvus tree-duck, spur-winged goose, purple heron, night heron, egrets, spoonbill, anhinga, cormorants, and great bustard. Several species of crocodile and gazelle have been successfully reintroduced.

Iles de la Madeleine National Park (450 ha.) Altitude: 0 to 35 m. Location: about 4 kms to the west of Dakar in the Atlantic Ocean.

C
SEPT–APR

Les Iles de la Madeleine was established as a National Park in 1976 to protect the bird population on three islands of volcanic origin. The islands' vegetation includes the only dwarf baobabs in Senegal, and 101 recorded species of plant.

The birdlife is rich and varied including the magpie-crow, black kite,

West African red bishop bird, red-bellied tropicbird, and forty breeding pairs of *Calerida crishela mesaunauta*. 300 pairs of the great cormorant breed on five sites on the islands. Osprey and peregrine hunt the waters and the skies. Among the seabirds are populations of northern gannet, bridled tern, and brown booby.

The marine fauna is rich with many species of fish, cetaceans and shellfish.

Langue de Barbarie National Park (2,000 ha.) Altitude: sea-level. Location: at the north of the Senegal River, 25 kms from the country's ancient capital, Saint Louis.

B/C
SEPT–APR

Langue de Barbarie is a 20-km stretch of a spit on the Senegal River, washed by both fresh and sea water. It was established in 1976 to protect the population of seabirds.

The resident seabirds include the grey-headed gull, Caspian tern, royal tern at its northern breeding limit, slender-billed gull, gull-billed tern at its southern breeding limit, sooty tern, and the little tern, also at its southern breeding limit. The Park is also an important roosting site for many Ethiopian species. The osprey can be seen, and there are herons, egrets, and sandpipers. The marine fauna includes green turtle, the endangered leatherback turtle, and dolphin.

Niokolo-Koba National Park (913,000 ha.) Altitude: 16 to 311 m – Mont Assirik. Location: on the River Gambia close to the Guinea border in southeastern Senegal.

B
DEC–mid-
MAY

Niokolo-Koba National Park was established in 1954 and gradually expanded to its present size. It was listed as a Biosphere Reserve and World Heritage Site in 1981. The Park's landscape is relatively flat with vetiver grass prairies merging into flooded grassland and marsh, and dry forest in other places. There are areas of bamboo, and tall trees and lianes in the ravines and gallery forest. The Park is watered by the River Gambia and its two tributaries, the Niokolo Koba and the Koulountou. It has a single wet season from June to October, when an average of 1,000–1,100 mm of rain falls; the rest of the year is dry.

The area is very interesting botanically as the wide variety of soil and irrigation conditions has stimulated great plant diversity. A multitude of annuals, which disappear when the water rises, occur in the periodically flooded sands near the rivers. The marshes are mainly in abandoned riverbeds. By 1981, 1,500 plant species have been identified and the listing continues.

Wildlife numbers 80 species of mammal, including the two big cats, lion and leopard, and the Park provides the last refuge for elephant in Senegal. The different habitats support populations of antelope, buffalo, roan, about a thousand giant eland, hunting dog, Guinea baboon, and green monkey. The rivers are frequented by all three African crocodiles: Nile, slender-snouted, and dwarf. All three watercourses have populations of hippo, and there are four species of tortoise. Some families of chimpanzee inhabit the gallery forest and, on Mont Assirik, overlap with the southern limit of the Patas monkey.

By 1970, 350 species of bird had been recorded, including Denham's bustard, the spectacular Abyssinian ground hornbill, the violet turaco, spur-winged goose, and white-faced tree-duck. Among the largest raptors are the bateleur and martial eagle.

The Park also contains 36 reptiles, 20 amphibians and over 60 species of fish.

Saloum Delta National Park (180,000 ha. of Biosphere Reserve, including 73,000 ha. of National Park.) Altitude: sea-level to 10 m. Location: 150 kms from Dakar close to the town of Kaolack. B/C DEC–APR

Saloum Delta was established as a National Park in 1976, and listed as a Biosphere Reserve in 1980. The Park and reserve, in the delta of the seasonally-flowing Sine and Saloum Rivers, contain many sand islands and lagoons together with the Sangomar point and its coastal waters, and the forests of Fathala. Most of the terrestrial area of the Park is covered by mangroves – the mangrove swamps are the most northerly in Africa – sand dunes, and open forest.

Large mammals were probably never very numerous, and many species have vanished. However the Sudano-Sahelian fauna is very varied, particularly in the dry forest of Fathala where the western red colobus monkey has made its home, and the list of small mammal species is long. Manatee are present and reptiles, among them the marine turtle, well represented. Dolphin also occur in the region.

The birdlife is mostly water and sea-based, and includes breeding populations of flamingo.

SIERRA LEONE

Sierra Leone is one of the smallest states in Africa, with its coastline deeply indented by the sea. The population is mainly rural and consists of two main groups, the Mende and the Temne. From the early days of the Portuguese presence in Africa the country was a centre for the slave trade.

Outama–Kilimi National Park (98,000 ha.) Altitude: 50–300 m. Location: two separate units in the Tambatcha Chiefdom of Bombali district in the northwest of the country.

C
DEC–MAR

Outama–Kilimi was established under provisional legislation in 1981. The western boundary is the Great Scarcies River, which forms the border with Guinea. The vegetation on the broad river plain ranges from moist, close forest, savanna, and boli grasses in seasonally flooded areas (bolilands), to riverine forest.

There are 125 recorded mammal species including eight primates:

Fringe-eared oryx

Guinea baboon, Campbell's mona monkey, green or vervet monkey, sooty mangabey, chimpanzee, black and white colobus, red colobus, and spot-nosed guenon. Among other mammals are hippo, buffalo, elephant, bushpig, and duiker. Carnivores include leopard, side-striped jackal, genet, and golden cat. Crocodile are present and the birdlife is rich and varied, especially interesting being the wetland species on the bolilands.

Mamunta–Mayoso Swamp Nature Reserve. Altitude: up to 500 m. Location: near the town of Magburaka in central Sierra Leone.

C
DEC–MAR

The reserve still awaits official government protection. The area consists of swampland which supports a wide variety of mammals, birds, and reptiles, as well as two threatened species of crocodile.

Gola Forest Reserve (58,000 ha.) Altitude: up to 472 m. Location: on the country's eastern border with Liberia and contiguous with a Liberian forest zone.

C
DEC–MAR

The reserve constitutes the furthest extension north and westwards of the Congo–West African closed forest. The forest is virgin and unique both in the size and height of its trees, which include a high proportion of rare species and one endemic, *Didelotii idae*. The area was formerly almost inaccessible, but in recent times a road has been constructed and 40% of the forest has been logged. There is scant information available on the current status of Gola's wildlife.

SUDAN

Sudan, the largest country in Africa with an area almost as big as western Europe, became an independent republic in 1956 after the deposition of King Farouk of Egypt, then its suzeraine. The country is particularly rich in wildlife, and its vast size accommodates a wealth of different habitats. The best season for visitors is during the Sudanese winter from November to March. The hottest month is June and the rains fall in July and August.

Boma National Park (1,750,000 ha.) Altitude: 400 to 1,100 m. Location: close to the Egyptian border in Jonglei province.

B/C
NOV–MAR

Boma was declared a National Park in 1979 to protect the richest variety of fauna in the Sudan and possibly in Africa. The Park has five ecological zones: montane forest, deciduous woodlands, semi-arid short grass plain (in the south), seasonal swamps, and tall grass floodplain. Numerous rivers meander across the Park's landscape on their way to the Nile.

Among the many species of mammal present in the Park are elephants, giraffe, buffalo, roan antelope, zebra, oryx, hartebeest, reedbuck, mongalla gazelle, giant gazelle, and white-eared kob – the dominant species of the Guom swamps. There are also large populations of leopard and cheetah.

Dinder National Park (639,700 ha. with a buffer zone of 277,300 ha.) A/B Altitude: 700 to 800 m. Location: in the northeast corner of the Blue DEC–APR Nile Province at the frontier with Ethiopia, approximately 500 kms south of Khartoum.

Dinder, which was proclaimed in 1935, is the most famous of the Sudan's National Parks. It was declared a Biosphere Reserve in 1979, and a buffer zone was added in 1980. The Park is on a low-lying floodplain with thornbush savanna sloping gently down from the Ethiopian highlands. The Rahad and Dinder Rivers, flowing through on their way to the Blue Nile, support gallery forest on their banks. The main source of food for the herbivores grows in and around the ox-bow lakes, or mayas, which gradually silt up. Rainfall ranges from 800 mm in the south to 600 mm in the north, and falls mainly between June and October. Temperatures are from 20°C in January to 44°C in May.

The fauna has been much reduced over the last couple of decades as a result of various problems, including over-grazing by nomads and their herds, and poaching. Quite recently the wild herds have been attacked by serious outbreaks of disease, which have been caused largely by infection from domestic livestock. Fires, both natural and man-made, have been another major factor in changing the Park's ecology through their effect on the vegetation.

However, representatives of most of the original inhabitants remain including lion, leopard, cheetah, giraffe, buffalo, roan antelope, greater kudu, topi, oribi, striped and spotted hyenas, reedbuck, waterbuck, and bushbuck.

The birdlife, headed by the ostrich, is extremely varied with eagles, vultures, guinea fowl, crowned crane, pelican, and bustard.

Nimule National Park (25,000 ha.) Altitude: 650 to 700 m. Location: C in the south of Eastern Equatorial Province, on the border with Uganda. NOV–MAR

Nimule was established in 1975 in hilly savanna woodland, with the White Nile flowing along about 48 kms of its eastern border. The River

Kayu runs through the Park, and in the east and west there are mountain ranges which include the Fula Rapids.

The area's mammals include elephant, Uganda kob, hippo, crocodile, warthog, waterbuck, and oribi. Unfortunately, the Park suffered severely during the recent civil war, and the white rhino was poached out.

Radom National Park (1,250,970 ha.) Altitude: 450 m. Location: in the southwestern corner of Southern Darfur Province, bordering the Central African Republic. B/C NOV–MAR

Radom was declared a Biosphere Reserve in 1979. It suffered during the recent Sahelian drought when tsetse flies and grazing by domestic stock moved southwards, and is likely to be important in the future as a study area for the process of desertification. The Park, whose vegetation consists largely of savanna woodland, occupies broken hilly country with two main rivers and numerous small streams flooding only during the wet season.

The area supports populations of elephant, hartebeest, waterbuck, kob, hippo, eland, giraffe, and a large number of carnivores.

Southern National Park (1,600,000 ha.) Altitude: 800 to 1,000 m. Location: in Lakes Province in the south of the Tonj district. B/C NOV–MAR

Southern, established in 1939, is an area of savanna woodland with a varying mixture of grass and trees. The Park is watered by three rivers: the River Sue, the main tributary of the Bahr Ghasal or Jur River on the western border, the River Ibba or Tonj, which flows through the centre, and the River Maridi or Gel to the east.

Wildlife is rich in quantity and variety, including elephant, buffalo, white rhino, hartebeest, waterbuck, tiang, kob, and giraffe. Carnivores include lion, leopard, and hunting dog. The forested areas shelter bongo while the marshes and watercourses are frequented by hippo, crocodile, and sitatunga.

TOGO

The Republic of Togo is a tiny country, only 600 kms long and 120 kms at its widest, with a seafront on to the Atlantic on the West African coast. Like all the neighbouring coastal regions, both its human and wild-

155

life populations were ravaged during the upheavals caused by the slave trade.

Togo is currently encouraging the growth of tourism. The climate is milder and more pleasant than on most of the Atlantic seaboard, the heat being tempered by sea breezes in summer and by the wind from the north in winter.

Keran National Park (109,240 ha.) Altitude: 140 m. Location: in the Kara region.

C

SEPT–MAR

Keran, an area of tree and grass savanna on floodplains, was established in 1950. The Park harbours a variety of mammals including elephant, buffalo, hippo, hartebeest, kob, warthog, and aardvark. The principal predator is leopard and there are several species of monkey.

The birdlife is interesting and includes Jbiru stork, crowned crane, marabou, ibis, herons, guinea fowl, bustards, and francolin.

Fazao–Melfacassa National Park (200,000 ha.) Altitude: 100–800 m. Location: in the central region.

C

SEPT–MAR

The Fazao–Melfacassa Park, established in 1950, lies in a mountain region with tree savanna and sparse forest. The Park contains a variety of mammals including elephant, buffalo, lion, and leopard. Bongo, sitatunga, yellow-backed duiker, hippo, kob, and several species of primate, including colobus monkey, are also present. Warthog, bushpig and great forest hog shelter in the forest, and packs of hunting dog swell the numbers of predators.

Among the avifauna are various species of guinea fowl and the splendid Abyssinian ground hornbill.

UPPER VOLTA (from August 1983 renamed BURKINA FASO)

Upper Volta is a landlocked and densely although patchily inhabited West African ex-colony of France. With very few natural resources, its chief export tends to be its own manpower. The country's poverty is in large part a result of its geography, as the only areas free from flood and disease are also those where the soil is least fertile.

Upper Volta is bisected by three rivers, the White Volta, the Red Volta, and the Black Volta, all of which flow sluggishly into Lake Volta in Ghana. The rivers' movement is slow because of the surrounding terrain, and the swamps which inevitably spread out round them are incubators for malaria, bilharzia, and river blindness. Most of the human population lives away from them. In the southwest the rainy season is May to October with an annual average fall of 1,000 mm. The rest of the country is much drier.

Arly National Park and **Arly Faunal Reserve** (76,000 and 130,000 ha. — contiguous with the Singou Strict Reserve.) Altitude: 300 m. Location: in the east of the country, on the border with Benin.
    C
    NOV–APR

Arly was established in 1954 and lies on a flat, flood-prone, lowland area bordered to the southeast by the Pendjari River. There are permanent ponds in the dry season. The vegetation is wooded savanna similar to that found in 'W' National Park.

Among the noteworthy fauna are elephant, lion, leopard, buffalo, and warthog. In addition, the Park contains several monkeys such as patas and the green or vervet monkey, waterbuck, hartebeest, topi, and hippo.

Deux Balés National Park (115,000 ha.) Altitude: 235 to 310 m. Location: in central western Upper Volta.
    C
    NOV–APR

Deux Balés was established in 1967 as a National Park, but was previously the *Forêt Classée des Deux Balés*. It occupies an undulating savanna plain with gallery forest along the river banks. Most of the larger animals, which formerly included buffalo, hippo, crocodile and several antelope, have apparently been wiped out by poaching and other human activities.

Po National Park (155,500 ha.) Altitude: 200 to 400 m. Location: in the centre of the country round the Red Volta River.
    B/C
    NOV–APR

Po was created as a *Forêt Classée* in 1936 and given National Park status in 1967. The Park's vegetation is mainly wooded savanna and gallery forest.

Among the noteworthy fauna are elephant, lion, buffalo, waterbuck, kob, Bohar reedbuck, warthog, roan, oribi, and bushbuck. Primates are represented by vervet and patas monkeys, and baboons.

'W' National Park (190,000 ha. — part of the international Park with a total area of 1,026,425 ha.) Altitude: 250 m on average. Location: in eastern Upper Volta on the borders with Benin and Niger.
    C
    NOV–APR

'W' in Upper Volta consists of open Sahel savanna in the north, and open wooded savanna in the south. It was established first in 1926 and declared a National Park in 1937. The Park's fauna includes elephant, lion, leopard, cheetah, and buffalo. Also present are waterbuck, kob,

157

Bohar reedbuck, roan, hartebeest, topi, warthog and bushbuck, red-flanked duiker, and yellow baboon. Hippo, crocodile, and tortoises can be found in well-watered areas.

ZAIRE

Zaire, formerly the Belgian Congo, is the third largest country in Africa. If its political problems had not made it effectively ungovernable during the post-colonial period, it would be one of the richest countries in the continent. It has immense natural resources, and the potential for hydro-electric power from the River Zaire, formerly the Congo River.

The capital, Kinshasa, is near the mouth of the Zaire where the country narrows to a bottleneck opening on to the sea. The central zone is covered by dense tropical forest, which, along with the un-navigable nature of the river, acted as a barrier to human migration and exploration across the centuries. The interior still holds a small population of hunter-gatherer pygmies, who have largely escaped the attentions of civilisation.

Zaire has a beautiful and abundant wildlife, in spite of recent depredations, and efforts have been made to preserve it. There is an extra-ordinarily rich avifauna, with over 1,000 species of birds recorded. Many of them can be seen in the Parks, particularly at Virunga, the largest and most accessible, and in the Ituri forest at Mount Hoyo.

Garamba National Park (500,000 ha.) Altitude: 710 to 1,061 m. Location: in northeast Zaire on the border with Sudan. B/C NOV–MAR

Garamba was established in 1938 with the aim of protecting the populations of northern white rhino and northern savanna giraffe. It was declared a World Heritage Site in 1980. The Park is watered by three rivers, the Dungu, the Aka, and the Garamba. The vegetation ranges from densely-wooded savanna, gallery forest, and papyrus marshes to grassy savanna in the northern sector. The grass can grow to five metres in height, and is burned annually by the Park staff. The climate is tropical with a rainy season from December to March and a long dry period from April to November, during which temperatures range from 15°C to 35°C. The mean annual rainfall is around 1,500 mm.

Heading the list of noteworthy fauna are the square-lipped or white rhino, with 259 individuals counted in 1975, and the northern savanna giraffe. The elephant population is unique in that it represents an inter-mediary form on the cline between the forest and savanna sub-species.

158

Further mammals include hippo, buffalo, hartebeest, kob, waterbuck, two species of otter, five of mongoose, warthog, bushpig, giant forest hog, roan, and six other antelope. Primates are well represented and include chimpanzee, olive baboon, colobus, vervet, and five other species. Predators number leopard, lion, wild dog, and golden cat.

Kahuzi-Biega National Park (600,000 ha.) Altitude: 1,800 to 3,400 m.   B/C
Location: eastern Zaire, close to the Rwanda and Burundi borders.   NOV–MAR
    Part of Kahuzi–Biega was established as a reserve in 1960. The enlarged

Bush pig, or Red River hog, Zaire

159

reserve became a National Park in 1970 and was accepted as a World Heritage Site in 1980. It occupies part of the western mountains of the Great Rift Valley in the basin of the River Zaire. The vegetation is mainly dense primary mountain forest with some bamboo. The rest is woodland, swamp and peat bog. A recent enlargement of the Park has brought a vast undulating area of equatorial rainforest within its borders. Temperatures range from 10°C to 18°C. The mean annual rainfall is 1,800 mm, but there is a wide fluctuation from year to year.

The Park was set up to protect 200 to 300 mountain gorillas which are found mainly in the forests between 2,100 and 2,500 m, but also occur in the rainforest. Other primates include chimpanzee, black and red colobus monkeys, and owl-faced monkey. Among other mammals are elephant, forest hog, and many antelope and duiker.

There is abundant bird and insect life.

Kundelungu National Park (213,000 ha.) Altitude: 1,200 to 1,700 m. Location: in southeastern Zaire.

B/C
NOV–MAR

Kundelungu, established in 1970, is located on a plateau characteristic of the Shaba region. The vegetation is open woodland and grassy savanna, with some forest along the drainage lines. The western limit is formed by 400 m cliffs which fall perpendicularly to the valley of the Lufira River – the falls on the Lofoi tributary are thought to be the highest in Africa, with a 342 m drop.

The fauna is especially rich in ungulates, including at least 15 species such as zebra, duikers, klipspringer, roan and sable antelope, bushbuck, greater kudu, and eland. Accompanying predators include leopard and cheetah. There are also populations of savanna monkey, blue monkey, yellow baboon, and bushbabies or galagos.

Birdlife, as everywhere in Zaire, is very rich and includes wattled crane and ground hornbill.

Maiko National Park (1,083,000 ha.) Altitude: 700 to 1,300 m. Location: in eastern Zaire, in the regions of Kivu and Haut-Zaire.

C
NOV–MAR

Maiko was established in 1970 in a region of dense humid primary equatorial forest and the fauna includes the classic elements of forest fauna. The Park's rainfall is the highest in Zaire, with almost no dry season. The whole area is extremely remote and has few human inhabitants.

The most important faunal species are the populations of the endangered mountain gorilla, the okapi, and the Zaire peacock. Elephant, duikers, and Cape buffalo are also present.

160

Giraffe in Ngorongoro Conservation Area, Tanzania

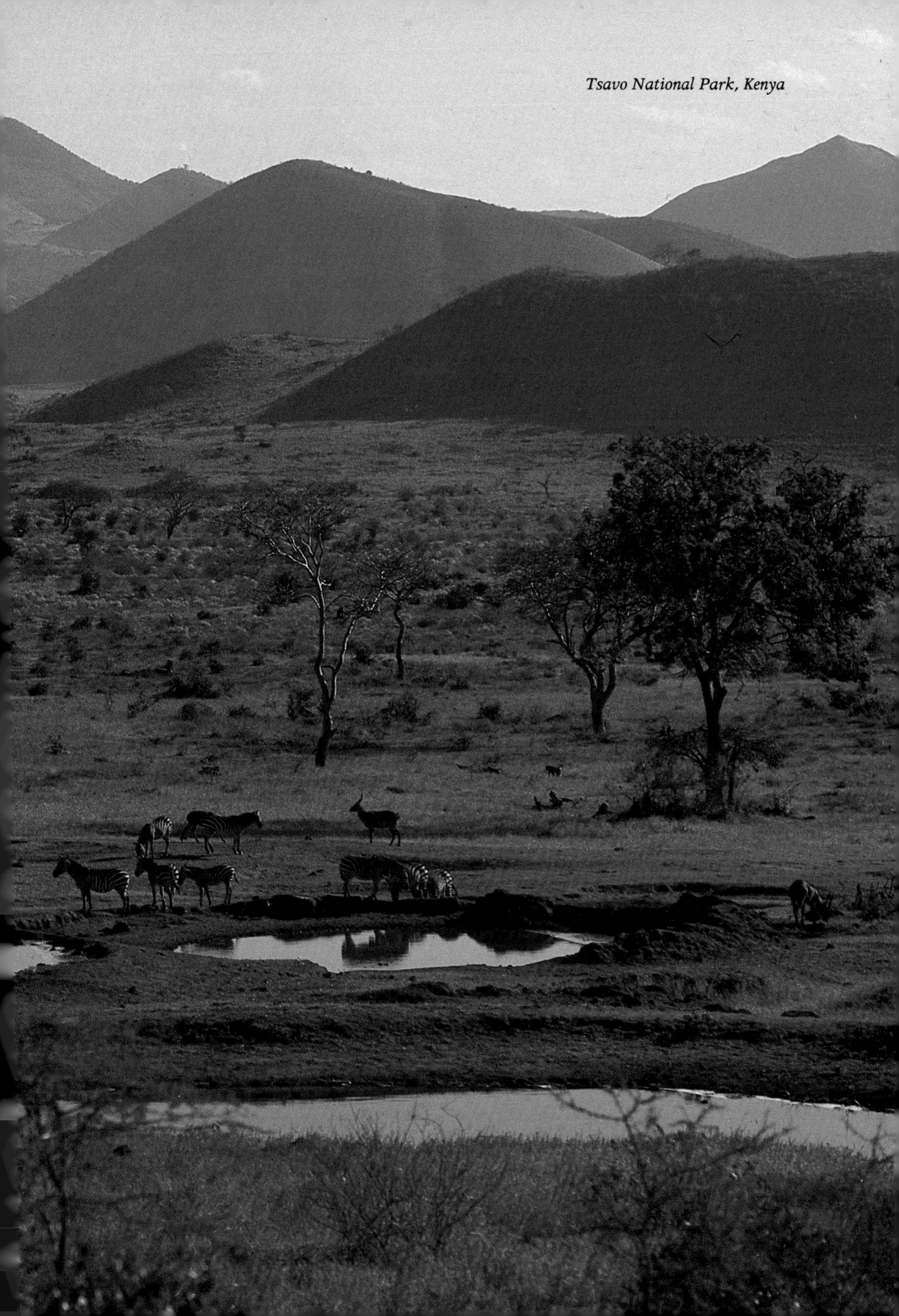

Tsavo National Park, Kenya

Black-backed jackal, Kenya

Salonga National Park (3,656,000 ha.) Altitude: 350 to 700 m. Location: in the central Zaire basin.

B/C
NOV–MAR

Salonga was established in 1970 and encompasses a large section of the central basin of the River Zaire, a very isolated region only accessible by water transport. Temperatures are stable at around 20°C at night and 32°C by day. The area is almost entirely covered with equatorial forest: swamp forests, riverine forests, and dry-land forest. There is some grassland in the northern sector.

Most of the forest animals appear to be present, although no systematic survey has been made. The fauna should include the pygmy chimpanzee, which is endemic to Zaire, although it could not be found in 1981. Among the other mammals are colobus monkeys, various other species of monkey, leopard, yellow-backed duiker, water chevrotaine, sitatunga, bushbuck, and bongo. Two other pygmy species are noteworthy: pygmy elephant, both *Loxodonta africana cyclotis* and the controversial subspecies *pumilio*, and the pygmy Cape buffalo. Reptiles feature among their number the African slender-snouted crocodile.

Birdlife includes herons, black stork, yellow-billed stork, and the Congo peacock, an endemic species.

Virunga National Park (780,000 ha.) Altitude: 798 m in the south, rising to 5,119 m in the Ruwenzori range. Location: in northeastern Zaire, on the border with Uganda and Rwanda. The Park is contiguous with the Gorilla Sanctuary in Uganda and Volcanoes National Park in Rwanda.

A/B
NOV–MAR

Virunga was first established in 1925 as Albert National Park, and accepted as a World Heritage Site in 1979. The Park ranges from Lake Edward to the high peaks of the Ruwenzori range, the fabled Mountains of the Moon, which are sited almost on the equator. The rainfall is equally diverse, measuring a yearly 500 mm at Lake Edward, and more than 3,000 mm on the slopes of Mt Ruwenzori. The Park contains lakes, marshy deltas and peat bogs, savanna and lava plains, equatorial forest, and high altitude glaciers and snow fields. Nyrangongo Volcano erupted in 1977.

The remarkable diversity of habitats is reflected in the richness of the fauna, and some of the largest concentrations of wild animals in Africa are found along the Virunga's rivers. There are elephant, lion, over 20,000 hippos (1979), buffalo, kob, topi, and Defassa waterbuck. Primates include a population of the endangered mountain gorilla in the Semiliki Valley and on the slopes of the Virunga Mountains. Also present are chimpanzee, the rare okapi, bongo, and forest hog.

161

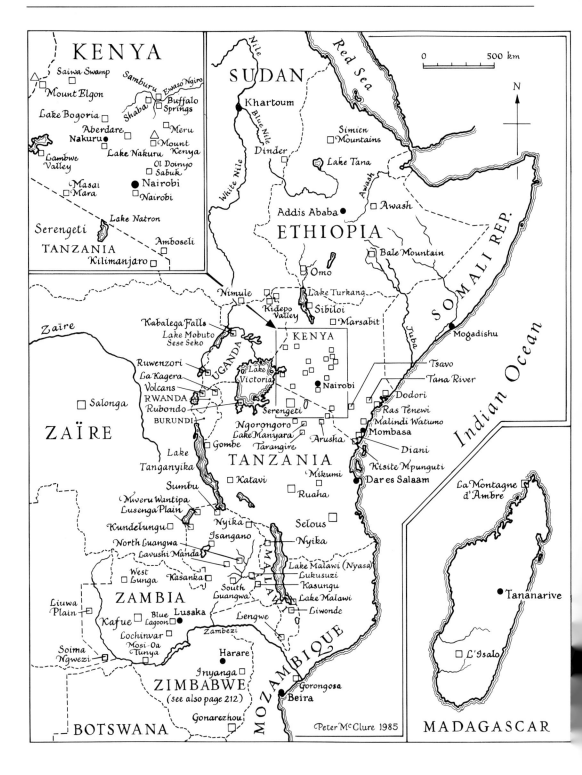

Peter McClure 1985

EAST AFRICA

East Africa's climate is predominantly tropical: the weather is dry and warm throughout the year with little difference in temperature between summer and winter. In most areas a long dry season is followed by intermittent and unpredictable periods of rain. The long rains in Kenya and Uganda tend to fall in April and May, the short rains in November and December. In Tanzania and Zambia the rains come between December and May. In Ethiopia the traditional rainy season lasts from February to April, and again from mid-June to September. Over the year the only significant temperature fluctuations are dictated by altitude. On the high Ethiopian plateau, for example, the nights can be bitterly cold whatever the season.

As a region East Africa is bisected longitudinally by the Rift Valley, which stretches from Ethiopia down to the far southern reaches of the Kalahari desert. The Rift Valley forms the great lake and river system bordering Uganda, Tanzania and Congo, and creates the vast expanse of Lake Victoria–Myanza before finally cutting through to Malawi. The landscape of Uganda, Rwanda and Tanzania is covered mainly by savanna woodland and scattered trees, although all three countries have some areas of dense forest. Kenya and the Horn of Africa consist principally of spiny steppe, desert steppe with occasional forests, and high altitude prairie–savanna. The grass grows rapidly on the rich plains during the rainy season, and dries out equally quickly. Animals are extremely numerous almost everywhere, particularly the herbivores and their accompanying predators. Until quite recently the region was one of Africa's prime hunting areas. Today trophy-hunting has largely been replaced by photographic safaris, although some of the Parks are re-introducing licensed hunting as a way of controlling animal populations and providing revenue for conservation measures.

ETHIOPIA

Ethiopia, the former Abyssinia in the Horn of Africa, was an ancient and legendary Christian kingdom in an area largely dominated by Muslims. Much of the landscape is mountainous, although denuded now of its former rich forests, and most of the present population lives in the highland areas.

Ethiopian wildlife is notably rich and varied, and in spite of the continuing strife in the country its conservation is recognised as being important enough to be part of declared government policy.

Awash National Park (72,000 ha.) Altitude: 1,000 to 1,200 m. Location: near the eastern margin of the Rift Valley, 225 kms east of Addis Ababa in Shoa Province.

B/C
ALL YEAR

Awash, in the Ethiopian highlands, established as a National Park in 1969, lies on a grassy plain crossed by the Awash River and graced by

Lesser kudu in Awash National Park, Ethiopia

the dramatic Awash Falls. There is a semi-dormant volcano, Mount Fantalle, in the southwest corner of the Park. Near the northern boundary is an area of hot springs and pools surrounded by palm groves. The climate is hot and dry with a low rainfall.

The mammal population includes the endangered Swayne's hartebeest, which was translocated to the Park in 1974, large herds of Beisa oryx and Defassa waterbuck, and a few Grevy's zebra. The principal primates are Hamadryas and Anubis baboon, and hybrids of the two species. Greater and lesser kudu are common.

For birdwatchers the checklist is 392 species, headed by the ostrich.

Bale Mountain National Park (167,500 ha.) Altitude: 3,000 to 4,500 m.   C
Location: 400 kms southeast of Addis Ababa.   ALL YEAR

Bale Mountain contains one of the best preserved mountain systems in Ethiopia. It contains several valleys and alpine lakes, and the tableland around Mount Batu and Mount Tullu Demtu. Close to the Park are the Sophomer Caves. The vegetation consists of low forest, giant heath, and some alpine bamboo.

The Park supports some 32 species of mammal including the endemic mountain nyala and simien fox. Other mammals include Menelik's bushbuck, klipspringer, olive baboon, warthog, Abyssinian hare, and hyrax. Among the predators are leopard, caracal, and golden jackal. The rivers have been stocked with brown trout and rainbow trout, which now breed freely.

The birdlife is notable and includes 12 of Ethiopia's 23 endemic bird species. Bale also has two controlled hunting areas.

Omo National Park (34,500 ha.) Altitude: 500 to 1,000 m. Location: in   C
the Kaffa Region in the southwest corner of Ethiopia, near the borders   ALL YEAR
with the Sudan and Kenya.

Omo, which was proclaimed in 1969, lies on an open plain by the banks of the Omo River. The vegetation consists of open grassland, savanna, bushland, and riverine forests. The climate is hot with a rainy season from April to July.

The area is rich in big game, some twenty-nine species being found in the Park. There are large herds of buffalo and eland, elephant and giraffe. Greater and lesser kudu, oryx, topi, and Lelwell's hartebeest swell the buck population. Hyrax are present in the rocky outcrops on the plain, and the carnivores include leopard and hunting dog, with crocodile in the rivers.

A few years ago an important archaeological discovery was made at

165

Omo, when the 2½-million-year-old jawbone of *Homo australopithecus* was discovered. Nomadic tribes inhabit the area.

The bird checklist is around 306 species.

Simien Mountains National Park (16,500 ha.) Altitude: 3,500 to 4,500 m. Location: in the western Simien Mountains, 120 kms northeast of Gondar in Bergemder Province.

C
APR–JUNE,
SEPT–JAN

Simien Mountains was established in 1969 and listed as a World Heritage Site in 1978. The Park occupies a broad undulating plateau with vast grassy plains on the Simien Massif and contains the highest peak in Ethiopia, Ras Dashan. The massif was formed some 25 million years ago as a 'Hawaiian type' volcano. Erosion has carved the landscape into steep cliffs up to 1,500 m high, and deep valleys. Two rivers, the Tekeze and the Mayshasha, cut through the landscape. There is a dry season from October to May, with two periods of rain in February and March, and again in July to September. Winds dry the air during the day and frosts may occur at night. Snow falls periodically on the summit of Ras Dashan.

The botany is interesting, with heath forest and montane moorland featuring tree heaths, giant lobelia, alpine flora, mosses and lichens. Forests of towering St John's wort 'giant heath' once flourished between 3,000 and 3,800 m, but few still remain.

Walia ibex and simien fox inhabit the north wall of the massif. The ibex is endemic to the Simien Mountains, while the fox is endemic to Ethiopia as a whole but only occurs in a few other sites. Other mammals include Gelada and Hamadryas baboons, colobus monkey, serval cat, and leopard. Bushbuck, duiker, and the elegant little klipspringer are among the species of buck present.

The area is excellent for birdwatchers, with a checklist of around 400 species, including the huge and beautiful lammergeyer or bearded vulture, Verreaux's eagle, kestrel, lanner falcon, and the augur buzzard.

KENYA

Kenya's landscape is spectacularly beautiful and varied, ranging from the pale coral beaches of Mombasa through the rolling grass plains of the south, up into the rainforest of the Aberdares and the bleak deserts of the north. The range of reserves, and the game-viewing facilities within them, is among the finest in Africa.

Aberdare National Park (76,619 ha.) Altitude: 1,829 to 4,000 m. Location: in the central highlands west of Mount Kenya.

Aberdare was proclaimed in 1950 and the well-known Treetops and Ark viewing lodges lie within it. In spite of being on the equator the Park's height means that the climate is always cool to cold. Heavy rain falls intermittently during most of the year.

The Park occupies an isolated range of volcanic mountains forming part of the eastern wall of the Rift Valley. There are two main peaks, Oldoinyo Lasatiem and Kinangop, which are separated by alpine moorland. Deep ravines cut through the forested eastern and western flanks and there are many clear streams and waterfalls. The flora is rich alpine and sub-alpine, including giant lobelias, giving way at lower altitudes to bamboo forests and then montane rainforest, with chestnuts, treeferns, camphor, and wild banana.

The fauna includes many mammals of the forest zone – Sykes' monkey, black-and-white colobus, leopard, elephant, buffalo, suni, red duiker, bushbuck, warthog, and giant forest hog. On the moorlands can be found black rhino, eland, grey and black-fronted duiker, and serval cat. There is also a population of 1,000–2,000 bongo, making Aberdare a stronghold of this buck of restricted distribution.

Birdlife is abundant and varied, numbering over 200 recorded species. These include the green ibis, cuckoo falcon, mountain buzzard, scaly francolin, Hartlaub's turaco, and the silvery-cheeked hornbill in the forest areas. The bamboo forest shelters Jackson's francolin, white-starred bush robin, and yellow crowned canary among others. Montane francolin, Montagu's harrier, great snipe, cape grass owl, and tinkling cisticola occur on the moorlands. Mountain chat and wing-snapping cisticola can be seen in the mountain zone.

Amboseli National Park (39,206 ha.) Altitude: rising to 2,760 m (Mount Oldoinyo Orok). Location: at the foot of Mount Kilimanjaro, Africa's highest mountain, on the Tanzanian border.

Amboseli was established as a National Reserve in 1947 and became a National Park in 1974. The Park occupies a dry lake basin of some 10,000 ha. formerly filled with saline water. There are two large swamps fed by underground springs from Kilimanjaro. The climate is generally hot and dry with only 305 mm annual rainfall. The two permanent swamps, Engonyo Naibor and Loginya, are major watering holes.

Apart from its animals, the Park has an extraordinarily beautiful landscape, and still maintains a large pastoral Masai population. Vegetation is divided between bush, salt grass plain, and acacia wooded grassland.

Tawny eagle in Amboseli National Park, Kenya

Elephant, lion, cheetah, Masai giraffe, Burchell's zebra (including several 'negative' examples), buffalo, black rhino, fringe-eared oryx, wildebeest, gerenuk, impala, Grant's gazelle, spotted hyena, baboon, and the lovely little bat-eared fox are all present.

The birdwatcher is well served as over 425 birds have been recorded. The list includes the southern banded harrier eagle and the golden weaver. Three species of sandgrouse visit the water-holes in the dry season, as do migrant waterfowl such as the squacco heron from Madagascar. Taita falcon is widespread but locally scarce.

Buffalo Springs National Reserve (33,915 ha.) Altitude: 900 to 1,000 m. Location: in the north of the country, on the south bank of Ewaso Nyiro River, 85 kms north of Mount Kenya. The reserve is contiguous with Shaba and Samburu.

A
JULY–MAR

Buffalo Springs occupies gently rolling lowland plain below the foothills of Mount Kenya. It has seasonal dry luggas and an average annual rainfall of 350 mm. Buffalo Springs itself is the dry season water source for myriads of sandgrouse and doves.

There are 22 large mammal species including elephant, Grevy's zebra, and reticulated giraffe. Crocodile are also present.

Birdlife is plentiful and includes the blue-necked Somali ostrich and martial eagle. There are also flocks of helmeted and vulturine guinea fowl, and the little pygmy falcon is widespread.

Diani Marine National Park Complex (Proposed 1982.) Location: south of Mombasa extending from Kya Punga in the north to Chale Island in the south.

B
JULY–MAR

The proposed Diani Marine Park would encompass Similani, Kya Punga and Chale Island, and include the bat caves at Similani. The vegetation is lowland rainforest with mangrove swamps along the seaboard.

The Similani bats, whose existence is threatened by habitat destruction, consist of eight or nine resident and migratory species, including the large fruit bat and the insectivorous *Hipposideros commersoni*. The Chale Islands are important nesting sites for several species of bird.

Dodori National Reserve (87,739 ha.) Altitude: sea-level to 100 m. Location: in the coastal zone extending to the Somali border.

B/C
JULY–MAR

Dodori was established in 1976 at the mouth of the Dodori River in the Indian Ocean. Behind the estuary are the Mundani Hills of pleistocene dune sand ridges. The vegetation is mangrove swamp along Dodori Creek and lowland dry forest inland. There are some marshes and seasonally flooded glades.

The area is a major breeding ground for topi, while the most common larger mammals are elephant and lesser kudu. The estuary formerly supported a substantial dugong population, and the tidal mangrove swamps are rich in birdlife, including pelicans and coastal waterfowl.

Kisite Mpunguti Marine National Park (2,301 ha.) Altitude: sea-level. Location: south of Wasini Island, off Shimoni on the south coast, near the Tanzanian border.

B
JULY–MAR

169

Kisite Mpunguti is a trapezoid section of the Indian Ocean encompassing four small waterless coral islands: Kisite, Mpunguti ya juu, Mpunguti ya chini, and Jiwe la Jahazi. The Park was established in 1973, largely to protect the islands' breeding colonies of birds, in particular the roseate and sooty terns on Kisite.

The marine fauna includes corals, money cowries, starfish, sea urchin, ghost and rock crabs, sergeant-major fish, butterfly fish, and parrot fish.

Lake Bogoria National Reserve (10,705 ha.) Altitude: 1,000 to 1,600 m. B
Location: 50 kms north of Nakuru in the Rift Valley. JULY–MAR

Lake Bogoria was established as a National Reserve in 1974. The shallow soda lake was previously known as Lake Hannington, and lies in the magnificent Rift Valley. The reserve embraces the entire lake, which is set at the base of the east wall of the highland escarpment and includes an area of hot springs, with steam jets and geysers. The vegetation is primarily thorn bush with small patches of riverine forest. The shoreline consists of alkaline grassland.

The area is known for its population of greater kudu which can be seen along the shore, and also for its large flocks of both greater and lesser flamingo which feed on the lake's diatoms and algae.

Lake Nakuru National Park (20,000 ha.) Altitude: 1,753 to 2,073 m. B
Location: in central Kenya, 140 kms northwest of Nairobi. JULY–MAR

Lake Nakuru was established in 1960 as a bird sanctuary. National Park status was conferred in 1967 and the Park's area enlarged in 1974. Lying in the central Rift Valley the lake water is shallow and alkaline with a pH of 10.5. The vegetation along the shoreline is swamp with an area of dry savanna behind. An average 965 mm of rain falls annually.

Lake Nakuru is chiefly known for what has been called 'the most fabulous bird spectacle in the world': the huge flocks, at times over a million strong, of greater and lesser flamingoes. There is also a flourishing colony of pelicans which colonised the lake after the introduction of an alkali-tolerant Tilapia fish. Other spectacular birds among the 450 species recorded are cormorant, night heron, and African spoonbill. The list of over 30 aquatic species includes cape wigeon and stiff-tailed Maccoa duck. Many migrants from Europe use the waters, and the birds of prey include the secretary bird and Verreaux's eagle.

The Park's fauna is also varied and interesting. The rare long-eared leaf-nosed bat is present, there are large numbers of springhare and rock hyrax, and the shallows support the clawless otter and some hippo. Rhino, leopard, Defassa waterbuck, Bohar and mountain reedbuck,

170

impala, and Thomson's gazelle are all resident too. A group of Rothschild's giraffe, with its curious horn formation, was successfully introduced in 1977.

Lambwe Valley National Reserve (30,814 ha.) Altitude: 1,200 to
1,600 m. Location: 10 kms east of Lake Victoria in west Kenya.

Lambwe Valley National Reserve was created in 1966 mainly to preserve the local population of roan antelope. The landscape consists of
rolling wooded grassland and thicket. The reserve is surrounded by high
density human settlement and there is no provision for tourism.

In addition to roan the common mammals include oribi and Jackson's
hartebeest. The birdlife is plentiful and varied with four species of stork,
white-faced tree-duck, blue-cheeked bee-eater, rufous-bellied heron,
Beaudouin's harrier eagle, and the banded harrier eagle. The African
marsh harrier and four species of sunbird can also be seen.

Malindi Watumu Marine National Parks and Reserves (21,309 ha.
of Marine National Reserve; 1,600 ha. of Marine National Park.) Altitude:
sea-level. Location: a strip of coast and sea, 30 kms long and four kms
broad and including Mida Creek, south of Malindi and 88 kms north
of Mombasa.

Malindi Watumu was established in 1968 and listed as a Biosphere
Reserve in 1979. Notable features of the landscape are the rock platforms
and cliffs. In the Watumu area there are caves or coral reefs inhabited
by fish. There is no continental shelf and the water depth drops sharply.
Between the limestone cliffs are beautiful sandy beaches. In Mida Creek
there are extensive mangrove areas. The best time to visit is January
to March and June to October, monsoon permitting. Temperature averages 26°C with no great variation.

Whale Island, at the entrance to Mida Creek, is the nesting ground
for roseate terns and bridled terns between June and October. Shore birds
include sanderlings, curlew sandpipers, whimbrel and three species of
plover: grey, greater and Mongolian sand. Non-breeding visitors include
lesser crested tern, Saunder's little tern, and the sooty gull. The birds
migrate in late April.

The rocks are inhabited by rock crabs, small rock gobies, anemones,
and the large, flat, six-plated barnacle. In the small caves with dripping
water is a dense population of the ghost crab. Near the foot of the cliffs
a red and white xanthid crab is common while below the porcelain crab
predominates. On the sandy beaches the hermit crab is found. Beyond
the water's edge are the coral gardens with their wealth of aquatic life:

brilliant fish, seaslugs, starfish, crabs, sea urchins, and molluscs, including the tiger cowrie.

Marsabit National Reserve (202,842 ha.) Altitude: 420 to 1,700 m. A/B
Location: in northern Kenya, 560 kms north of Nairobi. JULY–MAR

Marsabit, established in 1962, is a forested mountain oasis rising out of surrounding desert country. The mountain is comprised of a group of volcanic craters, several of which are occupied by freshwater lakes – the largest being Lake Paradise. The upper zone is forested and the lower consists of acacia grassland.

The fauna is rich and varied with populations of elephant, lion, leopard, cheetah, and reticulated giraffe. Ungulates include greater kudu, Beisa oryx, Grant's gazelle, klipspringer, and the little suni antelope. Primates number the olive baboon and diadem monkey. Other predators include striped hyena, caracal, and aardwolf. There are thirteen species of bat.

The checklist of birds is over 350 species, including fifty-two birds of prey. They include lammergeyer or bearded vulture, mountain buzzard, peregrine falcon, and swallow-tailed kite. Others listed are the Somali ostrich, purple heron, saddle-bill stork, black-faced Heuglin's bustard, cream-coloured courser, Somali bee-eater, masked lark, yellow-billed hornbill, trogon in the mountain area, and little grebe. Ibises and numerous duck species visit Lake Paradise.

Masai Mara National Park (167,274 ha.) Altitude: 1,500 to 2,170 m. A
Location: in southwest Kenya on the Tanzania border with Serengeti, JULY–MAR
250 kms approx. from Nairobi through the Rift Valley.

Masai Mara, established in 1948 as a Game Reserve and declared a National Reserve in 1961, is largely composed of undulating grassland with isolated rocky outcrops (kopjes) and several ranges of hills. The reserve represents the northern sector of the Serengeti eco-system, dominated by open grassland with some dense thickets and riverine forests down the Mara River.

A dry season concentration area for millions of migratory herbivores, including zebra, wildebeest and Thomson's gazelle, the most abundant fauna is plains game. Elephant, topi and buffalo are also numerous. Attendant predators include the largest lion population in Kenya, leopard, spotted hyena, and banded mongoose. Also present are giraffe, hippo, and black rhino.

The avifauna is profuse and includes fifty-three species of birds of prey. The peregrine falcon, African hobby, cuckoo-falcon, osprey, and

172

Pel's fishing owl patrol the skies. Ground hornbills and several varieties of bustard inhabit the plains. Open-billed stork can be seen, together with the crested guinea fowl, Ross's turaco, blue quail, flocks of red-headed quelea, and parasitic weaver.

Meru National Park (181,300 ha.) Altitude: 366 to 914 m. Location: northeast of Mount Kenya.

A
JULY–MAR

Meru, established as a Game Reserve in 1966 and straddling the equator, has as its southern boundary the Tana River, an important wildlife area. The Park's vegetation is mainly thornbush and thicket on a hilly upland drained by 15 streams in the west. The eastern sector consists of open plain. There are dense riverine forests, some swamps, and a small relic rainforest. The rainfall is 635–762 mm in the west and 305–356 mm in the east.

Lion, leopard and cheetah all prey on Meru's plains game. Elephant are present, as well as black rhino and some of the northern race of white rhino introduced from South Africa. Among other mammals are the reticulated giraffe, the elegant, finely striped Grevy's zebra, the southern race of zebra, hippo, lesser kudu, oryx, the gerenuk, hartebeest, and Grant's gazelle.

The Somali race of ostrich heads the list of 277 birds recorded. There are many other birds of restricted range including small brown-backed woodpecker and numerous golden-breasted starling. Found along the river are Pel's fishing owl, sacred ibis, shy African fin-foot, brown-hooded kingfisher, violet wood hoopoe, and scaly babbler, while mourning warbler, red-necked falcon and three species of courser, including Heuglin's, are present in the doum palms. Black-bellied sunbird, shrikes, starlings, and weavers inhabit the open scrubland.

Mount Elgon National Park (16,923 ha.) Altitude: 2,336 to 4,191 m. Location: on the western border with Uganda.

A/B
JULY–MAR

Established in 1968 Mount Elgon National Park is situated on the slopes of the east flank of a massive volcanic cone overlooking a huge caldera which, together with half the mountain, lies in Uganda. The vegetation is very varied and the Park contains a wide range of habitats including olive-studded wet montane forest, bamboo and gigantic podocarpus, moorland, and heathland. Mount Elgon is of great interest to botanists, with many alpines and both terrestrial and epiphytic orchids flowering during June and July. The annual rainfall is over 1,270 mm.

Mammals include elephant, leopard, eland, buffalo, black-and-white colobus, bushbuck, giant forest hog, duiker, and the rare golden cat.

173

Birds of the forest zone include crested guinea fowl, great blue turaco, and black-and-white crested hornbill. The moorland supports most of the species characteristic of such altitudes in east Africa such as mountain chat, an endemic form of highlands grass warbler. Raptors include crowned eagle, African hobby, and mountain buzzard, with Lanner falcon as the most common. Sunbirds are much in evidence when the nectar flowers are in bloom. The scarce swift nests in caves in the Park.

Mount Kenya National Park (Biosphere Reserve of 71,759 ha. and National Park of 58,800 ha.) Altitude: 1,600 to 5,199 m. Location: Mount Kenya straddles the equator about 193 kms due northeast of Nairobi and 480 kms from the Kenyan coast.

B
JULY–MAR

Mount Kenya was established as a National Park in 1949, and declared a Biosphere Reserve in 1978. The Park has several snow-covered peaks with glacial valleys radiating from them, and some 19 glacial tarns or small lakes. The vegetation is dominated by dense montane cedar forest in the east, south and west, with scrub and dense bamboo forest on the northern slope. Apart from the alpines and lichens at higher altitudes, the flora includes two terrestrial orchid species and a gladiolus.

In the lower forest and bamboo zone mammals include populations of elephant, black rhino, and leopard. Also present are suni, giant forest hog, tree hyrax or dassie, and white-tailed mongoose. Among the moorland creatures are the localised Mount Kenya mouse shrew, hyrax, black-fronted duiker, and common duiker.

Forest birds include the local Kenyan race of the green ibis, Ayre's hawk owl, the threatened Abyssinian long-eared owl, scaly francolin, Ruppell's robin-chat, and numerous sunbirds. Moorland species include scarlet-tufted malachite sunbird, montane francolin, Mackinder's eagle owl, and the locally threatened scarce swift.

Nairobi National Park (11,721 ha.) Altitude: 1,533 to 1,760 m. Location: 8 kms south of Nairobi.

A
JULY–MAR

Nairobi National Park, established in 1946, consists of a sloping grassland plain trenched by several deep river valleys. The vegetation is dry transitional savanna with forested upland areas. The Park is unique in that it supports a large variety of wildlife within a few minutes' drive of a major capital city. The annual rainfall varies from 889 mm in the uplands to 635 mm on the plain.

All the major game animals – over eighty species of mammal have been recorded – can be seen: elephant, lion, leopard, cheetah, black rhino, zebra, Masai giraffe, eland, bushbuck, Coke's hartebeest, wildebeest,

Black-backed jackal in Nairobi National Park, Kenya

dikdik, and many gazelle. The lions are a particular attraction for visitors as the prides are now used to vehicles. Buffalo has been introduced. There are various ponds, small dams and the Athi River to accommodate hippo and crocodile.

The birdwatcher's checklist includes some 500 bird species ranging from the Masai ostrich to the tiny 'kapok bird' or penduline tit, with its close-woven felt-like nest.

Ol Doinyo Sabuk National Park (1,842 ha.) Altitude: 1,524 to 2,146 m. Location: 50 kms northeast of Nairobi.

B/C
JULY–MAR

Ol Doinyo Sabuk, 'Buffalo Mountain' in its Swahili name, is an island mountain rising out of the surrounding plains. It was gazetted as a reserve in 1967, but has only recently been assigned National Park status. Apart from a bald patch at the peak, the vegetation consists of montane forest.

Mammals are not particularly numerous, but they include black-and-white colobus, Sykes' monkey, and black-faced remet monkey, as well as leopard, black rhino, buffalo, bushbuck, duikers, and impala.

175

Forest birds are well represented and include great blue turaco, Ayre's hawk eagle, African goshawk, lemon dove, Hartlaub's turaco, Narina's trogon, grey cuckoo-shrike, Abyssinian crimsonwing, and several sunbirds.

After the start of the seasonal rains butterflies are noticeably abundant, including species of charaxes and swallowtails. The threatened *Charaxes nandina* occurs in the Park.

Ras Tenewi Coastal Zone National Park (Proposed in 1982: 35,000 ha. — 10,500 land and 24,500 sea.) Altitude: sea-level. Location: north of the Tana River Delta on a headland south of the Lamu archipelago.
B/C
JAN–MAR,
JUNE–OCT

The proposed Ras Tenewi National Park includes extensive coral reefs and several rocky islands which are important bird breeding sites. The vegetation is lowland rainforest inland and mangrove on the seaboard.

Wildlife includes concentrations of elephant and topi, with dugong occurring in the nearby Tana River estuary. Three species of turtle are known to breed in the Park: the olive ridley, the green, and the hawksbill.

Among the migratory seabirds breeding in the Park are the sooty gull, noddy, roseate tern, and white-cheeked tern.

Saiwa Swamp National Park (192 ha.) Altitude: 1,860 to 1,880 m. Location: below the Cherangani Hills, 20 kms northeast of Kitale in west Kenya.
B/C
JULY–MAR

Saiwa Swamp was established in 1974 in a narrow basin of the meandering channel of the Saiwa River to protect the swamp's population of 80 to 100 sitatunga. This remarkable aquatic antelope submerges itself in water when surprised, and has splayed hooves enabling it to run on marsh vegetation. Other mammals include de Brazza's monkey, the nocturnal potto, spotted-necked otter, and giant forest squirrel. Leopard have been reported but are probably visitors.

The diverse avifauna includes eastern grey plantain-eater, go-away bird, great blue turaco, double-toothed and black-billed barbets. Ovampo sparrowhawk, fish eagle, and African marsh owl are among the raptors. Giant, striped and malachite kingfishers are all present, as are sunbirds and weavers.

Samburu National Park (22,510 ha.) Altitude: 800 to 1,230 m. Location: 90 kms north of Mount Kenya on the north bank of the Ewaso Nyiro River.
A
JULY–MAR

Samburu, contiguous with Shaba and Buffalo Springs, occupies 32 kms of wooded river bank. Away from the river the reserve is characterised

Warthogs, Kenya

TOP *Buffalo, Kenya*
BOTTOM *White rhino*

TOP *Eland, East Africa*
BOTTOM *Nyala in Mkuzi Game Reserve, Natal, South Africa*

Spotted hyena, Kenya

by steep gullied slopes and rounded hills with lava plains clothed in open woodland with some grassland. The annual rainfall is 350 mm.

There are twenty-two large animal species including elephant, Grevy's zebra, reticulated giraffe, and crocodile. The avifauna, as in the other two reserves, is rich and varied.

Shaba National Reserve (23,910 ha.) Altitude: 700 to 1,500 m. Location: 70 kms north of Mount Kenya, south of the Ewaso Nyiro River.

A/B
JULY–MAR

Shaba is part of the Samburu-Shaba-Buffalo Springs complex, and was established in 1974. All three reserves are in the huge empty region of what is known as the Northern Frontier Province, where travel remains difficult even today.

Both birds and mammals migrate from one reserve to the other, and all three reserves support much the same range of species. Shaba has 34 kms of Ewaso Nyiro River frontage producing a largely riverine vegetation together with acacia, doum palm, and some swamp. Seventeen large mammals are present including gerenuk, oryx, and Grant's gazelle.

Sibiloi National Park (157,085 ha.) Altitude: 500–1,000 m. Location: on the eastern shores of Lake Turkana (formerly Lake Rudolf), 720 kms from Nairobi.

B/C
JULY–MAR

Sibiloi, established in 1972 and the most remote of Kenya's National Parks, has been preserved in its original wilderness state. The vegetation is grassy with some doum palms on empty plains interspersed with luggas. There are also volcanic formations including Mount Sibiloi on which are the remains of a petrified forest, possibly seven million years old, and a volcanic island, Central Island, in the middle of Lake Turkana. The climate is hot and windy with fierce gales.

Game animals include Burchell's and Grevy's zebra, Grant's gazelle, Beisa oryx, hartebeest, and topi, together with populations of lion and leopard. The world's largest colony of crocodiles, around 12,000, breeds on Central Island.

Central Island is also favoured by migrating birds, including warblers, wagtails and little stints. Lake Turkana has over 350 recorded species of aquatic and terrestrial birds, including Egyptian goose, Lichtenstein's sandgrouse, chestnut-headed finch-lark, Heuglin's bustard, glossy and sacred ibis, yellow-billed stork, cormorants, and black-winged stilt.

Tana River Primate Reserve (17,807 ha.) Altitude: 40 to 70 m. Location: inland from the Indian Ocean, 120 kms north of Malindi on the Tana River between Hola and Garsen.

B
JULY–MAR

177

Tana River Reserve was established in 1976. Apart from its populations of primates, it is important as a major waterfowl sanctuary and wetland site. The reserve contains about 50 kms of the Tana River with its flood-plain and the adjacent dry plains. The vegetation is riverine with a high diversity of species.

The primates number seven and include two endangered species, the red colobus monkey and Tana mangabey. The other 43 recorded mammals include elephant, hippo, Peters' gazelle, red duiker, red river hog, giraffe, waterbuck, and squirrel. The Tana River has good point-bars for crocodile. Also present are a snake, *Aparallactus guenteri*, and a frog, *Hylarana bravana*, which are restricted to the Tana River delta and Mt Mbololo.

The birdlife is interesting and includes large numbers of breeding heron and other waterfowl, and the native warbler.

Tsavo National Park (2,086,844 ha.) Altitude: 229 to 2,238 m. Location: in southeast Kenya, inland from Mombasa.

A
JULY–MAR

Tsavo was established in 1948 and is one of the best known of all the African Parks. It occupies an area of volcanic hill and plateau watered by several rivers, including the Tsavo and Athi Rivers which join to form the Galana and flow through the centre of the Park.

The Park contains a diversity of habitats: thornbush, thicket, wood-land, and grassland. Tree species include baobab and doum palm. Big game is well represented – elephant, black rhino, buffalo, lion, leopard, cheetah, and hippo are all present. Also found are lesser kudu, eland, Burchell's zebra, gemsbok, waterbuck, Coke's hartebeest (kongoni), Thomson's and Grant's gazelle, and the graceful long-necked gerenuk.

The birdlife is rich and varied. There are numerous raptors, including fish eagle and osprey, eight species of hornbill, six species of nightjar, the sacred and glossy ibis, open-bill stork, black heron, weaver birds, the elegant little white-faced tree-duck, skimmer, and some twelve species of starling including Fischer's starling whose distribution is restricted.

MADAGASCAR

Madagascar is a remarkable volcanic island considerably larger than France, lying 400 kms off the east coast of Africa, from which it was

178

separated some 20 million years ago. The climate is tropical with a rainy summer from November to March and a dry winter from April to October. The island has many lakes and rivers, and a highly individual flora and fauna which had already evolved when the island broke away from the continent of Africa.

Isalo National Park (81,540 ha.) Altitude: 800 to 1,082 m. Location: to the west of Ihosey.

C
APR–OCT

Isalo National Park was established in 1962 in an area of steep and rocky mountains with spectacular scenery. There are many caves in the Park, including some where sixteenth-century shipwrecked Portuguese sailors are believed to have lived – the *Grottes des Portuguais*. The vegetation includes several endemic species.

The fauna includes many interesting mammals, such as the ring-tailed lemur and the endangered Verreaux's sifaka as well as the civet-like fossa and endemic herbivores such as the tail-less tenrec. *Acrantophis madagascariensis* is also present.

The birdlife is extremely interesting, again with many species endemic to Madagascar.

La Montagne d'Ambre National Park (18,200 ha.) Altitude: 1,000 to 1,446 m. Location: at the northern point of Madagascar.

C
APR–OCT

La Montagne d'Ambre was established in 1958 around a tertiary volcano whose massif has numerous crater lakes and waterfalls. The vegetation is upland tropical rainforest, rich in orchids, epiphytes and ferns, and the whole area is of great interest to the botanist. There has been little research in the Park, so the species lists are necessarily incomplete.

The fauna is equally remarkable, and includes the rare Perrier's sifaka and the endangered Sanford's lemur.

The birdlife is rich and varied. As Madagascar's fauna evolved before the island's separation from the mainland, there are many unique and ancient species which are found nowhere else in the world.

MALAWI

Malawi is the former British Protectorate of Nyasaland. From 1953–63 it was a member of the Central African Federation. Independence came in 1964, following the Federation's collapse. Lake Malawi (formerly Lake

Nyasa) dominates the country's geography, occupying the northern Malawi section of the Rift System.

Kasungu National Park (204,800 ha.) Altitude: 1,000 to 1,340 m. Location: west of Kasungu, 175 kms north of Lolongwe and extending along the Zambian border.

A/B
MAY–OCT

Kasungu was declared a Forest Reserve in 1922 as an anti-tsetse fly measure. The Park's landscape consists of some open and some wooded country embracing the higher catchment of the Swnagwa River. The daytime temperature from September to May can exceed 29°C. In winter, between June and August, the temperature drops to 4°C. The annual rainfall is highly variable averaging 750–1,000 mm over the years since records have been kept.

The Park contains a 1,500–2,000 population of elephant, which is conspicuous but thought to be decreasing. A few black rhino are present. The antelope include sable, roan, Lichtenstein's hartebeest, eland, greater kudu, impala, waterbuck, and oribi. Also present are reedbuck, duiker, Burchell's zebra, Sharpe's grysbok, warthog, bushpig, baboon, and vervet monkey. Numbered among the predators are leopard, cheetah, side-striped jackal, serval, and wild dog. In addition there are many small woodland mammals.

The checklist of birds records over 200 species.

Lake Malawi National Park (8,724 ha.) Altitude: 1,140 m. Location: the Park embraces the southern end of Lake Malawi and includes Nankumba Peninsula and three offshore islands.

B
MAY–OCT

587 kms long and up to 80 kms in width Lake Malawi, formerly Lake Nyasa, is more of an inland sea than a lake. It is the third largest area of inland water in Africa, and the ninth largest and third deepest in the world. Its shores range from low-lying swamps and sandy beaches to steep, rocky, and wooded hills. The surrounding vegetation includes baobabs and a wide variety of grasses and wild flowers. The area's mean annual temperature is 27°C and the annual rainfall, although erratic, is an average of 500 mm.

Lake Malawi contains the largest number of fish species in any lake anywhere, the total exceeding 450. 90% of these species are endemic. Particularly noteworthy are the 350 species of Cichlidae – representing 30% of all known Cichlidae. Elephant have been reported coming down to the lake between the Mwenya and Nkhudzi Hills. There are hippo, notably in the Monkey Bay area. Other mammals in the shore surrounds include leopard, kudu, impala, baboon, bushbuck, duiker, vervet monkey, bushpig, and warthog.

Fish eagles guard their territories along the shore, and the birdlife is rich. Several islands in the lake provide nesting sites for, among others, several thousand white-throated cormorants.

The lake has a population of crocodiles and there are abundant monitor lizards on Boadzulu Island.

Lengwe National Park (12,800 ha. – with recently-approved extensions 90,720 ha.) Altitude: 130 to 393 m. Location: 80 kms south of Blantyre to the west of the Shire River, extending along the Mozambique border.

B
MAY–OCT

Lengwe was established as a Game Reserve in 1928 and became a National Park in 1970. Various types of woodland and dry deciduous thicket cover the terrain, which is well watered by the Zambesi and Shire Rivers.

The Park is one of only two remaining sites in Malawi which shelters the Nyala antelope. Pre-1975 the emphasis was on the conservation of this species, but growth in the Nyala population since then has necessitated some culling. Other ungulates include greater kudu, buffalo, suni, Livingstone's suni, Lichtenstein's hartebeest, Sharpe's grysbok, a few sable, impala, bushbuck, and duiker. There are three primates: baboon, vervet monkey, and samango monkey. Among the predators are leopard, spotted hyena, and jackal.

The area's avifauna is very striking and includes many lowland tropical birds such as crested guinea fowl, Rudd's apalis (endemic), crested francolin, and the mouse-coloured sunbird.

Liwonde National Park (59,570 ha.) Altitude: 472 to 961 m. Location: on the upper Shire River plain, east of the river and 140 kms north of Limbe.

B/C
MAY–OCT

Liwonde, established in 1973, is primarily an area of plain with mopane woodland and grass bordered by Lake Malombe and the Shire River. The mean annual temperature on the plain is 13°C with extremes of 7°C and 39°C. Annual rainfall averages 650–2,250 mm.

The formerly-abundant game in the area is now much reduced, although nearly all the original species are still represented. Mammals include a declining elephant population (some 200 in 1983), lion, leopard, and buffalo. Also present are hippo, greater kudu, impala, waterbuck, Lichtenstein's hartebeest, duiker, Sharpe's grysbok, reedbuck, oribi, Livingstone's suni, bushbuck, and large numbers of sable antelope. A

181

few crocodile still inhabit the Park. There is a proposal to reintroduce the Johnston's race of wildebeest which used to be found in Malawi.

A preliminary bird checklist records 207 species, many of them aquatic. The rare (in Malawi) Nyasa lovebird occurs in the Park.

Nyika National Park – also known as **Malawi National Park** (304,385 ha.) Altitude: 1,600 to 2,606 m. Location: 480 kms north of Lilongwe and 35 kms west of Livingstonia. The Park extends along the border with Zambia.

A/B
MAY–OCT

Nyika was established in 1966, although part of the area was previously a game reserve. It consists mainly of a large, open grassland plateau. Temperatures can fall below 0°C in June–July, and rise to over 21°C in the warm season. The average rainfall is 1,140 mm.

Leopard, lion, hyena, and side-striped jackal are the large predators. There is a small and decreasing population of elephant, which totalled fifty in 1983. The most numerous ungulate is the reedbuck. Vervet and samango monkeys are present. Other mammals include zebra and the endemic species *Equus burchelli de winton*, also eland, roan, Lichtenstein's hartebeest, klipspringer, puku (rare in Malawi), warthog, bushbuck, and common and red duiker.

The birdlife is notable with seven species rare in Malawi and including wattled crane, Jackson's bustard, and red-winged francolin (with an endemic sub-species).

Fourteen botanical species are endemic to the area, as are two species of reptile, two amphibians, and seventeen butterflies.

MOZAMBIQUE

Mozambique has 2,500 kms of Indian Ocean coastline providing potential maritime outlets for several neighbouring countries. The land rises from the shore to high peaks inland, reaching altitudes of over 2,500 metres. The northern plateau dominates Lake Malawi, while the central plain is bisected by the Zambesi, the Rovuma, and the Limpopo rivers. Heavy monsoon rainfall contributes to the country's natural fertility. The vegetation varies from savanna in the highlands to thick rainforest along the rivers and mangroves by the coast.

Wildebeest in Gorongosa National Park, Mozambique

Gorongosa National Park (377,000 ha.) Altitude: around 200 m. Location: 150 kms northeast of Beira.

B
APR–DEC

Gorongosa, established in 1960, is considered one of the finest game Parks in this part of Africa. The Park occupies a large area of plateau watered by the River Pungue and its tributary. The vegetation ranges from savanna wood and grassland to forest, marsh, and riverbank.

The Park's fauna includes large populations of buffalo, elephant, kudu, sable, nyala, hippo, and Lichtenstein's hartebeest. Among the predators are lion and leopard.

183

RWANDA

Rwanda, landlocked in the central lakes of the Rift Valley, has a landscape of mountains, forest, and swamp. The country's inhabitants were largely isolated from the Zanzibari slave and ivory trade by the sheer impassability of the surrounding terrain. Although Rwanda has a low national wage, intensive cultivation of all the available farmland gives the mainly rural population a reasonable level of subsistence. The original human inhabitants of the area were probably the pygmy hunter-gatherers, the Twa people, who still survive in small groups.

Kagera National Park (280,000 ha.) Altitude: 1,400 to 1,825 m at the peak Mount Mutumka. Location: in the northeastern region, bordered by the Tanzanian and Ugandan frontiers.

B/C
NOV–APR

The Park was established in 1934 as a hunting reserve and can be divided into three main areas: the savanna hills of Mutara, the Kagera River depression and marshland, and the mountain ranges. The 90-km river depression contains the source of the Nile, sought for so long by European explorers. The Kagera fills six lakes and in places is 18 kms wide.

The wide range of habitats offers shelter to a variety of animals. The Park has more than 50 species of mammal, with lion, leopard, buffalo and rhino, waterbuck, roan, topi, and eland heading the list of big game. Hippo, zebra, impala, wild dog, oribi, sitatunga, hyena, and duiker are all also found. About 80 reptiles are numbered among the Park's residents.

The birdlife is magnificent and over 420 species have been recorded, including 44 raptors.

Volcans National Park (15,065 ha. – contiguous with the Virunga National Park in Zaire and the Gorilla Sanctuary in Uganda.) Altitude: 2,400 to 4,507 m. Location: 15 kms north of the town of Ruhengeri in the Virunga massif of northwestern Rwanda, on the borders with Uganda and Zaire.

B
NOV–APR

The Parc des Volcans contains five volcanic peaks which form part of the watershed between the Nile and Zaire river systems. The terrain is difficult and the rainfall, at just below 2,000 mm a year, high. The average temperature is 9.6°C. The vegetation is mainly forest with areas of bamboo. On the higher slopes it becomes sub-alpine, and there are some sections of heath.

184

The Park is best known for its population of the endangered mountain gorilla which numbered around 245 individuals in 1982. This gorilla sub-species, *Gorilla gorilla beringei*, is endemic to the Virunga Mountains conservation areas, and the Bwindi Forest in Uganda. The Park also supports a population of mountain elephant, buffalo, forest hog, yellow and black duiker, and bushbuck.

Birdlife is of interest, with 148 species recorded, including one endemic – Grauer's bush warbler. There are also at least six species which are endemic to the Virunga and Ruwenzori Mountains: the handsome francolin, Ruwenzori turaco and flycatcher, the strange weaver, the dusky crimsonwing, and Shelley's crimsonwing.

Visitors are being encouraged to come to view the gorillas by the Mountain Gorilla Project which is having some success in habituating gorilla families to the presence of humans. The project has been launched in order to give the Park some financial independence.

SOMALIA

Somalia occupies over half a million square kilometres of semi-desert on the Horn of Africa. Its coastline stretches 1,800 kms along the Indian Ocean and the Gulf of Aden, which gives the country considerable strategic importance.

Northern Somalia is extremely barren and dry. The south, which is crossed by two rivers on their descent from the Ethiopian highlands, the Juba and the Shebelle, borders on the bush country of northern Kenya. It is round these rivers that the country's wildlife is most numerous.

Lag Badana National Park (334,000 ha.) The Park was established in 1978, but no further information is currently available.

C
OCT–APR

TANZANIA

The United Republic of Tanzania was born of the union in 1964 of the recently independent republics of Tanganyika and Zanzibar, under the founding father, Julius Nyerere. The government has been strongly

185

socialist in direction ever since, promoting a self-help policy for an economy largely dependent on rural farming. With nearly a quarter of its area set aside as Parks or reserves, Tanzania has one of the best records for conservation in Africa.

Arusha National Park (13,700 ha.) Altitude: 1,525 to 4,565 m (summit of Mount Meru). Location: southeast flank of Mount Meru and 32 kms by road eastwards from Arusha.

A/B
JULY–MAR

Arusha consists of the former Ngurdoto Crater and Mount Meru National Parks, which were combined and renamed in 1967 and then enlarged in 1973. The Park contains three distinct habitats: the crater with its swampy floor, the rugged volcanic slopes of Mount Meru, and the seven Momela lakes at the northern end of the park, which were formed by subsidiary craters and the blocking of drainage lines by their eruptions. There are spectacular views of Mount Meru and Mount Kilimanjaro from the rim of the Ngurdoto Crater. Apart from the numerous craters and the higher elevations of Mount Meru, the Park is densely forested or covered with thicket.

Arusha has no lions, tsetse flies or mosquitoes. It does, however, have elephant, buffalo, black rhino, hippo, eland, and black and white colobus monkey. Remarkable views can be obtained from the Ngurdoto Crater rim of the animals feeding undisturbed below.

The water birds of the Momela lakes include flocks of greater and lesser flamingo, sacred ibis, Maccoa duck, and Egyptian goose. The Narina trogon and broadbill are among the many interesting species recorded in the forest.

Gombe National Park (5,200 ha. and formerly Gombe Stream Game Reserve.) Altitude: 750 to 1,500 m. Location: the eastern shore of Lake Tanganyika near Kigoma.

B
JULY–MAR

Gombe was established in 1968, replacing a Game Reserve created in 1943 to protect the area's population of chimpanzees. The vegetation is a mixture of miombo woodland and, along the Gombe Stream and its tributaries, gallery forest with oil palms.

The chimpanzee population is relatively tame since it has been much studied. Other mammals include several more primates: baboon, blue or diadem monkey, red-tailed monkey (which appears to interbreed with the blue monkey), and red colobus monkey. Leopard, buffalo, waterbuck, and bushbuck are also present.

Birdlife is interesting, with five species of barbet, the palm-nut vulture, and the very localised Forbe's plover among the more unusual species.

Katavi National Park (76,600 ha.) Altitude: 900 m. Location: western Tanzania, 40 kms along the road from Mpanda to Sumbawanga and the Zambian border. B/C JULY–MAR

Katavi Plain Game Reserve, established in 1951, became a National Park in 1974. The Park, which appears to have been considerably reduced in size in recent years, is situated on a high floodplain, well covered with miombo woodland and dominated by Lake Katavi in the northern sector and Lake Chada in the southeast. The two lakes are linked by the Katuma River and its vast associated swamps. The grasslands are punctuated by black cotton pans or mbuga, while the shores of Lake Chada are palm-fringed. The main rains fall between March and May.

The swamps contain large numbers of hippo and crocodile. The mammals of the drier areas include lion and leopard, elephant, zebra, eland, buffalo, puku, roan and sable antelope, and tsessebe at the northern margin of its range.

The avifauna is very rich and numerous with particularly large numbers of pelican in the waterlogged areas. Over 400 species have been recorded, including many waterfowl and birds of prey.

Kilimanjaro National Park (75,575 ha.) Altitude: 1,830 to 5,895 m. Location: upper levels of Mount Kilimanjaro, including corridors in the forest belt. A/B JAN, FEB, SEPT, OCT

Kilimanjaro, the highest mountain in Africa, is crowned by snow and ice fields. The mountain is volcanic, and one of its three peaks still shows minor signs of activity. The Park was established in 1973. The vegetation varies from montane rainforest, including a few tree ferns and cedar and olive on the drier northern slopes, to the moorland areas above with treeheaths and everlastings. There are two rainy seasons, the short rains of November and December, and the long rains of March to May. Average rainfall varies, in inverse ratio to height above sea-level, from 2,300 mm in the forest belt to 200 mm at 4,630 m.

The elusive Abbot's duiker is restricted to Kilimanjaro and a few neighbouring mountains, as is the Kilimanjaro tree-hyrax. There are two primates: the blue monkey and black and white colobus. Among the larger mammals, the most obvious are the populations of elephant, buffalo, eland and bushbuck. Black rhino is also present, and the major predator is the leopard.

187

For birdwatchers, the lammergeyer can occasionally be seen on the Shire ridge, as can the mountain chat, the duetting grass warbler, and the scarlet-tufted malachite sunbird. Below in the forest are several notable species, including two starlings of very restricted distribution, Abbot's and Kenrick's.

Lake Manyara National Park (32,500 ha. including the lake area of 22,900 ha.) Altitude: 960 to 1,828 m. Location: south of the Arusha to Ngorongoro road, 117 kms from Arusha, just before the road climbs up the western wall of the Great Rift Valley.   A JULY–MAR

Lake Manyara, created a National Park in 1960, occupies the Rift Valley salt lake which gives the park its name, and includes a patch of forest, two small rivers, and a section of the towering wall of the Rift. There are hot volcanic springs between the Rift wall and the lake towards the southern end.

The Park's vegetation covers a wide spectrum. Between the lake and the Rift wall are salt flats, reed beds, slatings, swamps, meadows, savan-

Waterbuck in Manyara National Park, Tanzania

188

nas, scrub, and dense forests. There is also groundwater forest with fig and sausage tree. Doum palms and thickets of raffia palm dominate the dense reeds where the rivers enter the lakes. The arrival of the rainy seasons, from November to December and March to May, are sometimes marked by spectacular dust-devils, when large areas of the soda-lake surface are still dry.

Manyara's best-known wildlife spectacle is its tree-climbing lions, but the Park also supports large herds of buffalo, sometimes numbering over 400 individuals, black rhino, leopard, zebra, hippo, giraffe, waterbuck, Bohar reedbuck, and impala. Elephant-caused destruction has opened up areas of dense forest, and plains game have begun to appear in increasing numbers. Many more animals migrate seasonally from the lake. Reptiles include cobras and monitor lizards.

Manyara's birdlife is magnificent, particularly the pale pink drifts of lesser flamingo, sometimes millions strong, which feed in the lake. Smaller numbers of greater flamingo and pelican keep company with them. Waterfowl of all sorts are numerous, often in huge flocks of individual species. A species of very restricted range which is common in the Park is the chestnut-banded sand plover. Such a large avifauna has its attendant predators, and 44 diurnal birds of prey have been recorded, including the palm-nut vulture and crowned hawk eagle.

Mikumi National Park (323,000 ha.) Altitude: 550 m. Location: eastern Tanzania, north of the main road between Morogoro and Iringa, and 280 kms by road from Dar es Salaam. A/B JULY–OCT, JAN–MAR

Mikumi lies in the arms of a ring of high mountains, the Uluguru range, and embraces the floodplain of the Mkata River. The vegetation is largely grassplain dotted with baobab trees, and dense forest growth around the river banks. The Park was established in 1964 and links up with the Selous National Park to the south. The plain is bisected by a main road and flanked in the south by the new Uhuru railway. Rainfall is variable, between 500 and 650 mm on the plain, and up to 1,000 mm in the hills.

Among the larger mammals the Park's populations of elephant, lion and buffalo are particularly striking, while the herds of giraffe are sometimes 50 strong. Also represented are leopard, rhino, zebra, eland, waterbuck, Bohor reedbuck, sable antelope, Lichtenstein's hartebeest, wildebeest, and impala.

Lying in the transitional zone between north and south, Mikumi's birdlife is rich and varied. There are typically southern species like Dickinson's kestrel, the Bateleur eagle and Boehm's bee-eater, as well as northern species such as the superb starling and the straw-tailed whydah. Among other birds recorded are crowned lapwing, flappet lark, the magnificent ground hornbill, and the tiny brilliant malachite kingfisher.

Ngorongoro Conservation Area (528,000 ha.) Altitude: under 1,500 to 3,648 m. Location: in the Arusha Region of northern Tanzania, southeast of Serengeti.

A
JULY–MAR

Originally proclaimed in 1959, Ngorongoro was accepted as a World Heritage Site in 1979 and as part of the Serengeti-Ngorongoro Biosphere Reserve in 1982. The reserve is one of the most famous in the world because of the extraordinary concentration of the habitat and its wildlife in a huge volcanic bowl, with a diameter of 16 to 19 kms and a rim soaring to 400 to 600 m above the crater floor. The crater itself spans an area of 26,400 ha., two thirds of which is covered with the short grass so attractive to plains game. The reserve contains a forest of fever trees; and at Enkoitoktok Springs, prehistoric boards for the game of *bau*, a pebble-game still played all over Africa, can be seen carved in the rock. The Conservation Area also includes the Olduvai Gorge, a rich source of fossil evidence for studies into man's origins. The climate is tropical, with a mean temperature of 20.8°C and annual rainfall of 1,210 mm.

All the big five of game-viewing are present: elephant, lion – the males growing long and magnificent black manes – rhino, leopard, and buffalo. The populations of ungulates are particularly large, including 10,000 to 14,000 wildebeest, numerous zebra, eland, and both Thomson's and Grant's gazelle. Cheetah, hunting dog, and hyena are the other major predators. Hartebeest, hippo, bushbuck, giant forest hog, mountain reedbuck, and common reedbuck are also represented. Serval cat and waterbuck inhabit the Lerai forest.

The birdlife is beautiful and varied, and periodically includes flocks of pale pink lesser and greater flamingo. Seven species of stork are found, including the European black, and the marshes are thronged with water birds. Ostrich and Kori bustard inhabit the plains. The occasional lammergeyer haunts the heights, as does a variety of eagles including Verreaux's, and the vultures include the Egyptian with its curious egg-yolk-yellow face. Of particular interest on the plains is the rosy-breasted longclaw, while the highland forest shelters the golden-winged sunbird and eastern double-collared sunbird among many others.

Ruaha National Park (1,295,000 ha.) Altitude: 750 m in the Great Ruaha River valley to 1,830 m. Location: west of Iringa in the southern highlands.

B
JULY–MAR

190

Although Ruaha was officially proclaimed a National Park in 1964, it was originally part of the Rungwa Game Reserve gazetted in 1946. Earlier still, it formed part of the Sava River Game Reserve which was created in 1910.

The valley of the Great Ruaha River is believed to be an extension of the Great Rift Valley, and the Ruaha flows for 160 kms along the eastern border of the Park through both rugged gorges and open plains. Beyond the river and its swamps lies a well-wooded undulating plateau which eventually turns into treeless grassland. The plateau rises to the peak of Datambulwa in the south and Ikungu Mountain in the west. Some of the woodland contains baobab trees and part consists of dense evergreen forest. The rainfall varies between 520 mm and 800 mm and is largely confined to December through to April.

The huge herds of elephant, which congregate along the banks of the Great Ruaha River, are both the Park's main attraction and also, in the damage they do to the habitat, its major problem. Greater and lesser kudu, sable, and roan are the other notable sights. Lion, cheetah, zebra, black rhino, buffalo, Grant's gazelle, bushbuck, Bohar reedbuck, and Lichtenstein's hartebeest are all also present. Nile crocodile inhabit the river pools.

The birdlife is rich and interesting. The migrant Eleanora's falcon has been observed in the Park on its way to Madagascar, while Pel's fishing owl haunts the densely wooded river banks. Dickinson's kestrel, violet crested turaco, pale-billed hornbill, and the racquet-tailed roller are among the many species found in the woodland.

Rubondo National Park (45,700 ha.) Altitude: up to 1,130 m. Location: an island in southwest Lake Ukerewe, formerly Lake Victoria. **B** JULY–MAR

Rubondo was established in 1977 for the introduction and conservation of threatened species, and was largely funded by the Frankfurt Zoological Society. Monitoring of the introductions has been carried out by Dr Markus Borner.

Indigenous species include bushbuck, sitatunga, hippo, vervet monkey, marsh mongoose, crocodile, and python. Among the introduced mammals are chimpanzee, elephant, black rhino, giraffe, roan, suni, and black and white colobus.

The Park's wide range of habitats supports an extremely diverse birdlife.

Selous Game Reserve (5,120,000 ha.) Altitude: 200-500 m. Location: southeast Tanzania. **B** JULY–MAR

Selous is at present (1985) the largest wildlife sanctuary in Africa. The Park is watered by the Rufiji River and its tributaries, and the vegetation ranges from dense thickets through riverine and ground water forests to open wooded grasslands. The landscape is outstandingly beautiful. The rainfall is a moderate 750 to 1,000 mm, with a temperature range of 13° to 41°C.

The Park was gazetted in 1905 for hunting, and by 1912 several reserves had been established in the region. In 1922 the reserves were gathered together and named after Frederick Courtney Selous (1851–1917), who spent most of his life hunting and studying the game of southeast Africa. In 1982 the Park was declared a World Heritage Site.

The immense size and remoteness of the Selous supports and protects vast herds of many of the larger species of mammal. At about 100,000 the elephant population in the areas of miombo woodland is the largest in the world. The Park also contains considerable numbers of Lichten-stein's hartebeest, around 7,000 of the beautiful sable antelope, some 200,000 buffalo, 98,000 impala, and 80,000 wildebeest. The numbers of many species seem to be increasing further still: the population of water-buck, for example, rose from five animals in 1969 to over 70 in 1982. As well as elephant, the Selous has the largest populations in Africa of hippo, crocodile, and black rhino. Other interesting fauna include leopard and wild dog, while cheetah and giraffe are found in the grasslands.

The Park's birdlife matches the richness and variety of its animals.

Serengeti National Park (1,476,300 ha.) Altitude: 950 to 1,850 m. Location: west of the Great Rift Valley, 130 kms west of Arusha with a corridor westwards to within eight kms of Lake Victoria and a northern sector extending to the Kenya border and the Masai Mara National Park.

A
JULY–NOV,
JAN–APR

The Park was established in 1951, having been a protected area since 1940, and in 1981 was named a World Heritage Site. The undulating plains of Serengeti are filled with the greatest concentration of plains game in Africa. Their annual migration takes place in May or June, when huge herds of wildebeest, zebra and other game stream westwards across the grasslands in search of water – in drought years the plains become virtual desert. The rainfall is largely restricted to November to May, with peaks in December and March to April, and the mean annual temperature is 20.8°C.

Wildebeest, zebra, and Thomson's gazelle are the most obvious animals, together with their accompanying predators: numerous prides of lion, leopard, cheetah, hunting dog, and spotted hyena. There are

Topi in Serengeti National Park, Tanzania

populations of elephant, black rhino, hippo and giraffe, and also of buffalo, topi, eland, sitatunga, bushbuck, oryx, roan antelope, Grant's gazelle, and reedbuck. The Park contains seven species of primates, seven species of mongoose, two otters, warthog, dozens of species of rodent and bat, striped hyena, and two species of jackal. Also present are the shy and elegant little bat-eared fox, and the brave and powerful ratel or honey badger.

Over 200 species of bird have been recorded, including the kori bustard, ostrich, and lesser flamingo. Several of Serengeti's birds, such as the grey-breasted spurfowl, Fischer's lovebird, and the rufous-tailed weaver, are of restricted distribution.

193

Tarangire National Park (260,000 ha.) Altitude: 1,100 to 1,500 m.Location: 114 kms from Arusha and about 20 kms southeast of Lake Manyara, east of the Arush-Dodoma road.

Tarangire was established in 1970 and serves as a dry-season retreat for many plains game. It is watered by the Tarangire River which bisects the Park from south to north, and dries back to a series of deep pools at the height of the dry season in July to October. The rains continue sporadically from November to May, with a total rainfall of around 600 mm. The mean afternoon temperature of 27°C falls to 16°C at night, but a minimum of about 4°C has been recorded at night in July, and a maximum of 40°C by day in January. Humidity is very low. The vegetation is arid and thorny, with baobab trees, parkland and some woodland. There are various euphorbia and succulents in the deeper gullies and rocky ridges.

Tsetse fly infests much of the Park and, combined with the dense thorny vegetation, probably explains why the most numerous mammal species is the impala. However, most other African plains species are also present including lion, elephant, zebra, eland, lesser kudu, buffalo, and the Beisa oryx.

The birdlife, mainly composed of typical northeast African species, reflects the arid vegetation. Species such as the rosy-patched shrike and the golden-breasted starling are present near the southwesterly extremity of their range. Ostrich, pelican, and a wide variety of raptors are resident, together with herons, spoonbills and storks. Bee-eaters, kingfishers, and rollers add their brilliance to the avifauna, and the river supports many water-based species.

UGANDA

Uganda is an extraordinarily beautiful country, fertile enough, before its recent problems, to be self-sufficient in food, its people gifted and hospitable, its scenery and wildlife magnificent.

Its population is concentrated round the shores of Lake Victoria in the south, but the centre and west of the country are well provided with lakes and rivers, including the White Nile, which flows out of Lake Victoria. The climate is tropical but tempered by altitude. English is the official language and Swahili is also spoken.

Uganda has all the natural advantages for a healthy tourist trade, which was of course non-existent during the Amin period.

Kabalega (formerly Murchison) Falls National Park (384,000 ha.) Altitude: 500 to 1,292 m. Location: upstream of the point where the Victoria Nile flows into Lake Mobutu Sese Seko, formerly Lake Albert.

B
DEC–APR

Kabalega was gazetted in 1952 and takes its name from the spectacular falls on the River Nile within its boundaries. The river below the Falls has one of the largest crocodile populations in Africa, albeit somewhat depleted by poaching in recent years. The Park lies in an area of rolling grassland and savanna with some isolated forest patches, bisected by the Victoria Nile from east to west. The Kabalega Falls, emerging from a rocky cleft only seven metres wide, constitutes an important ecological barrier for aquatic fauna. Damage by elephant has destroyed much of the original woodland, although in 1980 there were signs of regeneration after the elephant population had been reduced by poaching.

In the same year, well over 1,000 elephant were recorded in the northern half of the Park and the total today, 1985, is probably higher. Numbers of buffalo and kob are relatively large and there are good populations of several other game species. Lion and hippo are present, and there is a population of Rothschild's giraffe, often gathering round the Karuma Falls. The status of the two species of rhino is not good. Black rhino are decreasing and the white rhino, reintroduced in the 1960s, has not been seen recently. Chimpanzees are present in the Rabongo forest.

The bird checklist records over 350 species, including the rare whale-headed stork. Most conspicuous among the other birds present are the Goliath heron, saddle-bill stork, open-bill stork, fish eagle, and 49 species of raptor. Water-based birds include skimmers below the Falls and pratincoles above them. The beautiful little malachite kingfisher is among the Park's seven species of kingfisher. 10 varieties of sunbird sparkle on their nectar plants.

Kidepo Valley National Park (134,400 ha.) Altitude: 900 to 2,750 m. Location: extreme northeast of the country along the border with the Sudan.

B
DEC–APR

Kidepo Valley, established in 1962, is watered by the seasonal Kidepo and Larus Rivers. The rivers themselves are normally dry apart from a few permanent pools. The vegetation is arid savanna, with some high level forest savanna in the mountain areas. The scenery is magnificent, wild and unspoiled. The best time to visit is in the dry season from December to early April.

The fauna is very varied and includes species protected nowhere else in Uganda, among them lesser kudu, a local race of Grant's gazelle (Bright's gazelle), Burchell's zebra, eland, roan, klipspringer, bushbaby, and the little bat-eared fox. Predators include striped hyena, aardwolf, caracal, and cheetah. The greater kudu, elephant, hartebeest, oribi, Rothschild's giraffe, Chanler's mountain reedbuck, and long-snouted dikdik are found. The numbers of black rhino are much depleted.

Birdlife is abundant and among at least 50 birds of prey, both migrant and resident, are numbered Verreaux's eagle, swallow-tailed kite, and pygmy falcon. Ostrich, the magnificent ground hornbill, and five species of bustard are among the larger birds. Others include the stone partridge, standard-wing nightjar, the endemic warbler *Apalis karamojae*, fan-tailed raven, and piapiac.

Ruwenzori National Park (197,800 ha. of Park and 220,000 ha. of Biosphere Reserve.) Altitude: 1,000 to 5,110 m. Location: on the equator in western Uganda, between Lake Edward (for a time Lake Idi Amin Dada, now Lake Rutanzige) and Lake George on the Zaire frontier.
B
DEC–APR

Ruwenzori, which lies in the western arm of the Rift Valley, was established in 1952 as Queen Elizabeth National Park with an area of 76,700 ha. In 1978 it was nominated a Biosphere Reserve. The Park contains a wide range of habitats – within its boundaries there are tropical forests, undulating euphorbia-dotted grasslands, acacia savanna and swamps, and the tundra belt of the Ruwenzori range – and consequently supports an extremely varied fauna.

The Maramagambo Forest area contains several primates, including chimpanzees, the rare red colobus, black-and-white colobus, the blue, and the red-tailed monkey. The elephant population has been devastated by poaching in recent years, but the population, down to 150 in 1980, appears to be recovering. There are around 20,000 kob, and good numbers of buffalo, hippo, waterbuck, topi, and giant forest hog. Tree-climbing lions inhabit the Kigezi section, and leopard is by no means rare. There are notable and odd gaps: for example, there are no impala and no zebra, and no crocodiles in the lakes.

The bird checklist records a remarkable 543 species, and numbers such rarities as the whale-headed stork, the beautiful black bee-eater, and eleven kingfishers including malachite, pied, blue-breasted, and shining blue. Sunbirds and waterbirds abound round the small lakes, and there are many species of raptor.

ZAMBIA

Zambia, occupying a huge and thinly-populated plateau in the heart of Africa, takes its name from the Zambesi River which flows across the south of the country. Altitude tempers its climate to near-perfection. Zambia's main natural resource consists of copper, although some other minerals are also mined. As the country has no access to the sea, it is dependent on its neighbours for its trade routes, in particular on the Chinese-built TanZam Freedom railway. During the colonial period, Zambia was the British colony of Northern Rhodesia.

Blue Lagoon National Park (45,000 ha.) Altitude: 970 to 1,010 m. Location: west of Lusaka in Central Province.

B/C
JULY–MAY

Before being established as a National Park in 1972, Blue Lagoon was a private ranch. The Park consists of the north bank of the Kafue Flats, part of the southeast boundary being formed by the Luwato Lagoon – an oxbow lake which tends to dry out only at the end of the dry season. The vegetation varies from floodplain grasses and sedges, to a narrow belt of termitaria grassland and open woodland with abundant fig trees. In June, 30% of the Park is flooded.

The most noteworthy mammal is the threatened Kafue lechwe, of which the Park contains a population around 100,000 strong. The Kafue lechwe was formerly much hunted by the indigenous human community, and the books of the early European explorers are full of accounts of its slaughter. The most common carnivore is wild dog, and there are occasional cheetahs. Also present are zebra, bushbuck, kudu, roan, and sable antelope.

The Park is an important feeding ground for waterfowl, including the glossy ibis and spur-winged goose.

Isangano National Park (84,000 ha.) Altitude: about 1,100 m. Location: at the northeastern edge of Lake Bangwelu flats, Northern Province.

C
JULY–MAY

Isangano was established in 1972, having been a game reserve under previous legislation. An area of flat and floodplain, its eastern boundary is formed by the Chambeshi River, while the Lubansenshi River runs through the Park's heart. The vegetation is largely swamp forest, with some tall grasslands and watershed plain grasslands. Along the rivers reeds and papyrus flourish. The heavy rainfall reaches 1,500 mm or more in some years.

The mammal population is somewhat reduced through poaching, bush fires and the attendant problems of low priority game reserve status. It does, however, include elephant, buffalo, zebra, bushbuck, eland, and warthog. The rare black lechwe enters the Park seasonally, although most remain outside its borders in the Bangwelu Game Management Area to the southwest. Reedbuck, roan, and hartebeest are also present. Nile crocodile inhabits the rivers.

Waterbirds are well represented by many species of heron, ibis, and duck.

Kafue National Park (2,240,000 ha.) Altitude: 970 to 1,470 m. Location: south-central Zambia, west of Lusaka.

A/B
JULY–MAY

Kafue was established as a National Park in 1972, but has existed as a reserve since 1951. Covering an area as large as Wales on the plains round the Kafue River, its vegetation consists of open grassy floodplains or 'dambos' with sections of miombo and mopane woodland and patches of teak, including the Ngoma forest. In the northwest there is perennial swampland which supports a population of red lechwe, a species only found in Zambia.

Noteworthy fauna includes numerous large mammals such as an increasing elephant population, well-distributed black rhino, abundant buffalo, including a herd of over 2,000 in the Busanga area, numerous waterbuck, puku, the rare red lechwe, yellow-backed duiker, reedbuck, and Lichtenstein's hartebeest. Lion are also present, and primates are represented by yellow and chacma baboons, which occur within a few kilometres of each other with no signs of interbreeding.

For birdwatchers, the Kafue Flats are a paradise, with over 400 recorded species including large numbers of waterfowl. The Kafue River is well stocked with fish.

Kasanka National Park (39,000 ha.) Altitude: 1,100 to 1,300 m. Location: in Serenje district, Central Province.

C
JULY–MAY

Kasanka, previously a Game Reserve, was established as a National Park in 1972. It lies on a plain with extensive wetlands supporting papyrus and reeds. There are some areas of 'dambo' grassland and 'mushitu' swamp forest, otherwise the area is dominated by miombo woodlands.

The most noteworthy large mammals are the sitatunga, seen here more easily than in any other Park, and numerous puku. Elephant, hippo, buffalo, waterbuck, hartebeest, warthog, and grysbok are all present. The blue monkey and its sub-species, Moloney's monkey, are also found.

198

The most obvious feature of the rich birdlife is the abundance of waterfowl.

Lavushi Manda National Park (150,000 ha.) Altitude: 1,100 to 1,800 m. Location: southwest of Mpika, Northern Province.

B/C
AUG–APR

Lavushi Manda, formerly a Game Reserve, was established in 1972. The rugged Lavushi Manda hills run along the southeastern side of the Park, and a fair-sized river, the Lukulu, flows through its northern half. The vegetation is miombo woodland, interspersed with dambo plains. Dense gallery forest occurs along the rivers with palms in the canyons, while on the hills there are numerous euphorbia and aloes.

Large mammals are not numerous but include leopard, lion, elephant, common duiker, waterbuck, reedbuck, roan and sable antelope, and hartebeest. Klipspringer also occurs, and the rock rabbit or Smith's red hare should be found in the hills, although it has not yet been reliably recorded.

Although there are no spectacular concentrations of birds, there are some interesting species, such as the bar-throated apalis and the double-collared sunbird.

Liuwa Plain National Park (366,000 ha.) Altitude: about 1,000 m. Location: in the Western Province, Kalabo district.

C
AUG–APR

Liuwa Plain was established in 1972 and lies on a flat and sandy grass plain, flanked by the Luambimba River to the east and Luanginga River to the west.

Mammals include the largest population of wildebeest in Zambia, herds of zebra, some buffalo, the rare red lechwe, roan antelope, and lesser numbers of tsessebe.

Birdlife includes a variety of waterfowl on the pans together with such species as the secretary bird, crowned crane, and wattled crane.

Lochinvar National Park (41,000 ha.) Altitude: 970 to 1,038 m. Location: northwest of Monze, Southern Province.

B/C
JUNE–NOV

Lochinvar, established in 1972, was previously a game management area and before that a privately-owned ranch. The Park's primary purpose was to protect the local population of lechwe. The northern third forms part of the Kafue Flats and is flooded in December. The water reaches a maximum depth in May and gradually recedes to its lowest level by November. The rest of the Lochinvar consists of termitaria grasslands with euphorbia and some woodland.

199

The population of Kafue lechwe is around 35,000 (1977). The Park also contains zebra, eland, wildebeest and oribi. In the southern woodlands, kudu, bushbuck, duikers, and impala are present.

The area has a rich birdlife with almost 400 species recorded. These include white and pink-backed pelican, Goliath and purple heron, fish eagle, darter, secretary bird, Swainson's francolin, and helmeted guinea fowl; also, the magnificent crowned crane, wattled crane, Denham's bustard, wattled plover, and red-billed hornbill.

Lukusuzi National Park (272,000 ha.) Altitude: 800 to 1,240 m. Location: in the Eastern Province plateau, between Lundazi and Chipata.

C
MAY–NOV

Lukusuzi was established in 1972, having been a Game Reserve under previous legislation. It comprises an area of level plateau, with hilly broken country on the west leading to an escarpment overlooking the Luangwa valley. The vegetation is largely miombo woodland with some grassland. There is a long dry season from May to November, and a short, hot wet season.

Elephant, rhino, buffalo and zebra, eland, roan and sable antelope, and hartebeest are the principal mammals. Spotted hyena is present and Cookson's hartebeest occurs sparsely. The rocky outcrops in the Park afford the klipspringer one of its principal Zambian habitats.

Lusenga Plain National Park (88,000 ha.) Altitude: 800 to 1,300 m. Location: north of Kawambwa, Luapula Province.

B/C
MAY–OCT

Lusenga Plain, formerly a Game Reserve, was established in 1972. The plain's vegetation is 'dambo' grassland, with remnants of 'mishitu' swamp forest and dry evergreen forest round the edges. The Kalugwishi River, with its three large waterfalls, borders the north and east of the Park. The annual rainfall totals 1,400 mm and falls mainly between November and April.

The fauna is depleted, but numbers remnant populations of a considerable variety of species. These include elephant, buffalo, leopard, roan and sable antelope, zebra, warthog, bushbuck, eland, yellow-backed and blue duikers, waterbuck, reedbuck, and hartebeest.

There appears to be no account of the birdlife available.

Mosi-Oa-Tunya National Park (6,600 ha.) Altitude: 790 to 900 m. Location: on the southern border with Zimbabwe, Victoria Falls.

A
NOV–SEPT

Mosi-Oa-Tunya, formerly a trust area, was established as a National Park in 1972. The Park occupies the left bank of the Zambesi River and half of the Victoria Falls, together with a series of deep gorges below the falls. The maximum height of the Falls is 108 m, with a water flow of 540 million litres a minute around March and April. Above the Falls the river is 1,690 m wide. There are archaeological remains of stone- and iron-age man nearby. Dominant vegetation is mopane forest, and the 'rainforest' below the spray of the falls is rich with ferns and a profusion of flowering plants.

A 1,000-ha. fenced Zoological Park, upriver from the falls, contains some exotic species as well as native animals. The natural wild fauna includes elephant, leopard, hippo, buffalo, bushbuck, common duiker, waterbuck and warthog. Vervet monkey and baboon are common.

Birdlife is interesting, including the rare Taita falcon, a black swift, and the beautiful carmine bee-eater in the gorge; also shrikes, flycatchers, and sunbirds, taking advantage of the nectar in the flowering plants in the spray forest.

Mweru Wantipa National Park (313,400 ha.) Altitude: 900 to 1,400 m. Location: close to the northern border, between Lakes Mweru and Tanganyika.
B/C
MAY–OCT

Mweru Wantipa, established in 1972, was formerly a Game Reserve. The eastern half of the Park changes periodically from grassland and swamp to a large open lake, Lake Mweru Wantipa. The cycle is erratic, but the water level appeared to reach its recent high point in 1974. The swamp and lake area are dominated by dense papyrus thickets with some reed. The remainder is covered with miombo woodland. The wet season generally occurs between November and April, and one year in five produces a rainfall as high as 1,300 mm.

Mammals include large numbers of the blue monkey, baboon, and possibly occasional vagrant colobus monkeys from Zaire. The scarce bush-tailed mongoose has been collected in the area. The big five, lion, leopard, elephant, rhino, and buffalo, are also present. Hippo is found in the lake and swamps. Other ungulates are plentiful and include zebra, sitatunga in the smaller Kabwe marsh, eland, yellow-backed duiker, blue duiker, klipspringer, grysbok, puku, waterbuck, and reedbuck. The Nile crocodile is common.

Among the more spectacular birds are concentrations of pelican, several species of heron, shoebill, saddlebill, openbill (found and described nesting here by Livingstone), and greater and lesser flamingoes.

North Luangwa National Park (463,600 ha.) Altitude: 500 to 1,100 m. Location: in east central Zambia, in the upper Luangwa valley.
B/C
MAY–OCT

201

North Luangwa, a former Game Reserve, was established as a National Park in 1972. The Park extends from the 1,400 m Muchinga escarpment in the west to the northern part of the Luangwa River in the east. The river is seasonally flooded and there are no grassy plains. The vegetation is miombo woodland and scrubland with riverine forest on the meander belt. The mean annual temperature is 22°C, and the annual rainfall of 88 mm comes in a single wet season from November to April.

Caracal, East Africa

202

Mammals include elephant, leopard, lion, black rhinoceros, and buffalo. Also present are zebra, kudu, eland, puku, hippo, Cookson's wildebeest, and impala. Primates are represented by Chacma baboon and vervet monkey. The river provides a habitat for Nile crocodile.

Nyika National Park (8,000 ha.) Altitude: 1,295 to 2,225 m. Location: the extreme northeast of Zambia, adjoining the border with Malawi.

B
MAY–OCT

Nyika was a controlled hunting area until it became a National Park in 1972. It occupies the small Zambian portion of the high Nyika plateau, a steep and undulating area which slopes sharply down to the lower Shire river valley. The vegetation is miombo woodland with relict patches of forest. The Park is very rich botanically, with many species of orchid. The rainfall is around 1,000 mm, but cloud and mist at ground level in summer between June and September keep the landscape well watered. Frost of $-5°$ to $-10°C$ can occur between May and October.

Moloney's monkey is the most numerous of a very varied small mammal fauna, which includes the bush squirrel, four-striped rat in its only Zambian locality, long-tailed pouched rat, three species of vlei rat, a sun squirrel, two-spotted palm civet, and yellow-spotted hyrax or dassie. Larger mammals are infrequent, but include bushbuck, blue and, very rarely, red duiker, reedbuck, and klipspringer.

The butterfly populations are particularly splendid, the most notable species being two swallowtails, *Papilio phorcas* and *Papilio bromius*.

Among the birdlife is the secretary bird, white-necked raven, and a variety of sunbirds.

Sioma Ngwezi National Park (527,600 ha.) Altitude: 900 m. Location: in the southwest of the country, bordering the Caprivi Strip.

C
MAY–OCT

Sioma Ngwezi was established in 1972, having previously been the Paramount Chief's Game Reserve. It occupies a relatively flat area west of the Zambesi and bordered by the Mashi River to the southwest. The vegetation is Kalahari sandveld, with good stands of teak and areas of mopane.

The mammal population includes a particularly large group of giraffe, one of only two populations in Zambia. Elephant, lion, cheetah, and buffalo are the other large mammals present. Among the ungulates are roan and sable antelope, tsessebe, and the seldom seen steenbok.

While there are no obvious concentrations of large birds, a number of interesting and varied dry country species can be found including the greater kestrel, Bradfield's hornbill, pied barbet, Burchell's glossy starling, and the blue-cheeked waxbill. The ostrich formerly occurred, but is now locally extinct.

South Luangwa National Park (905,000 ha.) Altitude: 500 to 1,100 m. **B/C**
Location: in the central eastern section of the country, northeast of **APR–OCT**
Lusaka.

South Luangwa, formerly a Game Reserve, was established in 1972. It is remarkable for the abundance and variety of its fauna, and is widely considered as one of the best Parks in Africa. Lying along the River Luangwa, a tributary of the Zambesi, the Park's vegetation consists of woodland savanna, floodplain, and grassland, with some riparian forest. The mean annual temperature is 25°C, and the wet season runs from November to March when heavy storms give a rainfall of 832 mm a year.

The Park has plentiful elephant and good numbers of black rhino. The giraffe species present – Thornicroft's giraffe – is endemic to the valley and found mainly in the southern sector. There are huge herds of impala, some greater kudu, buffalo, puku, hippo, sable and roan antelope, Lichtenstein's hartebeest, and Cookson's wildebeest – a local subspecies present in small numbers. Predators are well represented, including leopard, lion, cheetah, wild dog, and hyena. Primates are highly characteristic of the fauna, including vervet monkey, Moloney's monkey, and chacma baboon. The Luangwa River provides one of the last remaining refuges for the Nile crocodile.

Birdlife is prolific and particularly noted for storks, geese, cranes, and the colonies of carmine bee-eaters which nest in the river banks.

Sumbu National Park (202,000 ha.) Altitude: 800 to 1,250 m. Location: **B**
in the Northern Province on the southwest shore of Lake Tanganyika **MAY–OCT**
– the second largest lake in Africa.

Sumbu, a former Game Reserve, was proclaimed a National Park in 1972. It follows 100 kms of the rocky shoreline of Lake Tanganyika, interspersed with small beaches on which are many small sites of considerable archaeological interest. In the hinterland is the Lufubu River plateau, and there are two steep escarpments to the east and west. The vegetation ranges from miombo woodland to thicket, grassland and gallery forest. The annual rainfall of around 1,400 mm falls mainly between November and April.

A varied fauna includes elephant, zebra, hippo, eland, buffalo, yellow-backed and blue duiker, puku, waterbuck, reedbuck, roan and sable antelope, and hartebeest. There are also grysbok and klipspringer. Predators include lion and leopard. The lake contains Nile crocodile, and the Tanganyika water cobra is common.

The birdlife is interesting and includes grey-headed and lesser black-backed gulls, fuscus, white-winged and whiskered terns, and skimmers among the more obvious species along the rivers and shores of the lake.

West Lunga National Park (168,400 ha.) Altitude: 1,120 to 1,200 m. Location: in Mwinilunga district, North Western Province.

B/C
MAY–OCT

West Lunga, a Game Reserve under previous legislation, was created in 1972. It occupies a flat area between two rivers, the East Lunga and the Kabompo Rivers, which join at the southwest corner of the Park. Most of the vegetation is dry evergreen forest, with some open grassland and permanent swamp.

Noteworthy fauna includes elephant, particularly in the evergreen forest, and most major carnivores. The blue monkey is found along the rivers. Among the other mammals are zebra, a few hippo, numerous bushpig, sitatunga, eland, buffalo, yellow-backed and blue duiker, puku, hartebeest, klipspringer, oribi, and impala. Crocodile are also present.

The birdlife is varied and abundant and includes a local red-throated sub-species of crested guinea fowl.

ZIMBABWE

Zimbabwe, formerly Rhodesia, is a large and beautiful landlocked country which was, from 1972 until 1980, torn apart by internal strife. Since settlement of the independence issue under the Lancaster House agreement, tourism, which was almost non-existent during the period of the war, is being encouraged again. The country has much to offer, not least of which is a fine and temperate climate and some of the most spectacular tourist attractions in the whole continent, including such marvels as the Victoria Falls, the Hwange Game Park, and the Zimbabwe ruins.

Chimanimani National Park (17,100 ha.) Altitude: rising to 2,400 m. Location: eastern Zimbabwe, 75 kms south of Mutare on the border with Mozambique.

B/C
APR–OCT

Chimanimani was established in 1953 and includes the main massif within Zimbabwe of the Chimanimani mountain range. The landscape is rugged and dramatic, with mountain peaks and deep gorges through which cascade magnificent waterfalls. The area is subject to sudden storms and mists. The vegetation is largely montane, with some grassland and relict forest patches. The flora includes some Cape specialities and interesting low-altitude rainforest.

A mountain wilderness area Chimanimani's fauna includes sable and eland, and the variety of the birdlife is unique in Zimbabwe.

Chizarira National Park (191,000 ha.) Altitude: 648 to 1,433 m. Location: in the central Binga district of Matabeleland North Province.

B/C
APR–OCT

Chizarira was set aside as a reserve in 1963 and granted National Park status in 1975. The area is a well watered 'island', cut through by river gorges on their way to the Zambesi River in the relatively arid Zambesi Valley. Mount Tunduzi is the prominent feature in the northeast. Due to the 'island' effect and the generally higher rainfall of the plateau, the vegetation is dry miombo woodland with mopane or open grassland. The gorges support riverine plant communities.

The Park shelters a wide spectrum of large mammals, among them elephant, buffalo, black rhino, zebra, warthog, and a whole range of antelope including roan and tsessebe.

Birdlife embraces, once again because of the 'island' effect, a westerly extension of the range of several species. The taita falcon, nowhere common in Zimbabwe, occurs in some of the gorges. Other birds include crowned eagle, fish eagle, brown hooded kingfisher, red-billed wood hoopoe, golden-tailed woodpecker, and Meyer's parrot.

Gonarezhou National Park (505,300 ha.) Altitude: 162 to 578 m. Location: on the southeastern border of Zimbabwe adjacent to Mozambique.

C
APR–OCT

Gonarezhou was established in 1968 in a well watered area encompassing the valleys of three rivers, the Lundi, the Nuanetse, and the Sabi. The south bank of the Lundi has the spectacular backdrop of the Chilojo cliffs for about half its distance through the Park. The rainfall is light, but there is a wide variety of vegetation types, ranging from mixed woodland and dry evergreen forest, to aloes and thicket.

The fauna includes several species of the Mozambique plains which are threatened or absent elsewhere in Zimbabwe, among them a soaring population of elephant. The reintroduced black rhino appears to be prospering and hippo are breeding so successfully that the population has to be periodically reduced. The area is also the stronghold in Zimbabwe for nyala, suni, and Lichtenstein's hartebeest. An unusual and possibly unique cohabitation of smaller antelope includes steenbok, grysbok, grey

duiker, Livingstone's suni, and oribi with klipspringer on nearby hills.
Other species include red squirrel together with common bush squirrel.

The water fauna is of particular interest, with freshwater turtle, lung
fish, and a threatened top minnow. Common river fish include tiger fish
and bream. Marine tarpon and sword fish have been taken in the Lundi
river many kilometres from the sea. There is also a significant crocodile
population.

The Park's avifauna includes crested guinea fowl.

Hwange (Wankie) National Park (1,465,100 ha.) Altitude: 938 to
1,152 m. Location: on the border with Botswana in the south of the
country, contiguous with Matetsi and 200 kms northwest of Bulawayo.

A
APR–OCT

Eland in Hwange National Park, Zimbabwe

207

Hwange, formerly Wankie, was established as a Game Reserve in 1928 and the area it occupies spans the transition between dry Kalahari sand and moist savanna woodland. The country is gently undulating, with 'fossil' river lines draining towards the great Makgadikgadi salt pans in Botswana. In the north of the Park, streams and rivers flow down towards the Zambesi River, watering great teak forests and moist woodland. The south is a mixture of grassland, thicket, and dry mopane woodland. The climate is dry and tropical, with an annual rainfall of around 655 mm, declining towards the south and west.

The Park contains some 35 recorded species (1981) of large mammal (jackal-sized or bigger), and the fauna represents a mixture of southern savanna and southwestern arid species. There are substantial populations of elephant (15,000) and buffalo (30,000). Also present are giraffe, zebra, hippo, warthog, and a wide range of antelope including wildebeest, kudu, impala, eland and sable. Black and white rhino have been reintroduced and appear to be prospering. The larger predators number lion, leopard, cheetah, wild dog, and two species of hyena.

Over 400 bird species have been recorded in the Park. These include the magnificent Bateleur eagle and several vultures – lappet-faced, white-backed, cape, white-headed, and hooded – as well as a great variety, changing with the season, of smaller birds. Among these are the flocks of waxbills, canaries, doves, francolins, guineafowl, sandgrouse, and starlings during the dry season. The wet season brings migrant cuckoos, swallows, swifts, warblers, nightjars, Egyptian goose, red-billed teal, and knob-billed goose on the pans.

62 artificial waterholes, rendering an otherwise seasonally waterless area suitable for year-round occupation, have brought problems, in particular an explosion of the elephant population.

Inyanga National Park (33,000 ha.) Altitude: 880 to 2,595 m. Location: on the Mozambique border, about 200 kms east of Harare.

B/C
APR–OCT

Inyanga has been protected since 1902. Most of the area, which includes the Mtarazi Falls National Park, was set aside under the will of Cecil Rhodes for the people of Zimbabwe. The Park takes in part of Mount Inyangani, the highest peak in Zimbabwe, and is the source of several important streams and rivers. It contains a number of waterfalls, of which the Mtarazi is the most spectacular, and many of its rivers have been dammed to form small lakes. The vegetation is stunted woodland and montane grassland, kept at a chosen level by the use of fire, but includes reintroduced conifers and alien pines and wattles. The Park is

208

an important mountain sanctuary for wildlife in a region where plantations of these aliens dominate the landscape.

There is an interesting mountain fauna unique in Zimbabwe, albeit with very few large herbivores, and lions occur occasionally.

Birdlife includes buzzards and eagles. Among the smaller birds are cisticolas, waxbills, mannikins, and widow-birds.

Kazuma Pan National Park (31,300 ha.) Altitude: 900 to 1,200 m. Location: on the border with Botswana – the Park forms part of the Hwange, Matetsi, and Victoria Falls complex.

B/C
NOV–MAR

Kazuma Pan, an area of flat open grassland fringed by mopane and Kalahari woodland, was proclaimed a National Park in 1949, deproclaimed in 1963, and reinstated in 1975.

There is a wide range of large mammal species, but populations are generally sparse and seasonal. Locally threatened species present include gemsbok, oribi, roan, tsessebe, and cheetah. This is the only area in Zimbabwe where the western populations of the southern African oribi occur.

The seasonally inundated areas are important to waterfowl.

Mana Pools National Park (219,000 ha.) Altitude: 500 to 1,062 m. Location: in the Zambesi Valley, northeast of Lake Kariba and on the south bank of the river which forms the border with Zambia.

B/C
APR–OCT

Mana Pools was created a National Park in 1963. The adjacent safari areas were established at later intervals, the last being the Urungwe in 1976. The vegetation is well-grassed in the mountainous escarpment, with mopane woodland on the valley floor, or dry, highly deciduous thickets known as 'jesse'. Along the fertile floodplains beside the Zambesi itself there are Natal mahoganies and lush grassland.

The complex formed by the Park and surrounding reserves has a rich and varied fauna with large mammal populations, which tend to concentrate on the floodplains during the dry season when water elsewhere is scarce and the *Acacia albida* trees shed their protein-rich pods. The mammals include a significant population of black rhino, elephant, whose numbers threaten the habitat, hippo, zebra, warthog, bushpig, and a wide range of antelope species. These last consist of mixed herds of puku, eland, bushbuck, nyala, waterbuck, grysbok, and steenbok. Among the attendant predators are lion, leopard, and spotted hyena. Also present is one of the bush animals most renowned for courage and ferocity, the ratel or honeybadger. Crocodiles inhabit the rivers which are well

209

stocked with fish, including tiger fish, bream, bundu, kupi, chessa, and cornish Jack.

Birdlife along the river and on the land is prolific, with notable species including Nyasa lovebirds, yellow-spotted nicator, white-collared pratincole, banded snake-eagle, and Livingstone's flycatcher.

Matopos National Park (42,500 ha.) Altitude: 1,300 to 1,466 m. Location: about 32 kms south of the city of Bulawayo and contiguous with the 2,900-ha. Lake Matopos Recreational Park.   A/B
APR–OCT

Matopos was established as a National Park in 1902 and a Recreational Park in 1926. The complex is partly on Trust Land bequeathed to the nation by Cecil Rhodes, and occupies the heart of the Matopos hills. The hills are composed of granite kopjes interspersed with deep valleys in which many Bushman paintings can be found. The flora is very diverse with wooded kloofs, grassy vleis, open woodland, and swamps. There are various winter-flowering plants, and a singular species of ground orchid.

The fauna includes at least 88 mammals, including 71% of the hare-sized and larger species recorded in Zimbabwe. There are many leopards, klipspringer, two species of hyraxes, and red hare. At least a dozen species of large mammals have been reintroduced. Also present are more than 70 reptile species, 30 amphibians, and 16 fish, including several exotics introduced to the streams and dams, among them bream and black bass.

Over 300 bird species have been recorded – half the number known for Zimbabwe. These include 40 species of raptor, with the highest density in the country of black or Verreaux's eagle, Wahlberg's eagle, tawny eagle, banded harrier hawk, secretary bird, black-shouldered kite, snake eagle, little sparrowhawk, Gagar goshawk, peregrine, and lanner falcon.

Matusadona National Park (137,000 ha.) Altitude: up to 1,201 m. Location: on the southern shore of Lake Kariba.   A/B
APR–OCT

Matusadona was established as a non-hunting reserve in 1963, but was managed as a National Park from the start and formally elevated to its present status in 1975. The Park is largely inaccessible and extends over the upland area high above the man-made Kariba lake. The numerous bays of the lakeshore are formed by drowned valleys. The Bumi River forms the western boundary and the flooded Sanyati gorge the eastern border. The vegetation is grassland on the upper slopes, with the lower woodland modified by the activities of elephant. The shore communities are still evolving.

Noteworthy fauna includes elephant, black rhino, buffalo, sable and roan antelope, kudu, waterbuck, hippo, eland, and impala. Among the predators are lion, leopard, and hyena. The lake supports, among other fish, bream, vundu, tigerfish, and Tanganyika sardine.

The birdlife is abundant and varied and includes fish eagle, African darter, cormorants, heron, stork, plover, lilytrotter, and numerous woodland species.

Zambesi National Park (56,400 ha.) Altitude: 1,000 m. Location: western Matabeleland Province, in northwest Zimbabwe, on the south bank of the Zambesi which forms the border with Zambia. The Park is contiguous with Victoria Falls National Park, Mtetsi-Kazuma Pan National Park, and Hwange (Wankie) National Park – a total conserved area of nearly 2 million ha.   A/B   APR–OCT

Zambesi has been part of Victoria Falls National Park since 1931. In 1979 it was subdivided into its present form. The vegetation is typical Kalahari woodland, with acacia and tamarind along the streams and the river and some papyrus swamp.

Mammals, birds, fish, and invertebrates are all well represented in the Park. Large mammals include elephant, hippo, black and white rhino, giraffe, zebra, warthog, and some dozen species of antelope. Among the predators are lion, leopard, and spotted hyena.

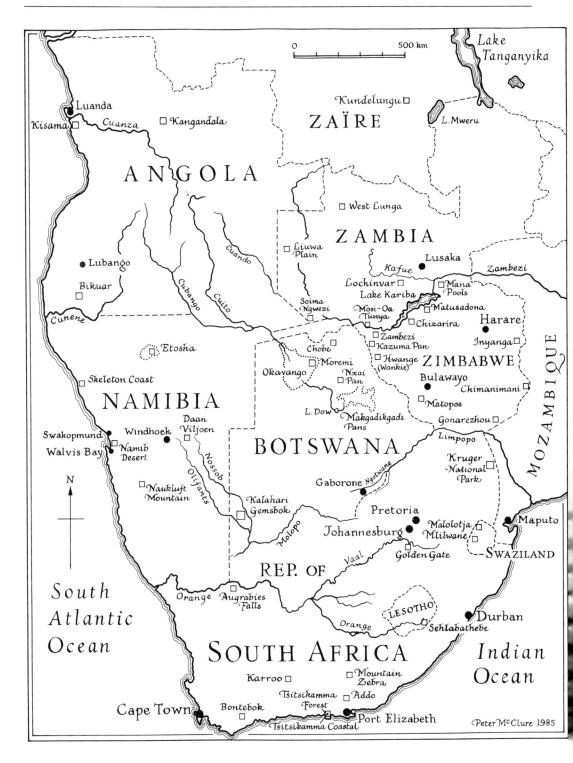

Peter McClure 1985

SOUTHERN AFRICA

The dominant geographical features of central and southern Africa (as defined on the map opposite) are the great adjoining dry plateaux of Angola and the Kalahari in Botswana. These are bordered along the Atlantic coast by Namibia's barren Namib desert, by the Great Karroo in South Africa's Cape Province, and by the Drakensberg range of mountains which ridge the province of Natal. The central eastern sector is watered by two major river systems, those of the Zambesi and the Limpopo. The Zambesi, 2,700 kilometres long, has its sources in the highlands of Angola to the west, and in the last of the Rift Valley lakes, Lake Malawi, to the north. Much of the region is high with huge expanses of arid semi-desert in the west and centre, and more fertile zones to the south and east – the climate of the Cape is similar to the Mediterranean. The rains, when they come, fall between October and March.

The region's wide range of landscape, vegetation and habitat supports a large spectrum of Africa's wildlife. The Parks in northern Botswana, which include the southern bank of a tributary of the Zambesi, the Chobe, are ancient Bushmen hunting grounds and remain particularly rich in antelope, elephant, giraffe, and the great carnivores. Within the borders of Botswana, too, is the inland river complex of the Okavango delta which offers a wealth of game-viewing of both dry-land and semi-aquatic species, including many birds. The great pans of the Namib, such as Etosha, provide magnificent sights of animal concentrations, particularly in the dry season.

Angola has a fascinating coastal fauna and some excellent inland Parks – all eminently worth visiting when peace descends on the troubled country and tourism becomes possible again. The two small states of Lesotho and Swaziland offer breathtaking mountain scenery, while Namibia, though frequently drought-ridden, is rich in all kinds of wildlife, especially birds.

South Africa, in particular the superbly-managed reserves of Natal, is the most obvious goal for visitors to the southern part of the continent who wish to see Africa's wildlife.

ANGOLA

Angola, which extends along the southwest coast of Africa for 1,600 kms, has the shape of a huge square with a single natural boundary in the Atlantic. Nearly two-thirds of the land consists of highlands which are the source of the water supplies for most of southern Africa.

Naturally Angola is immensely rich in wildlife, although the political turmoil since independence has made several of its Parks and reserves inaccessible to visitors for some time. Along the coast the cold Benguela current influences both marine life and the climate, making coastal areas warm in winter and hot in summer. The grass savanna between Luanda and Lobito has magnificent giant baobab and euphorbia trees.

Bikuar National Park (790,000 ha.) Altitude: 1,150 to 1,350 m. Location: 135 kms south of Lubango in the province of Huila.

C
MAR–OCT

Bikuar was established as a hunting reserve in 1938 and was given National Park status by the Portuguese in 1964. Its boundaries were redefined in 1972. An area of South African woodland and savanna on a gently undulating plain, the reserve is crossed by the Kunene and the intermittently-flowing Bikuar Rivers. Its vegetation consists principally of deciduous woods and high forest. The average temperature is 18.7°C with 50% humidity. Rainfall can be expected on 101 days a year. The coldest month is June, and September/October are the warmest.

The Park has very few human inhabitants. Elephant, buffalo, kudu, eland, roan antelope, and wildebeest are the larger animals, while the predators include cheetah, spotted hyena, hunting dog, lion, and leopard. Also to be found are impala, duiker, oribi, steenbok, bushpig, bushbuck, reedbuck, and warthog.

Kangandala National Park (60,000 ha.) Altitude: 1,040 to 1,157 m. Location: 55 kms east-southeast of Malange in Malange Province.

C
MAR–OCT

Kangandala was declared a Nature Reserve by the Portuguese in 1963, had its boundaries redrawn in 1964, and became a National Park in 1970.

The Park lies on gently sloping hills drained by four permanent rivers, the Cuque, Cuike, Maubi and Dmbe, which empty their waters into the marshes below. The average temperature is 21.3°C, with the coldest month June and the warmest February. The mean annual humidity is 73%.

The hill slopes are covered with thin woodland and savanna which support a mammal population including leopard, hunting dog, roan and giant sable antelope (both well represented), bushbuck, common duiker, bushpig, and warthog. Also present in the marshy areas are the elusive sitatunga, hippo, waterbuck, and reedbuck.

Kisama (also known as Quicâma) National Park (996,000 ha.) Altitude: sea-level to 265 m. Location: on the coast in Bengo Province, 45 kms south of Luanda.   B/C MAR–OCT

Kisama was originally established as a hunting reserve by the Portuguese in 1938, and became a National Park in 1957. An area of Congo woodland and savanna, the Park consists of extensive floodplains, gently undulating hills, and some raised plains. The climate is generally hot and humid with a mean annual temperature of 24.6°C. Rain falls on average 54 days a year. The coolest months are July and August, and the warmest March.

Five main types of vegetation cover the Park: dry, mainly deciduous forest mosaic with savanna at lower altitudes; coastal mangroves; 'steppes' near the coast with thickets and savanna; a savanna mosaic further inland with scattered trees; and marshy plains. There are two long and meandering permanent rivers, the Kwanza and Longa, which flood periodically and fill numerous lagoons on the plains.

Among the Park's common mammals are buffalo, roan antelope, eland, and bushbuck. Others include cheetah, spotted hyena, hunting dog, lion, leopard, manatee, hippo, warthog, bushpig, reedbuck, blue duiker, and common duiker. Of particular importance are the populations of manatee, roan, marine turtle and talapoin monkey.

Botswana

Botswana, the former British Protectorate of Bechuanaland, occupies much of the huge dry plateau which forms the Kalahari Desert – the legendary 'Great Thirst'. The landscape is harsh and flat and large tracts of the country are still almost uninhabited, except by the few remaining groups of nomadic San Bushmen. Unlike the Sahara, the Kalahari is a desert only in the sense that it has little permanent water. It is, however, fed by the rains. As in other parts of Africa the climate goes through cycles of drought, but in good years the rains nourish a rich layer of vegetation which supports large numbers of animals even in the heart of the desert.

Although increasingly encroached by ranching and mining, Botswana offers some of the finest game-viewing in Africa.

Chobe National Park (1,087,800 ha.) Altitude: 900 m approx. Location: in northern Botswana near the borders with Namibia, Zambia and Zimbabwe. The Park can be reached from Victoria Falls in Zimbabwe.   A/B JAN–MAY

Chobe was established in 1967 and borders the Chobe River, which forms a 35-km stretch of the Park boundary and derives from the Linyanti River on its way to the Zambesi. The Park encompasses the Nogatosau floodplains and their pans, and the sandy Mababe Depression which includes the Savuti Marsh. Rainy season is from June to December. The vegetation ranges from dry savanna grassland to mopane woodland and riverine forest. Maximum temperatures in January can reach 32°C.

Noteworthy fauna includes large herds of elephant, buffalo and zebra which gather on the plains and near the pans. Other mammals include giraffe, black rhino, oribi, roan, sable, tsessebe on the plains, waterbuck, and puku on the flats near the river. Among the predators are lion and leopard. The most dense faunal population is in Savuti.

Birdlife is diverse, including fish eagle, banded harrier hawk, guinea fowl, and carmine bee-eater, which nests in the banks of the Chobe.

Moremi Wildlife Reserve (800,000 ha.) Altitude: 900 m approx. Location: in the eastern area of the Okavango Delta in Ngamiland, northwest Botswana.   A/B JAN–MAY

Moremi occupies part of the inland delta of the Okavango River which rises in Angola. The reserve (which has National Park status) embraces numerous rivers, lagoons, papyrus and reed beds, and islands, including the 100 by 15-km wooded Chief's Island. There is extensive flooding between mid-November and March during which the rivers are clear and fast flowing. During the dry season much of the area dries out. Vegetation includes papyrus and reed, lily pads, dense mopane woodland with sausage trees, fig, leadwood, crotons and knobthorns, sycamore fig, and fan palm.

216

The diverse range of habitats supports hippo, over 20,000 buffalo, the semi-aquatic red lechwe, the shy sitatunga, kudu, roan, impala, tsessebe, elephant, bat-eared fox, lion, and spotted-necked otter. There are many amphibians, and the reptiles include crocodile. Among the fish are tigerfish, barbel and bream.

The birdlife is magnificent and species include lily-trotter or jacana, wattled crane, sacred ibis, squacco heron, marabou, yellow-billed stork, kingfishers, Pel's fishing owl, barred owl, fish eagle, bearded woodpecker, rollers, and bee-eaters.

Nxai Pan National Park (259,000 ha.) Altitude: 900 m approx. Location: north of the Makgadikgadi Pans complex in northern Botswana.

B/C
JAN–MAY

Nxai Pan was established in 1971 and contains two salt pans: Nxai Pan and the smaller Kgama-kgama Pan thirty-five kilometres to the north. The vegetation is primarily forest and woodland savanna, although Nxai Pan is covered with short grass. The rainy season is from December to March.

Mammals include large herds of giraffe and migratory zebra and wildebeest, which concentrate at the water-filled depressions during the summer season. During the rainy season the herds move to the Boteti River. Among the predators are lion, cheetah, bat-eared fox, and aardwolf.

Avifauna includes vultures, goshawks, and Bateleur eagle.

LESOTHO

Lesotho, formerly the British Protectorate of Basutoland, is a tiny, mountainous and densely-populated country landlocked by South Africa. It occupies the highest part of the Drakensberg Mountains and has magnificent scenery.

Sehlabathebe National Park (6,500 ha.) Altitude: 1,250 m. Location: in the southeast corner of the country, bordering on the Drakensberg mountains in the Republic of South Africa.

B
OCT–NOV,
FEB–APR

Sehlabathebe was established in 1970 in a mountainous landscape containing grassveld studded with striking outcrops of sandstone. The Park is crossed by the Tsoelikana River and snow falls regularly in winter. Access is by horse or four-wheel drive vehicle.

217

Game is not numerous. The Park contains a few black wildebeest, some mountain reedbuck, occasional eland and oribi which leave when the winter snow arrives, baboon, black-backed jackal, wildcat, and otter. The Tsoelikana River harbours the threatened minnow-like fish, *Oreodaimon quathlambae*, formerly thought to be extinct.

NAMIBIA

Namibia, or South West Africa, is a huge, sunbaked stretch of the south-western coast of the continent, and in 1985 was the last African country still under colonial rule. Drought, which can continue for seven years without break, is a constant threat to the landscape's inhabitants, but the area has always supported abundant wildlife and also, for thousands of years before the arrival of black or white colonists, a human population of hunter-gatherer San Bushmen.

Daan Viljoen Game Reserve (3,953 ha.) Altitude: 1,800 to 2,000 m. B/C
Location: in the Khomas highlands 39 kms west of Windhoek. MAR–OCT

Daan Viljoen is a National Park located in hilly broken country, crossed by the Augeigas River and its tributaries. The reserve was established in 1967. The vegetation is open montane savanna, with the endemic green-flowered aloe. Temperatures can rise to 39°C in the summer, and drop to near-freezing at night in the winter. About 375 mm of rain falls during the summer months.

The reserve's larger mammals, some of which have been reintroduced, include mountain zebra, kudu, eland, gemsbok, hartebeest, wildebeest, klipspringer, steenbok and springbok, baboon, and dassie.

The area has a very rich avifauna with breeding populations of black eagle and the African hawk eagle. Rare endemic species include Monteiro's hornbill, rock-jumper, short-toed rock thrush, and white-tailed shrike.

Etosha National Park (2,227,000 ha.) Altitude: 1,000 to 1,500 m. Loca- A/B
tion: about 400 kms northwest of Windhoek and 120 kms south of the MAR–OCT
Angolan border.

Etosha was established as a Game Reserve in 1907 and declared a National Park in 1958. The saline Etosha pan at the eastern end of the Park is an inland drainage area of the great African plateau. A system of channels or omurambas run down towards the pan, which covers an

218

Ostriches in Etosha National Park, Namibia

area of 4,800 sq kms. In the wet season water reaches it from as far away as Angola. The vegetation is arid savanna with some tree and shrub acacia. Temperatures range from below freezing at night in winter to a summer high of 43°C. Rainfall totalling 300 mm on average falls between January and March, and between September and December.

Most of the large mammals of the southern savanna plains are found in the Park: lion, leopard, cheetah and other cats, abundant elephant,

219

distinctive races of Burchell's zebra and mountain zebra, black rhino, and giraffe. Ungulates include eland, kudu, roan, gemsbok, red hartebeest, wildebeest, steenbok, black-faced impala – whose declining numbers are limited to this region – and a few Damara dikdik.

The wetlands of the pan support enough waterfowl, including the largest known breeding population of the greater flamingo, to be classified as of international importance. Ostrich and red-crested koorhaan are among the many other species present.

Namib Desert National Park (2,340,100 ha.) Altitude: sea-level to 1,500 m. Location: in the Swakopmund and Walvis Bay region between the Swakop and Kuiseb rivers.   B/C MAR–OCT

The Namib Desert was first established in 1904 as 'Game Reserve No. 3'. It forms part of the only true desert in southern Africa, which is also the oldest desert in the world. The river courses are sand-filled with a few scattered water-holes. Within the Park is Sandwich Harbour, an internationally important wetland consisting of saline lagoons. The Park's vegetation consists of true desert plants, with algae and lichen making use of the dew and succulents prevailing on the inselbergs and dykes. Tamarind grows down the riverbeds towards the coast, while giraffe acacia and ebony appear along the inland riverbeds. The unique fog-dependent gymnosperm (*Welwtischia mirabilis*) was first discovered in the region in 1863 and is still the only known species of its family.

Mammals include cheetah, mountain zebra, gemsbok, springbok, hyena, bat-eared fox, three species of elephant shrew, desert golden mole, three species of gerbil, and the black-backed jackal. Among the reptiles are the sidewinder snake, lizards, and geckos.

The birdlife includes some 20,000 Cape cormorants which frequent Sandwich Harbour together with large numbers of flamingoes, herons, egrets, gulls and terns, a high breeding concentration of lappet-faced vultures and red-necked falcons, and a smaller population of martial eagles. There are large colonies of the endemic Bradfield's swift, and on the gravel plains another endemic, Gray's lark. Also found are local races of the Karroo lark and the dry country chats, as well as the extremely localised Herero chat, first described in 1931 and whose nest was not discovered until 1969. Several unusual species of Palearctic shorebird winter in Sandwich Harbour.

Naukluft Mountain Zebra National Park (21,986 ha.) Altitude: 1,000 to 2,000 m. Location: about 170 kms inland and 200 kms southwest of Windhoek.   B/C MAR–OCT

Naukluft Mountain Zebra National Park, proclaimed in 1967, consists of a mountain massif in the western escarpment, overlooking the Namib Desert, 1,000 m below. The vegetation is varied. Scrub and perennial grasses predominate, but there are also larger trees, including fig and acacia, several rare species of aloe, and the endemic resurrection plant. The summers are hot with a maximum temperature of 35°C, and the winters cool with occasional frosts. Summer storms produce 200 mm of rainfall.

Mammals include the eponymous mountain zebra, leopard, kudu, klipspringer, baboon, and dassie.

Among the numerous birds the black eagle, largely a predator on the dassie, is especially interesting.

Skeleton Coast National Park (1,639,000 ha.) Altitude: sea-level to 500 m. Location: a stretch of coastline 190 kms north of Swakopmund.

B
DEC–JAN

Skeleton Coast has been protected since 1916, but the size of the Park was doubled in 1967. The shoreline is relatively regular, with sandy beaches and isolated rocky stretches, backed in the north by high dunes. Large tracts are covered with sparsely vegetated white sands. Several intermittent rivers run through the area, their blocked mouths resulting in the formation of freshwater pools. The Park falls within the fog belt so the temperature range is small and the rainfall low.

Species present on the beaches include black-backed jackal, brown hyena, and occasional seals. The marine fauna is particularly interesting and is the result of an overlap of cold and warm water masses, only paralleled in other continents off the west coasts of South America and Australia.

The freshwater pools in the river mouth are used by migrating shorebirds.

SOUTH AFRICA

The Republic of South Africa occupies a vast plateau, high at the edges and dipping to the Kalahari in the centre, on the southernmost tip of the continent. It is divided into four provinces: Cape Province, Transvaal, the Orange Free State, and Natal. The climate is Mediterranean in the south, humid and tropical (the country is on the same latitude as the Sahara) in Natal and the eastern parts, and dry and variable in temperature in the central highlands and plateaux. The vegetation is,

221

in general, grassland, with scrub bushveld in the north Transvaal and dry thornveld in the southwest.

The black and white populations of South Africa probably arrived at about the same time, the blacks from the north, skirting the Kalahari Desert, the whites from the Atlantic, mainly via the Cape. The original inhabitants were the San Bushmen, nomadic hunter-gatherers now only found in the central Kalahari.

The Republic of South Africa is by a large margin the richest and most developed country in the continent. There are very few large wild animals except those in the protection of the excellent system of Parks and reserves.

Addo Elephant National Park (7,735 ha.) Altitude: 60 to 180 m. Location: 72 kms north of Port Elizabeth in the Sundays River Valley.

B
OCT–MAR

Addo Elephant National Park was founded in 1931 to protect the last of the Eastern Cape elephants. It forms part of the dense Addo Forest whose vegetation is unique. A tangle of creepers and trees – none more than 3.6 m high and including such species as spekboom, sneezewood, Karroo boer-bean, and guarri – the forest can support three times as many elephant as any other habitat in Africa.

Apart from the herd of over 100 elephant, there is a notable population of Cape buffalo. Other mammals include black rhino, eland, kudu, mountain reedbuck, springbok, red hartebeest, bushbuck, grysbok, duiker, porcupine, bushpig, and antbear. Among the predators are caracal and jackal.

The Park's birdlife is rich and varied and more than 170 species have been recorded, among them ostrich, several raptors, finches, starlings, francolin, and various waterbirds.

Augrabies Falls National Park (9,000 ha.) Altitude: 500 to 1,000 m. Location: 120 kms west of Upington in northwest Cape Province.

A/B
OCT–MAR

Augrabies Falls was established in 1967 to conserve a part of the Orange River landscape which includes the magnificent Augrabies Falls. The vegetation includes the 'kokerboom' or tree aloe, many other varieties of aloe and succulents, camel thorn, white karree, wild olive, and Karroo boer-bean. The area is arid and the rainfall, mainly during Jan–April, is low. The waterfall itself drops over solid granite into a ravine 56 m deep.

The Park's fauna includes the little klipspringer, steenbok and several other small antelope, baboon, monkey, wild cats, and plentiful lizards. Giant mud barbel up to two metres in length inhabit the pool and gorge.

222

Bontebok in Bontebok National Park, South Africa

Bontebok National Park (2,586 ha.) Altitude: 60 to 200 m. Location: B
southwest Cape Province, 5 kms south of Swellendam on the Bree River. OCT–MAR

Bontebok was established in 1960 to accommodate a small and dwindling herd of the endangered bontebok, translocated from a private reserve at Bredasdorp. The area is very interesting botanically with more than 470 plant species, including 52 species of grass. Among the Park's trees are the Bree River yellowwood, wild olive, and white milkwood with scattered groves of sweet-thorn. The climate is temperate with an average annual rainfall of 511 mm.

223

The herd of bontebok has grown from the 17 individuals originally translocated to more than 300 — in all there are now about 800 bontebok in South Africa. The Park also contains grey rhebuck, Cape grysbok, steenbok, and grey duiker, while eland, red hartebeest, and springbok have been reintroduced. There is also a large reptile population.

The bird checklist numbers 184 species.

Golden Gate Highland National Park (4,792 ha.) Altitude: 1,892 to 2,770 m. Location: in the northeastern Orange Free State, 200 kms south of Johannesburg.

A
OCT-MAR

Golden Gate was established in 1963 to conserve a beautiful range of golden sandstone mountains together with their fauna and flora. The vegetation is largely upland grassland with a magnificent array of flowering plants including lilies, red-hot poker, and watsonias. The climate is cool in summer, with snow on the higher slopes in winter.

Among the Park's noteworthy mammals are eland, red hartebeest, springbok and wildebeest, blesbok, grey rhebuck, oribi, mountain reedbuck, and zebra.

The birdlife is particularly interesting and includes the increasingly rare lammergeyer vulture, with its habit of cracking bones for their marrow by dropping them from a height onto rocks, the secretary bird, black eagle, blue crane, rock pigeon, guinea fowl, and many waterbirds.

Kalahari Gemsbok National Park (959,103 ha. contiguous with a further 1,087,000 ha. in Botswana.) Altitude: 1,200 m. Location: in northwest Cape Province, bordering Namibia and Botswana.

B
JUNE–SEPT

The Kalahari Gemsbok National Park was established in 1931 and occupies a vast area of red Kalahari sandveld scattered with grass and occasional trees, such as silver cluster-leaf or terminalia, shepherd's tree, grey camel-thorn, black thorn, and raisin bush. Two dry river beds bisect the Park, the Nossob and the Auob, which meet near the southern entrance gate and administrative headquarters at Twee Rivieren. These two river beds act as 'roads' for both man and wildlife and are punctuated by a few boreholes. Although a little water from the unpredictable summer rainstorms accumulates in some of the many shallow pans, the area is largely dry wilderness.

The local fauna has adapted to the arid conditions and includes such dry country species as gemsbok, springbok in large numbers, blue wildebeest, hartebeest, eland, and kudu as well as small numbers of steenbok and duiker. Also present are Cape pangolin and springhare.

Predators include lion, leopard, cheetah, hunting dog, jackal, spotted and brown hyena, bat-eared fox, and black-footed cat.

The birdlife is plentiful with 215 species recorded including ostrich and secretary bird. The birds of prey are particularly interesting with giant eagle owl, and Bateleur, martial and tawny eagles among them. Camel-thorn trees support the massive communal nests of sociable weavers.

Karroo National Park (18,000 ha.) Altitude: 1,000 to 1,500 m. Location: near Beaufort West in southwestern Cape Province, on the Great Karroo.   B/C   OCT–MAR

Karroo was established in 1979 to preserve the unique flora and fauna of the arid landscape of the Great Karroo. The area is low-lying and hilly with a wide variety of grasses, bushes and other plants including the wild currant, the sweet thorn, several species of lily, and many other flowering bulbs. The climate is hot in summer but cold at night in winter, and the Park has an average annual rainfall of 250 mm.

The fauna includes 50 species of mammal, the larger of which – among them a herd of mountain zebra, gemsbok, red hartebeest, black wildebeest, and springbok – have been reintroduced. Other species include the fierce little black-footed wild cat and the porcupine.

Kruger National Park (2,000,000 ha.) Altitude: 200 to 900 m. Location: northeast Transvaal, 400 kms northeast of Johannesburg on the Mozambique border.   A   JUNE–SEPT

The immense Kruger National Park, whose history is outlined earlier in the book, is probably the best-known wildlife reserve in the world. Watered by six rivers the Park's landscape and vegetation varies widely: the western central zone, south of the Oliphants River, is acacia scrub and red bush-willow veld; the eastern central zone has knob-thorn and marula veld which provides good grassland; north of the Oliphants river, in the west, is red bush-willow and mopane veld; the northwest of the Park is covered by shrub mopane veld, with baobabs in the Pafuri region. The rainfall varies between 375 mm and 750 mm annually, and summer temperatures often exceed 40°C.

The Park provides sanctuary for 122 species of mammal, 109 species of reptile, and 55 species of fish. The mammals include populations, according to the 1980 census, of 7,500 elephant, 27,000 buffalo, 120,000 impala, and 22,000 zebra. There are many antelope species including kudu, waterbuck, sable, reedbuck, tsessebe, eland, roan, and klipspringer. Also present are crocodile, hippo, introduced black and white

Greater kudu bulls in Kruger National Park, South Africa

rhino, wildebeest, suni, oribi, warthog, a large giraffe population, diadem and vervet monkeys, and Cape hedgehog. Predators include lion, leopard, cheetah, jackal, hunting dog, bat-eared fox, Meller's mongoose, and brown and spotted hyena.

The bird checklist numbers 422 species including marabou stork, ground hornbill, secretary bird, vultures, Cape glossy starling, lilac-breasted roller, woodland kingfisher, and fish eagle.

The Kruger has excellent facilities for more than 2,500 visitors with fourteen restcamps offering accommodation in rondavels. The larger camps have restaurants and shops, and the Park is criss-crossed by more than 2,000 kilometres of road. There are also campsites, picnic spots, and guided 'Wilderness Trails', walking tours lasting three nights and two days. The best time for seeing the Kruger's wildlife is during the June–September dry season when the animals congregate at the water-holes. The north of the Park is only open from May to October, although the south is open all year.

Mountain Zebra National Park (6,536 ha.) Altitude: 1,000 to 2,000 m. Location: 27 kms west of Cradock in Cape Province.

B
JUNE–SEPT

Mountain Zebra was established in 1937 to ensure the survival of the threatened Cape mountain zebra. The Park is on the Great Karroo and embraces a hilly landscape covered by the characteristic karroo vegetation, which includes thick patches of sweet-thorn with wild olive groves in the ravines. There is a wide variety of flowering plants among them succulents, mesembryanthemums, and blue tulip.

As well as the small and beautifully-striped mountain zebra, the fauna includes large herds of eland, springbok, blesbok and black wildebeest, kudu, duiker, steenbok and red hartebeest. Predators include wild cat and black-footed cat, black-backed jackal, bat-eared fox, Cape fox, and aardwolf.

Birdlife is abundant with over 170 species recorded.

Tsitsikamma Forest National Park (478 ha.) and **Tsitsikamma Coastal National Park** Altitude: sea-level to 300 m. Location: on the coast of southern Cape Province, on the 'Garden Route' by the Paul Sauer Bridge over the Storms River, between Humansdorp and Knysna.

B
APR–AUG

Tsitsikamma Forest was established to protect an area of thick natural forest peculiar to the southern Cape. The Park, named after the local word for clear water, is located inland and does not adjoin the Coastal National Park. It contains much to interest the botanist, including thirty

227

different tree species, with ancient specimens of the 'Big Tree' or yellow-wood, stinkwood, candlewood and assegai. The 'fynbos' forms a rich scrub vegetation. Shrubs, creepers, ferns, including tree ferns, white alder, moss and lichen, all flourish. There are also several species of protea, orchids and lily. The area has a temperate climate and plentiful rainfall averaging 1,200 mm per year.

The Coastal National Park, which was established in 1964, stretches inland for 80 kms from the mouth of the Groot River near Humansdorp. In addition, the Park reaches 800 m out to sea as well as taking in the shoreline and the magnificent coastal cliffs. Iron oxide and vegetable matter colour its waters a deep brown.

The fauna includes the elusive clawless otter, rock-rabbit, bushbuck, Cape grysbok, blue duiker, the nocturnal bushpig, baboon, and vervet monkey. Marine fauna includes dolphins, whales, stonefish, starfish, sea-anemones, sponges, sea cucumbers, and sea slugs.

210 species of bird have been recorded, among them the rare Knysna lourie and the narina trogon, several protea-loving sunbirds including the malachite, and 35 species of seabird, including the southern black-backed or kelp gull.

SWAZILAND

Swaziland, formerly a British Protectorate, is a small, landlocked, and well-watered kingdom bordered by Mozambique and South Africa. Fertile and prosperous with magnificent mountain scenery, it is sometimes called the 'Switzerland of Africa'. Swaziland's ground-based wildlife was originally very rich, but long years of uncontrolled hunting have almost wiped out the larger species. Birdlife has been less affected.

Hlane Game Reserve (14,164 ha. contiguous with Mlawawulu and Ndzindza National Reserves.) Altitude: 500 m approx. Location: 75 kms east of Mbabane.   B OCT–MAR

These reserves are set in a lowveld landscape watered by the Black Mbuluzi River. The winters are dry and the summers, during which the game herds migrate south, wet. The vegetation is extensive grassland vlei with woodland along the watercourses, where the impala lily grows. There are over 10,000 animals in the Park including zebra, blue

wildebeest, kudu, waterbuck, steenbok, common duiker, the reintroduced white rhino, giraffe, and cheetah. The annual Butimba, a week-long
hunt, takes place every year. Hundreds of Swazis in traditional dress,
led by the king, hunt with spears, knobkerries and guns. At the end
of the hunt all the game killed is given to the king.

Malolotja Nature Reserve (18,000 ha.) Altitude: 500–1,000 m. Loca-   B/C
tion: in the northwest highland on the border with South Africa.   OCT–MAR

Access to the reserve is by vehicle from the Motjane-Pigg's Peak road.
The area is watered by tributaries of the Komati River and includes the
steep-sided Komati Gorge, the Malolotja Falls, and the abandoned
Ngwenya iron-ore pit where middle Stone-Age utensils have been found
nearby.

Mammals include the indigenous oribi and bushbuck, zebra, white
rhino, buffalo, blue wildebeest, impala, red hartebeest, black wildebeest,
and blesbok.

Among the resident birds are two colonies of bald ibis.

Mlilwane Wildlife Sanctuary (4,545 ha.) Altitude: 500 m approx. Loca-   B
tion: in the Ezulwini Valley in the eastern region south of Mbabane.   OCT–MAR

Established in 1960 and opened to the public in 1964, Mlilwane was
Swaziland's pioneer reserve. Set on the escarpment that divides the
lowveld from the highveld, it is watered by four rivers, including the
Little Usutu with its spectacular Mantegna Falls. Twin sharp-peaked kopjes rise to the north.

Before the establishment of the sanctuary, the area contained only
steenbok and duiker. Animals reintroduced since 1960 include white
rhino, hippo, giraffe, buffalo, sable, eland, kudu, blesbok, blue
wildebeest, zebra, impala, and warthog. There are plentiful waterfowl,
among them the blue crane, on the dams and vleis left by flooded mining
pits.

The bird checklist records over 240 species, including Verreaux's
black eagle, the plum-coloured starling, and several sunbirds.

INDEX

Page numbers in *italics* refer to black and white photographs

231